ב״ה

VISUALIZATION

AND

IMAGERY

Harnessing the Power of
Our Mind's Eye

RAV DOVBER PINSON

RAV DOVBER PINSON

VISUALIZATION
&
IMAGERY

Harnessing the Power of Our Mind's Eye

THE JEWISH MEDITATION SERIES

THE EXPERIENCE & PRACTICE OF KABBALAH

IYYUN PUBLISHING

Published by IYYUN Publishing
232 Bergen Street
Brooklyn, NY 11217

http:/www.iyyun.com

Iyyun Publishing books may be purchased for educational, business or sales promotional use. For information please contact: contact@IYYUN.com

cover and book design: RP Design and Development

pb ISBN 978-0-9890072-9-0

Pinson, DovBer 1971-
Visualization and Imagery: Jewish Meditation, Vol. 2
1.Judaism 2. Spirituality 3. Philosophy

DEDICATED

—— *to* ——

MR. MORRIS & DANI SAFDIE שיחי׳

————

REB BURICH & FALI KLEIN שיחי׳

————

MR. GREG (GERSHON) & CHANIE BELL שיחי׳

————

DR. HANA & DR. MORDEHAI WOSK שיחי׳

May they experience a constant Shefa/flow of blessings in a revealed and expansive way.

TABLE OF CONTENTS

PART ONE:
CREATIVE

PART TWO:
IMAGERY

//

PART THREE:
AWARENESS

PART FOUR:
ADVANCED VISUALIZATION

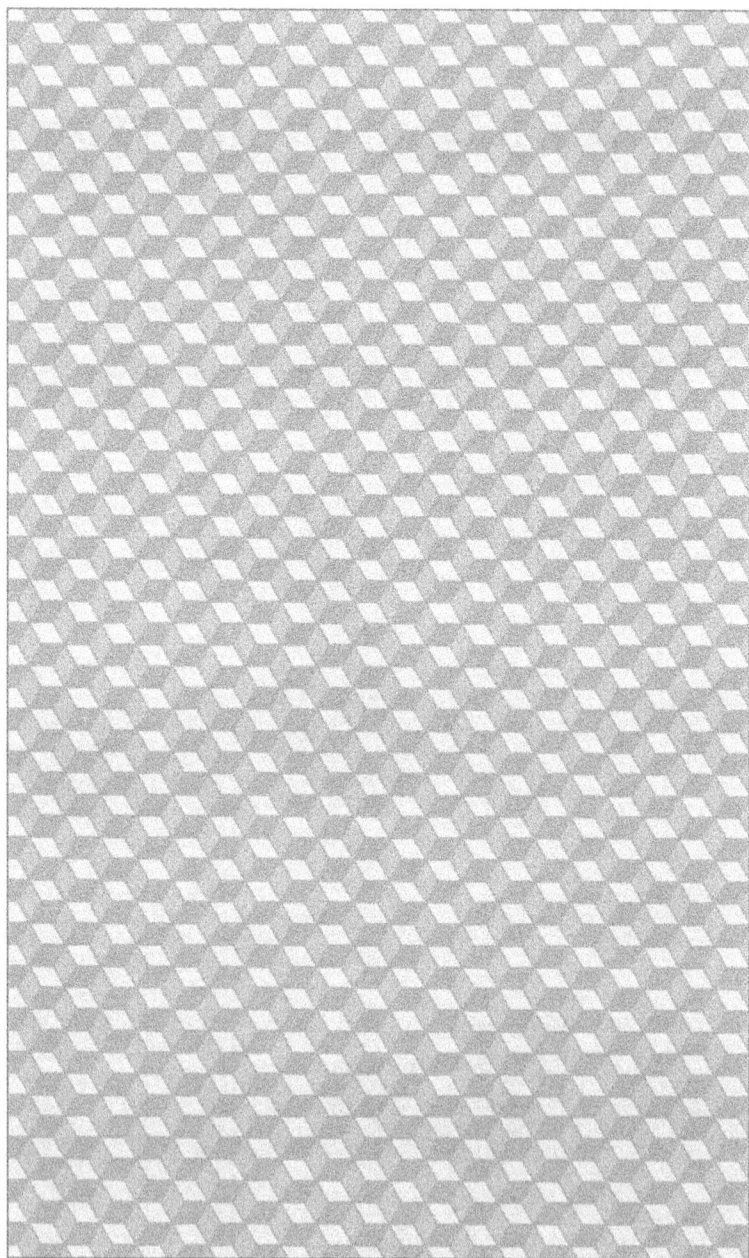

OPENING

....

THE CRISIS
OF IMAGINATION

THERE IS SO MUCH BEAUTY IN THE WORLD,
BUT THERE IS ALSO SO MUCH BROKENNESS.
For some people brokenness is manifest in the realm of relationships, for others it is present within their unrealized
goals, their "dreams deferred". For certain people brokenness is experienced physically in the form of various health
issues, while for others it is more psychological, exhibited
for instance in a lack of self-confidence or perpetual confusion. Additionally, brokenness is manifest on a societal level
in the forms of rampant poverty, bigotry, and war.

There are many people, even successful people (whatever that word means), who have the tendency to think of themselves as failures. Despite peak-moments wherein they experience real joy, most people are just going about their lives with a constant low-level sense of melancholy or depression.

Clarity seems hard to come by. Most people are walking around in a sort of existential daze with the overwhelming feeling that all decisions are daunting. For many there appears to be a sense of confusion and ambiguity in terms of career, relationships, life path, and certainly regarding the question: What is my true purpose and mission in this world?

Much of the mayhem and malaise that is rampant in the world can be traced back to a crisis of imagination. This is a result of most people's inability to exert conscious control over their subconscious mind, which speaks primarily in the language of images and impressions, rather than words or ideas.

Suffice it to say that much of the way we think, speak, act and live is but a reflection of deep-seated "imagery" implanted within our subconscious. We all have an inner, often unconscious narrative that informs our conscious self. But because of the apparent disconnect between these two parts of our psyche many people are internally conflicted.

Perhaps they have tried to change, attempted to start something fresh or different, like entering into a new relationship or shifting their perspective, but nothing has seemed to work. They may experience an initial boost of energy or momentum, but very quickly they fall back into old, negative patterns of unconscious thinking and being. They slowly lose all hope that it is even possible to live with more joy, clarity, openness or confidence. As a result they cannot even imagine an alternative.

This crisis extends into a person's spiritual life as well. So many people walk around with a sense of emptiness, fragmented and disconnected but burning with a desire to feel connected — connected with themselves, with others around them, with the world at large, and ultimately, the deepest desire of all is to sense some type of *Kirvas Hashem/* Connection to G-d. This is the sensation of being in touch with or touched by Transcendence.

Whether we know it or not, we are all affected by imagery. Sometimes these images are positive and sometimes they are negative.

Let's say a person is worried about his or her job or financial stability. Now, because of this worry they start imagining what it would be like if they lost their job. In a rapid unfolding their imagination runs wild and all types of morbid images come to mind. First it begins with the thought of losing their job, but then it quantum leaps into being homeless, completely alone and helpless, and so on. This type of negative, almost unconscious process of visualization can cripple a person. And then based on this defeatist imagery the person inevitably begins to expect negativity to follow. A certain negative image sinks in and then all future decisions are founded on this image, thereby unconsciously attracting that very type of projected negativity. In effect, this relatively unconscious imagery and narrative based on fear, worry and doubt ultimately becomes the foundation of our lives.

The beginning of healing this crisis of imagination and the apparent separation within the self is to secure a belief that it is possible to be healed and rectified. Yet, to begin this healing we need to somehow penetrate our subconscious mind and rewrite our inner narrative. We need to reclaim control of the subterranean regions of our mind, the deepest parts of the self that hold such sway over our lives, in order to consciously reprogram the system. We must learn in a conscious way to create positive imagery in the mind and thus to attract positivity.

There is incredible power contained within our subconscious mind but, for the most part, instead of being in control of our subconscious we are often enslaved to the reality it offers us unsolicited. Learning the language and methodology of the subconscious mind is the only way out of this choke-hold.

Mental imagery and other forms of non-verbal communication are the primary mediums to get to the subconscious. Our subconscious does not trade in the currency of words or language. It only understands the images that are consciously or unconsciously formed and fixated upon within our psyche.

Subliminal sights, sounds and other stimuli sneak into the deeper recesses of our mind and end up lodging themselves there. This could be in the form of something you saw, heard or experienced as a young child, or even today as an adult, but did not register in your conscious mind. Overtime such a bundle of unconscious 'images' forms a personality or identity, as it were. Often, without proper psycho-spiritual maintenance this haphazard collection of random imprints and experiences can result in an unhappy, insecure, negative or disconnected person. Ultimately, these images inform the way we think, speak and act in ways that we most often aren't even aware of.

THE FUTURE IS BASED ON OUR IMAGE OF THE PRESENT:

Our future is, to a large extent, a direct reflection of the images we hold and generate in the present. Whatever recurrent images are being displayed upon the inner screen of our mind in the present moment will be, for the most part, what we manifest in the future. If the screen shows you as a failure, or as unhealthy, perpetually trapped in bad relationships, impoverished, or unholy and spiritually immature, unfortunately your future will, most likely, be a materialization of this image.

The subconscious mind constructs a certain image of who you are and what you can expect of life, and automatically you are drawn to this image. You subconsciously imagine yourself as a failure and then you live up to that image, thereby self-sabotaging any possibility for success, be it physical, financial, emotional or spiritual.

For example, let's say that before you sit down to learn a difficult topic in Torah, or before you enter a business meeting, you think to yourself, "This is never going to work. Who am I fooling? I cannot do this." Then indeed you will almost certainly not be successful.

Every person has an inner image in their deeper subconscious that informs their life. If you believe deeply that you are a failure and think, "I can't do this. This is way beyond me. I don't have the ability," these thoughts will perpetually parade themselves across your inner screen and you will continuously fail. Conversely, if you believe deeply that you deserve goodness and blessings, you will open yourself up to goodness and blessings. "Think good and it will be good." Choose to imagine and create the image of empowerment: "I can do this. I may not be able to accomplish/afford/understand this now, but I will in the future." Goodness and positivity will follow suit.

The more times you mentally imagine something, the greater its chances of manifestation.

Just to be a little more clear. This is not simply a matter of entertaining a particular image and then having the image magically materialize. Of course one needs (as will be explored further on) the inner image to be attached to a deep *Cheshek*/Yearning, desire, and passion. And certainly one needs continuous *Tefilah*/Prayer. But also, one needs to add a good dose of hard work and healthy realism into the equation. Create positive imagery, whether in the realm of physical, financial, emotional, mental or spiritual success, and then imagine all the obstacles and challenges that may arise and stand in your way, then visualize overcoming them one by one.

BEING THE CAUSE OR EFFECT:

As mentioned earlier, for the most part the collective subconscious image of one's self and one's reality is not created by choice, but rather the world around you chooses it for you. It is, in effect, an externally generated and unconsciously projected image of who you are as a person. What adds insult to this injury is that not only do you not retain hegemony over your own life or identity, but furthermore because the stimuli by-passes your conscious mind you always end up feeling like a divided and fragmented person with two voices — the conscious ideals and the subconscious images.

Living this way means that we are constantly caught up in the 'effect' of choices/causes that are not our own. Therefore any conscious choice we do make today is nearly irrelevant in the face of such deep-seated impressions and, at best, can only exert an actual influence on our actions for a few moments until we inadvertently swing back to acting out the previously established unconscious self-image.

On a more spiritual level, due to this crisis of imagination and the lack of control over our own subconscious minds, many of us have absorbed a host of toxic ideas and images from our surroundings, which then become the imaginal seeds for many of our defeatist, materialist, overly competitive, carnally obsessed, money hungry, war mongering world-views. As a result, many people have become dulled to their more subtle spiritual imaginations and sources of intuitive wisdom. We have been tricked into thinking that if we can just take control of our conscious, logical, rational mind (which is itself a great accomplishment), we are all set. We have therefore been trained to ignore the other, deeper, murkier parts of our self and psyche.

Until we learn to train or retrain ourselves to consciously choose and form the inner images that make up the self we will be forever enslaved to the externally imposed images of our surroundings. When we learn to consciously craft the previously unconscious image of self that we desire — an empowered, connected, secure, confident and spiritually attuned person — we will then become that person.

This will help us liberate ourselves from all the confusion, distortion, melancholy and alienation that we so regularly experience. The goal of physical, emotional, mental and spiritual freedom is achieved through the cultivation of our capacity to consciously communicate and collaborate with our subconscious mind and imagination.

ALPHABET LANGUAGE
VS. PICTORIAL LANGUAGE:

In thinking about the mechanics of visualization and internal imagery, the Torah's story of the Jewish people's collective Exodus from the constraints of slavery experienced in Egypt comes to mind. Through this lens let us examine the relationship between cartographic and phonetic language systems as they are symbolically represented within this most well-known narrative from the Torah for the purpose of more fully understanding the inner mechanisms of the imaginal and ideational mind.

Language is generally understood to be a function of the left hemisphere of the brain, the rational part of the brain that thinks in linear sequence and logic. And yet, this is not necessarily the way language began. All known human languages began with depictions through images, a classically 'right-brain' function. Before communicating with written words, people communicated ideas with images.

The ancient Egyptians in fact had two separate languages. The first was used by the priests in their temples for idol worship and 'sacred' purposes only; this is known as Hieroglyphics — an abstract form of symbolic language, which is written using pictures and images. The second was the common, colloquial language used for ordinary conversation, which was written with an Alphabet. Being that the 'higher' sacred language was in Hieroglyphics, we can surmise that there was understood to be a deep relationship between icons and 'sacred' images

A profound paradigm shift of history began with the giving of the Torah. One foundation of the Torah is that the Creator of Heaven and Earth is image-less, Infinite, ineffable and not able to be depicted. Icons or any images meant to represent the Creator are thereby rendered as pure idol worship and utterly forbidden. Our connection with the Infinite One is not through perception, but rather through conception. This is a radical movement away from the world of depicted icons to the abstract world of ideas.

As a result we do not create sacred imagery, rather, our

language is holy. The Torah and the *Luchos*/Tablets were given to us in *Lashon Ha'Kodesh*/The Holy Tongue (Biblical Hebrew). This catalyzed the shift in cognitive emphasis from image to idea, from symbol to word. But an even more drastic shift is that there were no longer "two" separate languages — a language for the sacred and a language for the mundane. The Torah, through the medium of the Holy Tongue, bridged the worlds of sacred and mundane, spiritual and physical. Indeed, before the giving of the Torah, prior to the exodus from Egypt, there does appear to have been two distinct languages used by the Hebrews — one being the local language that was used by our Patriarchs and their families for mundane interactions *(Sanhedrin, 38b)*, and the other being *Lashon Ha'Kodesh* (Hebrew) that was used for sacred actions or interactions *(Kuzri, Maamor 8; 68)*.

But following the giving of the Torah there was, and is, only one Alphabetical language — Hebrew. *Lashon Ha'Kodesh* is an all-inclusive language used to both transmit prophecy and to order dinner. Even historically when Jews spoke other indigenous languages the Hebrew letters were always used to write in a regional dialect (i.e., Aramaic, Ladino, or Yiddish). The letters of *Lashon Kodesh* were always employed in whatever written language Jews were using at the time.

The shift from pictorial language to a phonetic Alphabet, from language that can only depict immediate reality to language that can intimate abstract ideas, brought about a revolution and paradigm shift in human thought and understanding. Some historians have called this the "Alphabetic Revolution." When letters and not images are employed to convey information this leads to abstraction, invention and innovation. Logical reasoning, scientific research and philosophical pondering are only possible in the world of alphabetical language. Only concrete reality or crude and highly anthropomorphic theology can be pondered or conveyed in a language of images. For example: There are two juxtaposed images, one image is a sheep and the other is a hand with a cow. This would roughly 'translate' as: You give me your cow and I will give you my sheep.

Modern Western civilization can be traced from Greece to Rome to continental Europe, but the roots of all this is founded on the Alphabetical revolution of the Ancient Near East. The same is true of the two largest groups of people who practice religion in the world. They too are most clearly rooted in and founded on the path of the "word", as evidenced by their self-identification with the Torah, the archetypal Holy Book. In fact, one could say that the giving of the Torah initiated this dramatic shift away from icons and imagery, leading humans and history into the world of the *Aleph-Beis*. As a result there emerged the possibility for deeper, abstract, meta-physical, philosophical and scientific exploration.

RIGHT-TO-LEFT
VS. LEFT-TO-RIGHT:

And yet upon closer scrutiny it becomes apparent that even within phonetic languages themselves there are two ways (at least) to read and write: Either from "Left to Right", such as Greek and English for example, or from "Right to Left", such as *Lashon Ha'Kodesh* and other Semitic languages.

As mentioned, the left-hemisphere of the brain is connected with analytical and sequential thinking as well as the function of speech. Alternatively, the right-hemisphere is connected with grasping whole patterns and visual concepts, apprehending shapes, images and pictures. Reading the Alphabet is therefore a predominately left-brain activity. And yet, when a person is reading Hebrew from right to left he begins by slightly tilting his head towards the right, thus stimulating, ever so gently, the right hemisphere of the brain. Conversely, when one reads from left to right, as is the case with Greek or English, the head is slightly shifted towards the left. Reading is then a completely left-brain activity.

Through this subtle somatic shifting of the head the Torah is intimating that we need to activate and incorporate the more associative and affective modes of cognition within the more textually based consciousness of alphabetic culture in order to approach any kind of integral understanding of the Infinite One. Yes, we do need to lift ourselves beyond the image, beyond icons and representation in order to truly assimilate the deeper message of the Torah. And yet, we ought not cut ourselves off from any and all connection with the right hemisphere of the brain, which supports the creative, imaginative and intuitive perceptive faculties, as these modes of perception add the elements of color, texture and emotion necessary to achieve a more mature and robust spiritual sensibility. And so when we read Hebrew we begin with a slight shift towards and stimulation of the right hemisphere of the brain in order to activate both sides of the brain, as it were.

LETTERS: LEFT-TO-RIGHT
WORDS: RIGHT-TO-LEFT:

If we delve deeper something even more interesting emerges. Most Hebrew letters are written from left-to-right. This is the case even though the words themselves are read from right-to-left. If a person were to write the word Av/Father, which is spelled with an *Aleph* and a *Beis*, they would begin to write the letter Aleph from the furthest top-left corner of the slanted line א and move towards the right. The same is true for the Beis- ב. One would begin with the left side of the upper horizontal line and move towards the right. And yet when one reads the word *Av*, one reads from right-to-left.

In short: While writing the Hebrew letters one moves from left to right, thus activating the left hemisphere of the brain; whereas, while reading the words one moves from right to left, thus stimulating the right side of the brain.

According to the deeper Kabbalistic teachings of the Torah, letters are rooted in the "left column" attribute of *Gevu-rah*/Strength, restriction and concealment, whereas words are rooted in the "right column" attribute of Chesed/Loving-Kindness, openness and revelation. As mentioned, letters are written from left to right (i.e., Gevurah to Chesed), and therefore they predominantly represent the quality of Gevurah. Words, on the other hand, are read from right to left (i.e., Chesed to Gevurah), and therefore predominantly represent the quality of Chesed. (Note- The structure and function of the Sefiros will be explored in greater detail in the following pages. If one is completely unfamiliar with the above concepts and wants to skip ahead for clarity, please do so.)

A letter on its own is meaningless, it does not convey any meaningful information, unless of course the letter itself symbolizes something or has independent meaning as a word on its own. Once a person attaches one letter to the next, thereby forming a word, the letters become animated and loaded with meaning; they are now conveying information and ideas. The letter Aleph on its own means nothing. Once the letter Aleph is joined with the letter Beis it becomes a word, *Av*/Father. The letters are then animated and the word is filled with an influx of Chesed.

In summary, alphabetical language in general, as opposed to cartographic communication, is more of a left-brain activity. Regarding Hebrew specifically, the letters are written from left-to-right, stimulating the left-brain, but read from right-to-left, activating the right-brain. This is a Divine hint encoded into the Holy Tongue itself that alerts us to the appropriate cognitive approach to Torah: As much as we need to be analytical and abstract thinkers while trying to wrestle with the text in order to 'grasp' the intangible and ineffable, we still need to stay connected to our affective, creative, imaginative and intuitive faculties as we engage the Torah's mysteries.

Reason, logic and critical thinking are the roots of philosophy. These processes of thought give prominence to the left-brain over the right. Revelation, prophecy and higher intuitive wisdom are more in the realm of the right-brain reality. Seen from this perspective, there appears to be a division between "Athens" and "Jerusalem" as it were, between the Greek philosophers and the Hebrew prophets. For the most part, Western secular civilization has followed the path of the left-brain. Over time, we have all become a little too "Greek", as it were. We need to reclaim our connection with the active and prophetic imagination. In order to do this we must reconnect with the faculties of the right-brain, what is called the Koach *Ha'M'damah*/Power of the Imagination, in order to visualize an alternate reality than what is currently seen as possible.

THE PROPHET &
THE POWER OF IMAGINATION:

Maimonides, the great 11th century Jewish philosopher also known as the Rambam, explains in the second part of his philosophical magnum opus, "The Guide for the Perplexed", that a prophet, which is the most advanced level a human being can reach, is somebody with both an exceptionally strong intellect and a highly developed imagination *(Morah Nevuchim, 2; 36)*.

The prophet is thus one who is in possession of a complex and complementary capacity to both think and imagine — to be critical as well as creative. Having achieved this pinnacle of human consciousness, it is possible, upon entering a prophetic state, for a deeper and higher aspect of Divine wisdom to be revealed to the prophet.

The normative/logical mode of thinking is to take images or impressions and attempt to discern and elucidate inherent patterns or principles by analyzing, comparing and contrasting these images or impressions. This is the essential scientific method of discovery — analyzing, comparing and contrasting the "imagery" of data until a breakthrough occurs, thereby revealing a new principle or underlying pattern. This is referred to as inductive reasoning. A more subtle or theoretical method of thought is to think in total abstractions, such as in numbers or pure ideas. This gives rise to what is known as deductive reasoning — the ability to recognize particular situations based on the assumptions of broader principles.

Intellectual rigor, logic, inductive and deductive reasoning, and the imaginative faculty are all very strong and symbiotic in the mind of the prophet.

Later on there will be an in-depth exploration of the nature of imagination and the contrasting qualities of "positive" and "negative" imagination. For now, let it suffice to state a few general principles and ideas.

Negative imagination is considered only "skin deep", as there is no substance beneath it. This form of imagination is mere fantasy. People with overactive "skin deep" imaginations create all types of "demons" and "monsters" that end up crippling them, not allowing them to function as healthy human beings. Or, alternatively, they create "messianic" grandiose illusions that put them totally out of touch with their own personal reality as well as reality as a whole.

The prophet, however, possesses an imagination that is able to develop from the inside-out. It emerges from the depths of his or her understanding and reaches all the way to the extremities of the mind, moving from the intellect to the imaginative faculty. This type of imagination is positive. Here the imagination is referred to as the "skin of the flesh", referring to its nature as being an external reflection of the inner mind; as opposed to the negative "skin deep" form of imagination, which has no substance or foundation beneath its outer appearance and luster.

Regarding the "skin of the flesh" form of imagination the movement is from the inside-out. First the intellect is stimulated and the prophet gains a deeper understating and higher awareness in the form of an abstraction. Only afterwards is the concept translated and expressed through his imaginative faculties. When the prophet experiences the concept as a kind of dream sequence, an image, he immediately recognizes the message or idea that it is meant to convey.

A sound intellect combined with the power of positive imagination is a requisite to receive prophetic influx. In very simple words, perhaps even a little oversimplified, a prophet is one who possesses two, often contradictory capacities: 1) A sane, rational intellect that can properly comprehend the world "as it is". 2) And a healthy power of imagination with which to envision the world or humanity "as it could be". In short, they are able to see life simultaneously as it is as well as how it could be.

Without a healthy and positive imagination the vision of the prophet would be acutely penetrating providing them with an excellent diagnostic understanding of how things are in their unredeemed state. But they would be stuck, as it were, in the world of "what is", and would therefore not be able to perceive and ultimately inspire the people to mend their ways and liberate themselves from blind causality in order to receive a "new light" and to "sing the new song" of a rectified future.

Today, in our own collective condition of exile our *Koach Ha'M'damah*/Power of Imagination is what is really in exile. Much like the time when we were stuck in bondage in Egypt and our imagination was so askew — as will be shortly explained — our power of positive imagination is similarly in exile. We are ruled for the most part by hollow fantasy and skin deep, shallow, empty imagery.

Our sense perceptions dictate our reality to us, and as a result, the images that guide our inner life are only skin deep. No wonder we are so lost in our personal and collective exile. We need to redeem and rectify our imagination by becoming more attuned to our powers of "prophetic" and positive imagination.

THE VISUAL REVOLUTION:

When we are able to reclaim our *Koach Ha'M'damah*/Power

of Positive Imagination we can open ourselves up to the possibility of experiencing some form of deeper, prophetic, intuitive insight. As we are moving closer to the ultimate redemption we need to once again focus on cultivating this imaginative faculty. We must do this in order to counter the tremendous *Kelipos*/Concealments and shallow temptations of fantasy and negative imagination that we are inundated with daily via the internet and all forms of media advertising, as well as to hone our imaginative abilities to enter more fully into a renewed prophetic era. This "medicine" is both a perfect remedy for our modern illness (i.e., fantasy and false imagination as a result of rampant negative imagery), and a perfect supplement to propel us onward towards higher levels of visionary consciousness through positive imagination.

We are nearing the Final Redemption, a time when we will all be seers with a perfected *Koach Ha'M'damah* as prophesied by the great Biblical prophets of old: "And it shall come to pass that I will pour out my Spirit on all flesh. Your sons and your daughters shall prophesy, your old men shall dream dreams, and your young men shall see visions" *(Yoel, 3; 1)*. Precisely during this time period, and more specifically over the last hundred years, there has been a proliferation of visual stimulation and information available through the optical sense.

Some five hundred years ago there was what was called the "printing press revolution." Due to the developments of technology that made popular printing possible and affordable there was a proliferation of printed material, which eventually ushered in the modern scientific age. A new type of revolution is now occurring as a result of radical advances in digital technology, what can be called a "visual revolution." Today we live in a world where most people, certainly the youth, get a majority of their information and ideas about the world through "visually" transmitted data, whether it be film, live news, or the internet. Our sense of the visual is stimulated, perhaps over stimulated, and yet, when channeled correctly we can evolve beyond mere fantasy into a higher form of positive, 'prophet-like' imagination.

Indeed, many great scholars and mystics, including the Rambam, have written that during the era shortly before the arrival of *Moshiach*, prophecy will return to Israel. The Rambam writes that he received a wonderful tradition from his father, and his father from his grandfather, going all the way back to the beginning of the current exile, that prophecy will eventually return and, "there is no doubt that the return of prophecy is an introduction to *Moshiach*" *(Iggeres Teiman, Chap 3)*. The closer we come to that time, which according to all opinions we are quite close, the more we move into a prophetic time, a time where, as quoted, "Your sons and your daughters shall prophesy, your old men shall dream dreams, and your children shall see visions."

DREAMS, IMAGERY
& PROPHETIC INSIGHT:

Every waking moment our senses are taking in literally billions of sights, sounds and smells. This is on the level of sense perception. If a person has a powerful imaginative capacity he can continue to see an image or hear a sound or smell a scent even after the actual sight, sound or smell is no longer physically present. During our waking moments this imaginative faculty is relatively quiet as we are continuously being bombarded with new and fresh stimulus. In sleep, however, when we are taking in less stimuli and our sense of sight is shut down, our imaginative faculty is heightened.

A dream is considered one-sixtieth of prophecy *(Berachos, 57b)*. Therefore, we can see that dreams, the creative imagination and prophecy are all interlinked and deeply related. In fact, besides Moshe, all prophets received prophecy in a dream-like state *(Rambam, Hilchos Yesodei HaTorah, 7; 2)*. Yet, it must be noted that whereas dreams may contain traces of prophetic insight, premonition, or precognition, most of the time they are mere nonsense burping up from the subconscious reflecting an overload of junk information that needs to get expunged and cleared from the brain and nervous system.

How does a person discern whether they are having a "pro-phetic" dream or a fantastical release of the subconscious? The illustrious son of the Rambam, Rabbi Avraham, writes that only a person who has total control over his mind, both the revealed intellectual mind and the more unconscious imaginative faculty, will experience prophetic dreams. For such a person, whose imaginative faculty is the most exter-nal aspect of mind, the movement is from the inside-out (i.e., the "skin of the flesh"). Their imaginative mind there-fore has no independent voice apart from their intellectual consciousness and is primarily used as a channel through which to express and reflect upon deeper truths. Otherwise, the fantasies of those who are crippled and controlled by their negative imagination cloud their intellect. In such a case, even if a "prophetic" image is revealed to him in his dream, the image will be entangled within the web of their un-redeemed unconscious and the nonsensical fantasies will surface and skew the transmission, so to speak.

We have our work cut out for us. We need to learn to har-ness and cultivate the power of positive imagination. The power for image-making is essential for our soul develop-ment and to experience any form of "soul elevation". To do this we need to create the conditions wherein we are able to access and choose our subconscious imagery. We will there-by develop the capacity to direct our "waking dreams", as well as being able to experience lucid, controlled dreaming while asleep by becoming more aligned with the prophetic-like, right-brain modalities of imagination and intuition. This again serves a double purpose — both as an antidote to the modern proliferated illness of fantasy and false imagination and as a catalyst that elevates us to a higher/deeper level of consciousness, where we can sense that which is normally beyond our basic sensory input.

BREATHING & QUIETING THE MIND:

This current book is the second volume to be released in *The Jewish Meditation Series.*

The previous volume focused on basic breathing techniques and methods of quieting the mind, titled simply, *Breathing & Quieting the Mind.* While each book is completely independent from the next, the books do proceed along a developmental trajectory. One cannot begin any type of meditative practice without first learning to quiet their mind and focus on their breath. This volume goes a step further, both inward and upward.

The previous volume dealt with a more passive form of meditation wherein the intent is to clear the mind of thoughts and content that crowd one's consciousness in order to create space within which to experience the Unitive Reality beneath all the apparent multiplicity; or at the very least to quiet the deluge of thoughts and the chaotic nature of the mind in order to allow one to more fully relax and restore equilibrium. This volume deals more with active meditation practices where one uses an actual image, whether it is literal or formed in the mind, to access deeper levels of consciousness wherein all imagery eventually dissolves and one is left with a sensation of "touching" the ineffable and utterly Transcendent aspect of Reality. In short, the first volume is more focused on emptying the mind, while this volume is focused on creative ways to fill and focus the mind.

In either case, the objective of the entire "Jewish Meditation Series" is to make information available that can be utilized as tools of transformation. What is of primary interest is not merely what the great sages and *Tzadikim*/Righteous Ones said or wrote, but rather, what they did. What were the techniques they used to become the people they were? What was the formula that transformed ordinary people into extraordinary teachers? Of course, it goes without saying that a general approach of disciplined inner-work, deep commitment to Torah, patience, perseverance and choosing to live large is essential — but was there something else? What were the actual practices used by the sages to expand their awareness and open their hearts?

One such practice, as evidenced in many traditional sources, is the practice of visualizations. This is the practice of actively engaging the power of *Tziyur*/Imagination to animate, expand and flesh out ideas of the mind. This type of practice is recommended by many great rabbis, mystics and teachers throughout the ages *(See e.g.; Kabbalah teachers; Pri Eitz Chayim, Shar HaShabbos, Chap 3. Mahara M'panu, Maamor Tikkunei Teshuvah, Chap 3. Shaloh, Asarah Maamaros, Maamor 10. Chassidic teachers; Tanya, Iggeres HaKodesh, 11. Noam Elimelech, Tzetil Katan. Beir Mayim Chayim, Parshas Titzavah. Moar Vashemesh, Parshas Miketz. Mussar teachers; Ohr Yisrael, p. 22. Sha'arei Ohr, p.17. Michtav M'Eliyahu, 4; 252).*

In the realm of visualizations there are both externally based visuals where one uses an actual external object as a focal point, as well as inner creative visualizations where one creates an image within the mind's eye. In addition, there are also awareness practices with which one learns to become aware of what already exists within the inner screen of the mind's eye. Each of these methods will be explored in greater detail throughout the rest of this book, along with explanatory ideas and anecdotal events meant to contextualize the practices within the broader framework of Torah thought and spiritual practice.

CHAPTER 1

....

THE POWER OF
A VISUAL

BEFORE WE BEGIN TO EXPLORE THE PATH OF VISUAL
MEDITATION, LET US FIRST LAY DOWN SOME FUNDA-
MENTAL CONCEPTS ABOUT THE POWER OF THE IMAGE.

There is immense power to a visual image, whether it is an
actual 'thing' one is seeing or a mental image. The truth is
that it is quite difficult for the mind to tell the difference
between the two. The world we observe is similar to looking at a screen or observing a film, the only difference is
depth and dimension. What is the difference, for example,

between watching a film depicting a building and seeing an actual building? The difference is, essentially, volume and depth. But if the "real" building is seen from a distance and appears flat or if the film is in three dimensions the difference becomes less apparent. The point is that a visual, even one that is produced within our own mind's eye, can be, and in many ways is, just as real to us as the "real thing", and effectively has the same impact on our psyche.

At times an image, whether real or imagined, has an even greater effect on our inner psyche then we can fathom. It can even have a tangible physical effect on the body. A classic exercise to experience this point is to visualize, as clearly as possible, biting into a lemon. Most people will begin to salivate when imagining this as if they were actually biting into a sour yellow lemon.

This is all testament to the deep seated power of the image within our subconscious. In addition to the physiological responses elicited by internally generated imagery, there are also psychological implications of our own sense of self-image.

When a person finds himself doing, saying, or even thinking negative thoughts for example, despite his best intentions not to think about them, it is often because of a subliminal self-image ingrained in the subconscious regions of the mind that informs and impresses itself upon one's thoughts, words and actions.

When we are in the presence of certain conditions or stimuli (social and/or environmental) that awaken this 'image', the subconscious then dictates our actions, words and thoughts, defying our normal conscious control. One might tell one-self very strongly to stop doing, speaking or thinking about something, but words may not have a lasting effect. And when the stimulus returns one may spontaneously resort to one's unconscious reactivity.

Western man tends to focus on the word as opposed to the image, especially since the seventeenth century with its attendant advances of science and reason. There is a great amount of cultural emphasis placed on the intellectual and analytic approach to knowledge, self-transformation and personal development. As a result we end up ignoring the more intuitive and embodied forms of wisdom. Yet much of who we are is not informed by the word or logic alone, but rather by images that have been either consciously ob-served or subliminally picked up by osmosis from our sur-roundings and experiences.

Life is a continuous tension between our conscious, logical or verbal self, and our deeper subconscious imaginative self — a tension between word and image, between the right and left hemispheres of the brain.

There seems to be an inner dichotomy or existential split between knowing something intellectually and acting unconsciously that allows one to behave in a manner completely contrary to what one knows to be true. For instance, say a person understands with their conscious mind that anger is negative, that it is a prohibition of the Torah, that it erodes one's integrity, that it not only hurts the other person one is angry at, but it also hurts oneself — and yet sometimes when challenged and provoked one becomes angry. It's not that one chooses to become angry. Rather, it seems that it is a reactive, almost instinctual behavior. The question is why?

Why would one flare-up in anger if one knows that anger is detrimental? The answer is quite simple: What we know on a conscious level of "mind" is just one level of self. There are deeper levels of self, such as what is popularly referred to as the subconscious, from where a person acts and reacts purely on instinct.

A lot of what goes on within the subterranean levels of the self is not based on intellect or words, but rather on images, impressions and instincts. The human being first learns by observing and seeing, then by listening to sounds and words. In this way images lodge themselves into our subconscious, and most often they burrow into a place deeper than words can reach. Just like it is hard to un-train oneself from intellectual mistakes or misconceptions learned from a young age (what our sages call, "the learning of our youth"), it is in a way even harder to unlearn one's self-image and recreate alternative imagery in order to rectify or purify what was previously seen or envisioned, whether consciously or subliminally.

The question is: How do we undo or transform our deeper self so that our instincts should be consistent with our ideals?

BRINGING THE FORCE OF THE SUB-CONSCIOUS UNDER YOUR CONTROL:

We need, in effect, to transform our subconscious self. But how do we do that?

As mentioned, in our Western culture the primary method of self-transformation and personal development is based on the intellectual or analytical faculties. But words and concepts are only one form of stimulus, and often it is a fleeting or unconscious image that lodges itself into our psyche and holds sway over us much more than a word or idea that is read, heard, or thought about consciously.

Imagery registers deeper than words do. An image lodges itself into the subconscious and informs our actions, even when we are uncertain as to what causes such behavior. Imagery influences our emotional responses, and thus our life, in hidden and mysterious ways beneath the surface of our conscious mind and projected identity.

How do we rectify negative imagery that has embedded itself into the very structure of our psyche?

One way to undo negative or destructive imagery is to supply the mind with positive, constructive, holy imagery.

In other words: We must fight fire with fire. Only an image can heal or repair an image.

CREATING AN INNER IMAGE:

If your internal self-image is negative - if you see yourself as unsuccessful, sinful, or incompetent - you need to supplant this defeatist image with an empowering image of yourself as a capable person, or even a *Tzadik*/Righteous Person. One method to do this is by actively envisioning yourself as successful, pure, or holy. And thus, through the power of the creative imagination you can generate a more positive self-image.

Take the liturgical phrase "The soul that You have given me is pure," for instance. One way of activating and integrating this teaching is by working with it on a verbal and auditory level. This would be the method proposed by Reb Yisrael Salanter, the founder of the *Mussar* movement of ethical development. According to this method one would take this phrase, set it to a *Nigun*/Melody, and repeat it over and over again like a chant so that it may thereby penetrate the subconscious level of mind through repetition and melody.

Alternatively, what we are suggesting in this text is to take the phrase or idea and make it a visual experience. Actually try to imagine yourself as a *Tzadik*, an angel, the *Cohen Gadol*/High Priest serving in the Holy of Holies, or whatever actualized image you are seeking to manifest in your life. As unusual as it may seem this is a traditional practice of character development as brought down in the *Reishis Chochmah*, the *Noam Elimelech*, the *Kav Ha'yashar*, and the *Chidah*, to name a few.

In general, we need to learn to utilize our *Chush Ha'tziyur*/Sense of Visualization, which can have a deeper effect on the subconscious level of the mind than conceptual or analytical learning. Therefore the power of *Tziyur*/Creative Visualization is a much more effective means of transformation than an approach predicated only on intellectual understanding. One can learn something on the level of ideas, but the developmental effect is much deeper when one is able to create an image within the imagination, as suggested in the writings of many masters of contemporary *Mussar*. Through the method of internal visualization what we know in our minds becomes animated within our hearts, and as a result the information is more fully integrated into the whole of our being *(R. Simcha Zisal of Kelm Kisvei Ha'Saba M'Kelm 1, p. 143-144. R. Eliyahu Dessler Michtav M'Eliyahu 1, p. 296. 4. p. 252-253).*

Essentially, what we need to do is to connect ideas with images. That way the concepts are able to enter into our whole being in a more profound and lasting way. Through a visual image we can take what we know intellectually on a conscious level, and make it "known" intuitively on an affective and even embodied level.

What we know intellectually becomes more real for us in direct proportion to the number of senses we are able to include in the act of integral apprehension. If you can touch a strawberry for instance, if you can smell or see it, it becomes much more real to you than simply hearing about it. Most of the intellectual information we retain is comprised of ideas that were somehow, either intentionally or accidentally, attached to visual impressions, or possibly to one of the other senses. Often, we remember what we learned because at the time we learned it we also saw something memorable, or even saw something related to the idea.

This understanding (i.e., that ideas are best retained when combined with some form of sensory input) provides us with a method to deepen any learning or experience we may have by coupling an idea with an image.

For example, one way to deepen our prayer practice is to re-live the experiences we are recounting as we are reciting the prayers. For example, when we are singing the song at the Splitting of the Sea we should, as the *Chidah* suggests

(Avodas HaKodesh, Tziporen Shamir, Chap 24. See also Hachsharas Ha'Avreichim, Chap 7), imagine as if we are standing on the shore and the sea is parting before our very eyes and we are passing through, being saved from the onrush of the water and the attacking enemies in pursuit. And thus in the process of harnessing our creative imagination every part of us is able to participate in the prayer experience — we are all accounted for, so to speak.

FOUR LEVELS OF AN IDEA: FROM INTELLECT TO IMAGINATION:

We will now explore the process of developing an idea or concept from an intellectual understanding to an animated image. There are ideas that we can conceptualize in our mind, this is the level of *Muskal*/Intellect. Then, once we truly secure the idea in our mind, the idea becomes *Mutba*/ Impressed or Imprinted within our minds. So much so that these ideas, when truly grasped, attain the level of *Murgash*/ Sense. We can actually sense or feel the ideas in a tangible way. And then, there is the fourth movement of ideational integration where ideas move from being felt into the state of *Temunah*/Seen, as in a picture. At this stage, the idea is so thoroughly ingrained and sensed so strongly that we start 'seeing' it wherever we look.

These are the four levels of integrating an idea, from intellect to imagination:

1) *Muskal* – Intellect
2) *Mutba* – Imprint
3) *Murgash* – Sense or Feeling
4) *Temuna* – Seen (Picture)

Ordinarily, a person may look at the surface of a physical object without registering any deeper significance, pattern, or narrative within which the object exists. But on a deeper level, as a result of going through the integral process outlined above, one becomes able to perceive the significance, pattern, or meaning inherent within the object itself. It is, in effect, a different way of seeing.

For example, say a person studies the laws of gravity. First he secures a solid understanding of the basic principle until the principle becomes ingrained. Then, through contemplation, he can literally sense this natural principle in his own experience of life. Until, finally wherever he looks he is able to see the laws of gravity in effect. He is so excited and senses the idea so deeply that he sees it everywhere and within everything.

Of course, a deeper example would be of a person who meditates on the idea that Hashem's 'hand' guides his life. He can understand this abstractly on an intellectual level; then, through contemplation it becomes imprinted progressively deeper until he can actually sense or feel it; and finally he sees this truth manifesting on every level of his life. So, while one person may see just a red light at a traffic stop for example, the person who has been meditating on the idea of Divine Providence 'sees' the guiding Hand of Hashem telling him to slow down or stop his trajectory along his current life path.

That's not to say that we should all be 'seeing signs' everywhere and in everything all the time, at least not in the literal sense. What we are suggesting here is the development of a more poetic sensibility in which one can appreciate and interpret the text of their life in a more symbolic, aesthetic and meaningful way.

The ultimate objective of this practice is for abstract ideas within the mind to be 'seen', and thus experienced, in real life. The *Zohar* tells us that the gate of *Kedusha*/Holiness is the power of imagination *(Zohar 1, p. 103b)*. A rectified and properly engaged imagination is holy and noble.

One definition of a *Chasid*/Pious Individual is one who maintains control over their mind. This includes, among other things, the power to visualize events or occurrences clearly; for example, the giving of the Torah or the construction of the Holy Temple *(Kuzari, Ma'amar 3; 5)*. R. Yechezkel Levenstein teaches that the difference between a *Tzadik* and the opposite of a *Tzadik* is that a *Tzadik* is someone who has the ability to visualize holy things in his mind as vividly as if they were real *(Sichas Musar, 26)*.

A *Tzadik* is one who has transformed, or, in reality — revealed, the innate conditioning of their consciousness. They are no longer slave to the mentalities and thought processes (i.e., the images) that they received, albeit unconsciously, while growing up. They have rewired their circuit board, so to speak. And through this process they have enabled their imagination to flow from the inside-out, rather than just chasing after that which is externally validated. In this state of mind one chooses the contents and functions of their imagination, not the other way around — as that would be mere fantasy.

In general, negative imagery functions from the outside-in, where the world around us chooses our imagery for us. This is the normal course of developmental growth and ideational integration, where outside stimulus impacts and imprints our internal screen, which has been unconsciously constructed and created through years of self-centered and ego-based reality.

Yet, once a person has truly substituted this (natural) negative imagery with creative, positive and consciously chosen imagery, thus transforming not just the contents of his or her mind, but the actual screen or context of the mind itself, then even impressions that come from the outside-in will be viewed and interpreted as positive, holy, and in alignment with the renewed foundation of one's perception.

In other words, once how we see the world has been purified and transformed it no longer matters as much what is being seen. This is only true regarding a fully evolved individual who has utterly transformed his or her way of looking at themselves and the world. For example, such a person can look at a strikingly beautiful person and only utter praise to Hashem for creating such beauty, rather than being consumed by illicit lust or repressed perversions.

But how does one begin to reprogram their subconscious self-image? How does one use their imagination to manifest a more redemptive reality?

THE MENORAH IMAGE:

Our personal/inner and collective/outer redemption begins with redeeming our imagination. In order to achieve this we first need to be able to use our imagination to create positive, holy and constructive imagery that will inspire us towards such a redeemed reality.

Jewish history from Avraham/Abraham up until the destruction of the second Temple has been characterized as the "action" period. This period was distinguished by the practice of bringing physical offerings to the Temple as a ritual method of transforming ourselves and absolving misdeeds. After the decline of the Temple period we have been bringing the "offerings of our mouths" (i.e., prayer) in place of material (i.e., animal or agricultural) offerings. Our main spiritual technologies for the past 2,000 years have therefore been prayer and study — i.e. text, speech and words. But the next phase, G-d willing, in our meta-historical journey is that of Redemption, and Redemption is connected to a subtler garment of thought — i.e., imagery and the imagination.

To provide an example of such a transformative use of the symbolic imagination, we will now explore some interesting and inspiring dimensions of one of Judaism's most recognizable symbols — the Menorah.

The Menorah is one of the most prominent symbols of Jewish culture and history. In fact for many years the most conspicuous art adorning synagogues was the image of the Menorah. Long before the symbol of the Six-Pointed Star, known today as the Magen David, the image of the Menorah was the popular Jewish symbol par excellence.

The Menorah was not only an image used to symbolize or define a Jewish space or person, but the Menorah was also used as a mental/visual aid. In some older *Siddurim*/Prayer Books chapter 67 of *Tehilim*/Psalms *(Lamnatzeich B'niginos)* is written out in the shape of a Menorah, which was, at times throughout history, also referred to as the Shield of David, the Magen David. It is taught that King David would go out to battle with this image (i.e., the Psalm in the shape of a Menorah) engraved on his shield *(Midbar Kadmos, Ma'areches Dalet, 22)*. In this way, the image of the Menorah, combined with the words of the Psalm, was accorded a kind of amuletic spiritual power. This is a prime example of the textual and literal cognitive capacities working together to create something 'magical' and transformative.

Chapter 67 is a very powerful chapter in *Tehilim*/Psalms and in fact throughout the ages many *Segulos*/Spiritual Omens were attached to its reading. Specifically, reading or writing it in the image of the Menorah was considered most efficacious, as there are essentially seven verses in the Psalm. Each verse is therefore another branch in the Menorah. This reading/visualization is considered a form of protection from all harm to ensure that one finds favor in the eyes of both G-d and man. The verses of this Psalm were therefore understood to take on a powerful protective energy when they were written out in the geometric pattern of the Menorah and used as a visual tool for meditation and focus in the face of danger or fear.

The image of the Menorah is also seen by the prophet Zechariah (Chap 4) and understood as a signifier of the second *Beis HaMikdash*/Holy Temple, as well as being an allusion to the Third and final *Beis HaMikdash*.

In this way, the Menorah is understood not only as a symbol of our ancient past (i.e., the glory of the First and Second Temples), but of our redemptive future as well, culmi-nating in the rebuilding of the Third Holy Temple, which will be, as prophesied by the prophets, "a house of prayer for all peoples."

Today, in exile, the Menorah is primarily related to as a sym-bol of *Chanukah*. Appropriately, Chanukah is a holiday that commemorates a past event by bringing it into one's pres-ent reality through a variety of symbolic and ritual actions, while at the same time it contains and communicates the prophetic anticipation of a brighter future and redeemed world.

The word *Chanukah* means "dedication", as it was following the defilement of the Temple that there was an eight-day re-dedication Ceremony with kindled lights and festivities *(Maharsha, Shabbos 21b)*. The root of the word *Chanukah* can also be seen as coming from the word *Chinuch*/Education *(Yavatz)*. Yet, *Chinuch* can also mean preparation and train-ing, being as it is the beginning of the revelation of these intense lights, which will only be fully manifest in the times of *Moshiach*, when the inner light of all existence will be revealed for all to see.

"In the time of ultimate redemption all Holidays will be rendered superfluous except for Chanukah..." *(See Yerushalmi Taanis 2:12)*. In this way both Chanukah and the Meno-rah can be considered as having the quality and symbolic charge of *Moshiach* energy and redemptive potential. They are both tangible and experiential symbols of our bright but broken past, and even brighter future. The Menorah is thus an image of hope, of light, and of the potential to light up the darkness in order to dispel negativity.

Interestingly, the Menorah is also one of the most prominent symbols of Judaism in the eyes of the outside world as it is publicly displayed throughout Chanukah in cities and capitals throughout the world. It is an image for Jews, and by extension for the entire world, of light over might, and a reminder of how a tiny amount of light can bring so much hope and joy even in the darkest times.

It is for all of these reasons that the Menorah is a perfect symbolic image with which to re-program our unconscious imagery and all of the negative narratives that come along with it. This may very well explain the Rabbi's insistence that the private practice of a family lighting their Menorah for Chanukah be made public by displaying the lit candelabra for all to see. In recent times this practice of public Menorah lighting has taken on an altogether different application, with Menorahs being placed in city squares and public spaces, not just being displayed in private windows. The initiator of this very contemporary practice of public Menorah lightings was the legendary *Tzadik*, the Lubavitcher Rebbe, may his memory be a source of blessings, whose life dream was to usher in a redeemed world, a *Moshiach* world. It could be that, on a deeper level, the initial opposition towards this initiative was a battle between the old and the new, between those who, while perhaps praying for a redeemed world, did not wish to facilitate its manifestation through tangible actions; believing instead that Jews were better off staying out of sight and out of the mind of the general public. In contrast to this way of thinking the Rebbe was strongly convinced that in order for this world and for us to be vessels to receive and reflect this 'new' reality, we as Jews must be proud and open with our Judaism. Thereby generating ritual and mythic 'images' that awaken the imagination and train people to think, feel, speak and act differently.

The image of a lit Menorah displayed publicly in the darkest time of the year is a perfect visual aid to help us all transition into a *Moshiach* world.

THE IMAGE VS. THE SOUND:

In addition to the specific image of the Menorah it is taught that the era of the *Moshiach* in general is connected with a visually stimulated and rectified imagination. It will be a time when we no longer have to 'hear' the Word of G-d to sense spirituality, but rather it will be a time when, "All flesh together will see the word of Hashem as it is spoken." We will actually 'see' the presence of Hashem.

The *Zohar* is essentially a *Moshiach* text, as it says that,

"With this book of the *Zohar* we will leave the exile with mercy" *(Zohar 3, p. 124b).* The formulaic opening of many passages in the *Zohar* begins with the words "*Ta Chazi/* Come and See.*" This is in contrast to the Gemarah, the Babylonian Talmud, which was a text created in and connected to the state of exile. Regarding the exilic energy of the Gemara it is understood that the scriptural saying, "He causes me to dwell in darkness," is referring to the Babylonian Talmud itself *(Sanhedrin, 24a).* Following this line of thought we can now understand on a deeper level why the standard opening of many passages in the Gemara is the well-known refrain, "*Ta Shema/*Come and Hear."

Now, as we are in exile we "hear" words of spirituality; higher awareness will emerge when we can actually "see" the reality of spirituality. Now we are able to "see" physicality and (only) "hear" about spirituality. But there will come a time when spirituality will be so real to us that we will "see" Hashem's presence in the world.

TAKING CONTROL OF OUR IMAGINATION:

As mentioned, a *Chassid* and a *Tzadik* is one who, among other qualities, has control over his or her *Koach HaD-imyon/*Power of Imagination and is in charge of their *Chush HaTziyur/*Sense of Visualization. Indeed, this is precisely the aspiration and goal of this book — to learn to control the power of our imagination through visualization, thereby not allowing ourselves to be completely powerless under the total control of our subconscious mind.

Most times, when imagery floats up to our consciousness it arises automatically and involuntarily. Seemingly random images appear to flow directly from the deeper recesses of our mind, which, as mentioned earlier, are connected with unconscious impressions and are therefore not necessarily chosen by us for conscious contemplation. It is most often not a choice a person consciously makes to visualize or imagine this or that; in fact, it is often as if a particular image is forced upon a person by their own subconscious. The aspiration of these visualization practices is to achieve some measure of hegemony over our power of imagination and our *Chush HaTziyur.*

AUTOMATIC IMAGINATION *VS.* ACTIVE IMAGINATION:

To clarify the issue a little further some new terminology will be offered and developed for the purposes of this text. A distinction must be made between what we will call "Automatic Imagination" versus what we will refer to as "Active Imagination."

Automatic Imagination is the level of imagination that

everyone experiences. Active Imagination is the level of imagination that these visualization practices seek to enable us to access and attain.

Even people who think they lack the ability to visualize are only referring to the "active imagination", and not the "automatic imagination" to which everyone has access to greater or lesser degrees.

Automatic imagination, which everyone has, is usually grounded in the ego and in what is immediately observed and experienced within one's environment. Active imagination is something that one needs to work on and develop; it is a reality that is created from within.

Let's explain:

Say that a person is an artist, musician, writer, or even business person. What drives the artist who is sitting alone in his or her studio to finish their painting, or the writer to get up early and plug away at their manuscript, or the business person to invest? At this point there is nothing yet to show for their effort and it will take some time before the project is finished and one can reap the benefits of their labor. Yes, of course we must take into account the reality that artistic people are often driven by an inner need to be expressive. But beyond that, or even before that, on a more ego-based and unconscious level, what inspires the drive to exercise one's will in any given direction?

To more fully understand this, let us first explore another process-oriented model of ideational development.

First, there is the sense of *Moach*/Mind and intellect. Then there is the *Chush HaTziyur*/the Ability to Visualize or the *Koach M'damah*/the Power of Imagination. This results in the activation of the *Cheshek*/the strong Desire to manifest that which has been imagined and/or visualized. One's aspirations and goals therefore move from the realm of being an idea, to being something that one can visualize, to a strong desire that impels one to act in order to achieve and manifest their initial idea.

The way it works is as follows. You have an idea or an idea is presented to you. The more you think about it the more your *Chush HaTziyur* is activated. If you are a writer, for example, this is what creates the pull that makes you sit down to write. You start to visualize or "see in your mind" how the end result of a project is going to look, or even how you are going to feel about it upon its completion, or how you are going to enjoy your next vacation with the money you earn. Some people, those more anchored in a fragile ego that needs constant boosting, will even envision how other people are going to complement their work, the applause and praise they are going to get. This kind of projective visualization often plays an initiatory role in inspiring one's actions or decisions regarding how they are going to direct their energy and resources. It is therefore of the utmost importance that one is in control, or at least in alignment, with their imagined desires, as these inner projections will most likely influence their behavior on a fundamental level.

EVERYONE VISUALIZES:

As mentioned, everyone has the power of *Tziyur*/Visualization to some extent. For instance, in the case of someone who sits and learns Torah all day, when they are unable to understand a particular concept or teaching and all the toil feels hopeless, the ego may step in and generate a beautiful *Tziyur*/Image of the pleasure they will receive when they finally understand what they have been learning. Or, if they are even more steeped in their ego, a visual may be generated within them of a future in which they have become a world-renowned Torah scholar. And if their ego is their primary level of soul, they may even visualize the accolades that they will receive because of their great scholarship.

Essentially, once you are committed to a project, whatever it may be, then your *Tziyur* generates imagery of the end result and how you are going to feel about it. And as a result your *Cheshek*/Desire is aroused to act in a manner that seeks to manifest that which has been visualized. The more active your *Tziyur*, the more forceful your *Cheshek*. The more you can "see" how it is going to look at the end, or how you are going to feel about it when it is done, the more impetus you will have to move forward. Principally, the more *Tziyur* one generates, the more *Cheshek* they will mobilize towards the manifestation of their imagination or desire.

This is all within the realm of the Automatic Imagination, based primarily upon externally induced *Tziyurrim*/Images. The idea is set in one's mind either from outside the mind, or because it was physically observed, and then the *Chush HaTziyur* takes over. This type of visualization is automatic and flows directly from the state you are currently at. If (as most people) you function primarily on the level of ego and your ego is attached to the narrative that you are an artist, you start painting and your *Tziyur* imagines the finished project and perhaps even the accolades you may receive from the future viewers.

But, the level of *Tziyur* that we are aspiring to achieve is one of Active Imagination. This level of awareness can be defined simply as that level wherein you have control over your power of *Tziyur*, and not that it has power over you. As a result your guiding imagery arises from within your own mind and value systems, and not from the outside world or environment.

Because Automatic Imagination is spontaneous and involuntarily so long as a person is still anchored in their ego, which most people are, their imagination will be filled with images concerned with bolstering their ego. Thus, the writer visualizes being published and praised, the artist being critically acclaimed and applauded, the business person becoming rich, and so forth.

Automatic Imagination is unconsciously imprinted and reactive and is thus not self-generated. The imagery attaches itself to a narrative, a sight or an experience. The writer has already defined himself or herself as a writer, the artist as an artist, and the Torah scholar as a student of Torah. The Automatic Imagination then confirms or reinforces, sometimes grandiosely, this already arrived at perception. The writer 'sees' himself writing the greatest book of the century and being recognized for such a feat, the artist 'sees' himself as a great artist, and the scholar 'sees' himself as a great scholar.

But the real *Chush HaTziyur* we are aspiring to acquire is self-generative and not automatic. It is the power to visualize 'anything', and does not need to attach itself to a narrative. It is completely free and not restrictive, as it exists within the person him or herself.

Many people who already have a narrative — be it an artist, writer, businessperson, or scholar — are basing their narrative on a set of influences and imprints chosen for them by their parents or society. Their Automatic *Tziyur* then merely serves to confirm or validate this story. Many people who have jobs will daydream vividly and visualize themselves becoming the boss of the company. Or if someone has met a person who they feel could potentially be their spouse, they will proceed to imagine a life together with that person. Again, the greater the *Tziyur* the stronger the *Cheshek*.

But how many people without a job can imagine themselves with a job? Or how many people who are not in a relationship can visualize themselves in a relationship? This is where Creative Visualization and the Active Imagination come in and can be immensely helpful.

Active Imagination is defined by the ability to imagine something that has no narrative as of yet. It is a method of visualization that does not inherently attach itself to what a person is doing or seeing in the immediate moment, it does not just arise automatically, and, most importantly, it is an art that needs to be practiced and mastered.

The more we practice the art of creative visualization, the more control we will gain over this limitless potential and the more we can use it for creating positivity and blessing in our lives and in the lives of others. For ultimately, the clearer the imagery that we are able to generate from within, the more *Cheshek* we will have to fuel the fires of our passions and dreams, making it that much more probable that we will actually be able to realize our goals.

THREE PURPOSES TO HARNESS THE POWER OF IMAGINATION:

In summation there are three overarching reasons for the need to work with and harness our power of *Dimyon*/Imagination.

1) One is so that intellectual ideas of the mind become experiential and fully integrated within one's whole being. When we can imagine in the mind's eye what we learn with the 'left-brain', the ideas become more alive and tangible. Visualization endows ideas with immediacy.

As a result, not only do the ideas themselves become more animated they also become more deeply ingrained into our subconscious, thereby penetrating the deeper recesses of our soul. When we connect an idea with an image the information permeates the psyche and is thus holistically transformative.

Imagination is a 'right-brain' activity that reaches the subconscious regions of the mind. In addition to creative visualizations and imagery, music, rhythm, chant, or for that matter any repetitive or ritual action can also penetrate the subconscious. But in our text we will be primarily concerned with the visual methods of accessing and influencing the deeper levels of the psyche using the power of visualizations and imagery.

2) The second benefit of the practice of creative visualization is that we can exchange unconsciously absorbed negative imagery with consciously selected positive imagery. By and large, life is a continuous struggle between the word (i.e., the revealed and comprehensible reality) and the image (the visual messages we take in, albeit mostly subliminally, that become deeply embedded within our subconscious). By proactively choosing to generate positive imagery we are substituting one set of uncontrolled, un-chosen, and mostly unhealthy images, with carefully chosen, creative, holy and healthy imagery. In this way we are able to 'design' a new 'set' within which our reality-play occurs.

All of the ingrained imagery we encounter and absorb collects in our subconscious and forms a backdrop and prism through which we apprehend and interpret the world around us. Unfortunately, for the most part this filter is naturally and biologically created (unconsciously) and stimulated by the ego, which is driven by the self-centered sense of survival and perpetuation. Keep in mind that this filter is being crafted and molded from the moment of birth, and even prior. For this reason, what this filter/prism sees when it looks around is a world full of possibilities to feed and aggrandize the ego. From a soul's perspective, rather than an ego's, these 'possibilities' are then characterized as temptations and distractions from one's ultimate purpose. These become, therefore, unhealthy, or at least spiritually unproductive stimuli in the form of images and impressions. The world then seems full of enticements and desires, in which the ego would love to partake and indulge.

Here is a simple daily life example of how this works. A person is walking down the street and sees a nice car, person, or object. At this point he does not only just see the "car", he sees the car through his projected filter and prism. And so, when he sees the car he sees a narrative attached to the car: How nice it would be to own the car. Or, perhaps he feels jealous of the person's wealth that is driving the car. Or, maybe he imagines what he would do with this car. This is our 'negative' ego driven prism that is projected and superimposed upon the object that is being observed. Yet, the object itself, like everything else in Hashem's creation, is perfect and holy. It is only the overlaid narrative of our unconsciously constructed screens, filters and prisms that render the object as negative in relation to what our soul really needs. A car is just a car, like a person is just a person.

There is what we see, and there is how we see. What we see is determined by how we see. How we see is influenced by what we have seen previously and unconsciously assimilated into our self-image. By consciously generating positive and healthy visual content for our mind to meditate on, we are, in effect, altering the very context through which we see in the first place. We will therefore be less victimized and tempted by the things we see in the world, as we will have transformed the very apparatus through which we encounter and interpret Hashem's creation, which includes everything, the beautiful as well as the apparent ugly. Once we have effected such a transformation of how we see, we will be able to see Hashem's presence in all things, rather than having to constantly hide and shield ourselves from the world. The primary method through which to initiate this shift of consciousness is through generating positive and healthy visual imagery to replace the unconsciously collected and constructed self-images that one has allowed to dominate and determine their existence up to this point.

The ramifications of this transformation are immense and all-encompassing, impacting one on all levels — physically, spiritually, mentally and emotionally. This positive imagination can have practical physical health benefits, as well as psychological, financial and emotional benefits. Since our future is largely contingent on the self-image and inner screen through which we see the world in the present, changing one's frame changes their story and self-image. And, as we have established, one's self-image determines the role they are empowered to play in their life story.

Instead of reinforcing negative, unconsciously constructed self-images based on one's past experience, one may replace these broken images with visions of wholeness, health, vitality, confidence and competence. Once you begin to proactively imagine yourself as healthy, happy, holy, and well-adjusted, goodness and blessing will surely follow.

This process will radically transform your spiritual make-up and self-image from the inside-out. By deliberately choosing to visualize positive, productive, holy, and empowering imagery one can begin to cancel-out all the previous negative imagery related to oneself or the world in general that one may have picked up subliminally over the course of their life. When one does this they are consciously counteracting the toxic and debilitating effects of the negative self-images they may have accumulated throughout the years. So now instead of helplessly projecting and living out the predictable patterns of a negative self-image, one may begin to live consciously and creatively from a place of health, wealth, and knowledge of self.

3) The third purpose for cultivating the power of visualization is to acclimate ourselves to be open and receptive to more prophetic-like intuition. Not prophecy in terms of predicting the future, or speaking in the Name of Hashem what should or should not be done; but rather, "prophecy" characterized as deep, penetrating, personal insight. Through this level of inner vision we are able to gain a deeper awareness into our soul, our purpose and our distinct mission in life. This will then help us co-create a life lived in deeper connection with Hashem from moment to moment.

In order to open ourselves up to such deeper/higher prophetic-like insight we need to first secure a complete hegemony over our power of imagination.

Imagination, left to its own devices, is "snake–like", empty, void of substance and overly exaggerated. It is thus the root of all temptation and negativity. This is the power of imagination when it has control over us. This is similar to the state of Adam and *Chavah*/Eve when the *Nachash*/Snake tempted them with grandiose visions of greatness that were completely unrealistic and totally within the realm of fantasy. Paradoxically, the *Nachash*, who is the source of humanity's (potential) downfall, is also connected to their ultimate redemption, as evidenced by the fact that it has the same exact *Gematria*/Numerical Equivalent as the word *Moshiach*/Messiah. We can see from this alphanumeric resonance that the power of imagination is the key to transformation, whether positive or negative. It is ultimately neutral, like any other power or energy. It all depends on the way it is wielded by the human being.

The Hebrew letters that spell the word *Nachash* are also the same letters that spell the word *Choshen*/The Mystical Breastplate worn by the Cohen *Gadol*/High Priest. Embedded within the breastplate were 12 different gemstones inscribed with the names of the Tribes of Israel. The breastplate, as detailed in the Torah, was used for 'visual' divination, as it were. When the leaders of the Tribes had an important question, such as whether or not to go to war, they would consult the Breastplate as it was worn by the High Priest. The letters on the *Choshen* would light up in a pattern to spell out an answer to their question. The *Chosh-*

en was therefore a visual divination device used by the High Priest to receive a form of prophetic insight and instruction.

In contrast to this kind of priestly divination that uses an external visual aid, the prophet, being the most spiritually evolved person, receives their prophecy through the medium of their own rectified imagination, often in the form of a *Chizayon*/Dream-like Vision.

Imagination is thus the medium through which prophecy flows. A flow of Divine intelligence emanates from the Creator, as it were. It is first absorbed by the mind of the prophet and then further assimilated into his consciousness through the power of his imagination *(Morah Nevuchim, 2; 36)*. For a transmission to be properly and accurately received the vessel that receives the transmission must be transparent. Humility is therefore a requisite for prophecy.

A prophet is one who harnesses and controls his imagination during the day, proactively and mindfully choosing the images that fill his inner vision and combine to create his self-image. In this way, rather than being a servant of his ego-oriented subconscious, the prophet is able to cleanse the doors of his perception rendering his self/ego transparent to his soul, and his soul transparent to Hashem.

Such is the positive power of imagination. When it is guided by reason, it can be the medium for prophetic insight, and the means through which all faith flows.

Ultimately, we are either riding the waves of our imagination, as it were, controlling and guiding their currents, in which case it is greatly valuable; or we are being uncontrollably pulled out to sea, so to speak, by our imagination, in which case it is less than valueless *(Morah Nevuchim, 2; 30)*. When we are able to steer our imagination it can be used as a springboard to catapult us beyond our ordinary rationality, allowing us to enter into a realm beyond mind, a realm of intuitive awareness and prophetic-like experience.

True prophecy is no longer readily available. Yet, the contemporary alternative to the prophet of old is the *Chassid/* Pious One. The *Chassid* is one who has control over his or her *Dimyon*. He is able to conjure up images in his imagination, such as meta- historical events like the exodus from Egypt or the Splitting of the Sea, with ease. And it is precisely through his imagination that he is able to truly experience Divine love and awe *(Kuzari, 3; 5)*.

Through the power of imagination and visualization the meditator taps into the actual Divine flow, as it were, and creates a fusion or channel between himself the Source. In the words of The *Recanti* (1223–1290), "When the *Chassid* would ponder the deepest secrets of the universe he would imagine, with the power of visualization, the ideas as being literally present. And when he would attach his soul to the One Above in a concentrated matter, the lofty ideas would overflow and become revealed to him automatically. This is similar to a person who taps a wellspring of water and then the water gushes forth in all directions" *(Ricanti, Parshas Vayechi (Levush Malchus), p. 37b).*

Although to clarify, there is a marked distinction between the prophet and the *Chassid*. Whereas the prophet experiences a *Chizayon*, an 'objective' image or a 'revelation,' perceived within his Imagination, the *Chassid*, by contrast, creates the image through his power of imagination. A *Chizayon*, while also observed as an image, does not come through the actions of the meditator. Rather, it is a form of 'revelation' observed within the imagination, as an image. In either case, both need to first gain hegemony over their imagination in order to achieve such heightened states of perception, as only one who has full control over his *Dimyon* can experience, observe and truly identify the image for what it really is.

All in all, by learning to harness, control and channel one's *Dimyon*, one learns how to authentically experience prophetic-like insight. By being able to control our imagination the imagination itself becomes a springboard to propel us beyond conventional rationality, and affords us the ability to enter into a realm beyond comprehension.

CHAPTER 2

THREE TYPES
OF VISUALS

1
CREATIVE
2
OBJECTIVE
3
AWARENESS-ENHANCING

VISUALIZATIONS ENCOMPASS VARIOUS FORMS. To further clarify and contextualize this we will posit that there are three primary types of visualization. There are self-generated visuals, object-oriented visuals based on actual images, and awareness-enhancing visualization practices.

1) Creative (Self-Generated)
2) Objective (Externally Focused)
3) Awareness

In the creative, self-generated visual you generate the image in your own mind using the power of *Dimyon*/Imagination. This is also referred to as imagining or creating an image in the mind and maintaining that image for a period of time, engraving it into the mind.

In the object-oriented visual you are actually using a physical image as a focal point, a stepping-stone, or a metaphor from which you move beyond the image itself. This can be a particular color, the Chanukah lights, the sky, a tree or river, and so on.

In the third form of visualization you are becoming aware of internal imagery or color patterns that already exist within the mind's eye. These patterns or palettes appear to you when you close your eyes. In this case, the purpose of the "visualization" is to become aware of what is already present.

PART ONE

CREATIVE

CHAPTER ONE

....

CREATIVE VISUALIZATION:

A TRUE MASTER OF LIFE IS ONE WHO HAS CONTROL OVER THEIR CONSCIOUS THOUGHTS, WORDS, ACTIONS *(AT LEAST MOST OF THE TIME)*, AND MOST IMPORTANTLY — HIS IMAGINATION.

In general, there is negative imagination and positive imagination. The essential difference between the two is whether the imagery comes from the inside-out, i.e., from a deep understanding of who we are and what we can achieve, which is noble and positive, or if the imagery and imagination is externally imposed from the outside-in, i.e., based upon the unquestioned norms or expectations of society, which is, in the contemporary world, primarily ego-driven and self-serving.

To illustrate this complex dynamic we must look no further than the first few chapters of the Book of Genesis in the Torah. Regarding the serpent from the Garden of Eden the text states that the snake was *Arum (Bereishis, 3; 1)*. Literally, the word *Arum* means 'sly', implying a type of manipulative sneakiness *(Berachos, 17a, Rashi)*. The snake, writes the Sforno, had an overactive imagination and was trapped in the world of fantasy.

Arum also means 'naked', as fantasy is based primarily on surface impressions and externally oriented imagery. Additionally, one's distorted fantasies are windows through which others can see where a person is truly at, as expressed through their naked imagination and distorted desires. This is hinted at in the Torah when one considers that it is only after Adam and *Chavah*/Eve have succumbed to the Snake's sneakiness and eaten from the Tree of Knowledge that they realize they are in fact naked.

The Snake (i.e., overactive fantasy) inculcates Chavah with grandiose visions, telling her that Hashem told her not to eat from the tree because, "Hashem knows that when you eat from it your eyes will be opened, and you will be like god" *(Bereishis, 3; 5).* The snake (i.e. false imagination) attempts to infuse Chavah with a pompous and presumptuous vision of self by telling her that the reason she is told not to eat from the Tree of Knowledge is because if she does, she will become all-powerful.

The Snake, which represents the over-active imagination, clouds Chavah's (and our) true vision of reality. And this voice, the voice of the snake, is an 'external' voice, a voice that does not come from deep within, but rather, a voice that comes from 'outside' the self — the voice of an external 'snake'.

The Snake, or the external image and voice of 'fantasy', distorts Chavah's imagination and instills within her a false self-image and illusory fantasy.

The 'Snake', and the world of negative/external imagination and fantasy, is all around us — all the time. We are continually being bombarded with unhealthy images and messages from the popular culture and mass media, whether through explicit advertisements or subliminal imagery. After many years of being bombarded with imagery and stimulus these images accumulate in the storehouse of our subconscious mind. As a result, certain experiences can trigger this imagery and bring it up into our conscious awareness like a belch or burp. These are messages or images that come from the outside and enter into our subconscious.

Healthy imagination, on the other hand, works from the inside–out. When our imagination is aligned with our inner understanding, wisdom, and experience, we can then be assured that our visions and desires are organically generated and authentic, and are, therefore, not externally 'implanted' within us from outside of ourselves.

Within the body there are four basic 'parts' as it were. They are the four vessels or structures of the body, from the most inner to the most outer. They are: the *Atzamos*/Bones, the *Gidin*/Sinews, the *Basar*/Flesh, and the (outer layer of) *Ohr*/Skin.

These four bodily dimensions are reflections of the four types of Mind, or the four forms of intelligence that guide the body. The first three types of intelligence are: *Chochmah*/Wisdom and Intuition, *Binah*/Reason and Cognition, and *Da'as*/Experiential Knowledge and Awareness. We will speak briefly about these first three before introducing the fourth type of Intelligence.

Chochmah is, essentially, the 'right brain' — the creative and intuitive aspects of mind. Binah is more representative of the 'left brain' — deciphering, understanding, and breaking down ideas into comprehensive language. Da'as is primarily located in the frontal lobe of the brain — it is the executive mind, the part of the brain that chooses, implements and decides. Overall, these are the three primary forms of intelligence.

In addition there is the fourth element of the mind and
that is the *Koach Ha'M'damah*/the Power of Imagination.
This fourth form of intelligence is the skin of the mind, the
external or most projective form of mind. In summary, here
are the four forms of intelligence and their corresponding
body parts:

Atzamos/Bones — *Chochmah*/Wisdom
Gidin/Sinews — *Binah*/Cognition
Basar/Flesh — *Da'as*/Knowledge
Ohr/Skin — *M'damah*/Imagination

In this model, the power of imagination is the most external capacity of the intellect, referred to as the skin of the
mind. The more core faculties of mind are a person's wisdom, his understanding, and his integral awareness. This
hierarchy is unrelated to another model of mind that deals
with the dialectic between surface conscious vs. deeper unconscious parts of the psyche. In that model, imagination is
lodged deeper within a person's psyche then mere intellect.
Rather, this schematic hierarchy is measured in terms of
evolution- i.e., what makes us human, the complexity of
our thought process. And from that perspective the model
moves from the inside-out —first from Chochmah, then
Binah, then Da'as, then *Dimyon*. This model is concerned
with the deeper structures that provide the underlying context within which one's unconscious images are interpreted
and assigned meaning based on one's worldview and perspective (i.e., upon their Chochmah, Binah, and Da'as).

Much like how the shape of the skin is formed by the flesh, the flesh, in turn, is formed by the sinews and bones of the body. Similarly, imagination without wisdom, understanding, and balanced awareness is empty of any true, lasting or constructive form. People who have overactive, "skin deep" imaginations create all types of "demons" and "monsters" crippling them or, alternatively, they create grandiose illusions that put them totally out of touch with reality.

In fact, according to the Rambam, the root of all negative behavior is when a person simply follows his (skin-deep) imagination *(Rambam, Morah Nevuchim, 2; 12. Likutei Moharan 1, 25; 5)*. This is the amoral compass of a shallow, skin-deep person who lives only "for" the immediate now (not in the now, but for the now). Whatever his eyes can see and his hands can touch is the extent of his reality. There is only the present moment with no larger picture or sense of consequence or causality. If something looks tempting in the isolated present, divorced from any sense of past or future, they pursue it. This is the essence of the skin-deep imagination; that events occur in a vacuum, with no connection to one's past or future. This results in the false fantasy that one bears no responsibility for the outcome of their actions.

Positive imagination, on the other hand, is the healthy "skin of the flesh", that is the external reflection of the balanced inner mind — the flesh, sinews, and bones. Positive imagination is also called the "vessel of the intellect" *(Eitz Chayim, Shaar Kitzur A'b'y'ah, 10)*. The movement, as mentioned, follows the trajectory from the inside, higher parts of the mind to the external, lower aspects of the ego. Negative imagination, which we will call fantasy, is only "skin deep", it only accounts for the external. It moves from the out-side-in, and ends up going nowhere.

Imagination without one's inner wisdom guiding it is an empty shell, both negative and potentially destructive. And then there is the fullness of imagination, which is positive, prophetic and insightful. The prophet, as mentioned, is one who has a secure, grounded intellect and yet also possesses a developed power of *Dimyon (Hosha, 12; 10)*. But healthy, positive and productive imagination is only possible when it is connected to one's inner wisdom, understanding, and knowledge; when it is not only "skin-deep", but is truly the skin of the flesh, i.e., the outer expression of the inner in-telligence. Otherwise, even the most beautiful vision is only "skin deep", as it were.

The snake functions in the world of fantasy and, indeed, when Adam and Chavah do eat from the Tree it says, "and their eyes were opened and they saw that they were *Arum*" *(Bereishis, 3; 7)*, literally 'naked'. And yet, this is also a clear allusion to the *Arum*/Trickiness of the snake. The verse could therefore also imply that instead of realizing they were naked, Adam and Chavah suddenly realized that they had been tricked. When they "saw", i.e. had a clear vision of reality, they were able to see that they were following their

false imagination and pursuing a fantasy; they thus instantly saw the emptiness of their actions. They were therefore
ashamed of being *Arum*, which is, as mentioned, often read
as "naked", but, seen from this perspective, one could also
deduce that they were in fact ashamed of being 'tricked' or
'tricky,' as they were trying to take a forbidden shortcut to
expanded consciousness.

SKIN OF LIGHT:

We learn from various *Medrashim* that the Snake damaged
the 'skin' of Adam and Chavah, both literally and figura-
tively. In the Garden of Eden, before the Snake convinced
them to eat from the Tree of Knowledge, the skin of Adam
and Chavah was transparent, like the fingernails we have
today *(Zohar 2, p. 208b. Yalkut Shimoni 15; 27. R. Moshe Alshich,
Torahs Moshe, Bereishis. Tola'as Yaakov, Sod Shabbos)*. They were
initially created with a shining, transparent skin *(Targum Yo-
nasan. Pirkei D'Rabbi Eliezer, Chap. 13)*. But read from a Kabbalistic perspective, the snake damaged the imagination,
the 'skin of the mind', of Adam and Chavah. From then
on, after eating from the Tree of Knowledge and Duality,
their garments were that of snake skin *(Pirkei D'Rabbi Eliezer,
Chap. 20)*.

In truth, the Snake continues to ruin the imaginations of
those who choose to listen to the external voice of fantasy
and false imagination. Therefore, the snake is punished in
a cosmic cause and effect manner known as *Midah K'neged*

Midah/Measure for Measure. And so, for damaging the 'skin' of Adam and Chavah, the snake must shed his own skin from time to time *(Medrash Rabbah, Bereishis, Tikkunei Zohar, 92b)*.

Fantasy and false imagination are the roots of all negativity and non-constructive thought, which lead to negative and non-constructive words and actions. To be non-constructive is essentially to be 'idle' — to go nowhere or do nothing. We can learn from this that distorted imagination can lead to "idle worship" — a type of religiosity or spirituality that only serves to bolster one's ego or insulate one from the realities of the world and of themselves.

Certain images of self, completely detached from actual reality, are often lodged deep within our subconscious. Many people walk around expressing this false image. They act, speak and think about themselves and their reality from a place of total illusion and fantasy. This is the work of the *Nachash*/Snake. The snake was *Arum*, which can be translated as 'sly', a type of sneakiness. From the Hebrew letters that make up the word *Arum*, one can also spell the word *Ohr*/Skin, as the snake represents a level of 'skin deep' fantasy. It is only external. The great commentator Rashi explains that the word *Arum* represents a situation wherein the exterior and interior are not consistent and aligned with each other *(Sotah, 21b)*.

Healthy imagination is only possible when the 'skin' is connected to the flesh, to the sinews, to the bones, and deeper, to the mind itself. When there is this kind of alignment our imagination is redeemed and there is an elevation of our self-image. Then we can truly say that we are transparent again, our outer imagination is an honest reflection of our inner understanding — in fact, they are one.

The skin we have today, which is the skin affected by the Snake and damaged by negative imagination, is appropriately called in the *Zohar, Mishcha D'Chaviyah/*Skin of the Snake. We strive to realign our consciousness in such a way that our skin is returned to its original transparency. In this way we are able to return to our primordial state of balance and harmony, such as a Tzadik with a perfected imagination. As a result we will regain our skin (*Ohr* with an *Ayin*) of light (*Ohr* with an *Aleph*).

The skin of light is a perfect reflection of what is going on internally, within the mind. This is the same skin of light that was experienced clearly by Moshe. When Moshe came down from the Mountain his face was radiant *(Shemos, 34:29)*. The skin of his face was similar to the skin of light that Adam and Chavah had before the episode with the Snake and the Tree of Knowledge and Duality *(Rabbeinu Bachya, Bereishis, 3; 21)*. His skin (*Ohr* with an *Ayin*) was shining; it was transformed into light (*Ohr* with an *Aleph*).

Yoseph/Joseph is called *"Yoseph the Tzadik" (Yumah, 35b)*. A *Tzadik*, as explained earlier, is one who is a master of his reality, as well as one who has the ability to visualize holy things in his mind as vividly as if they were real. *Yoseph* was given a beautiful coat by his father *Yaakov*/Jacob. The Kabbalists write that this coat was made from the skin of *Ohr/ Light* that Adam and Chavah had before being tempted by the snake *(Megalah Amukos, 176. Sefas Emes, Vayeshev)*. This means on a deep level that *Yoseph* had total control over his imagination and that his imagination worked from the inside-out. He was therefore able to conjure up images in his mind at will. Later on, in Egypt, when he was alone with the wife of his master and she tempted him to lay with her, our sages say *(Sotah, 36b)* that he looked and saw the image of his father *Yaakov*, and he fled. The image was enough to remind him of who he was and of what type of life he was meant to be living. Yet, a deeper reading *(Kav Ha'Yashar. Ohr Hachayim, Vayikra, 19; 3)* is that *Yoseph* himself called to mind the image of his father. It was not an external image that was miraculously projected to keep him away from temptation. Rather, he had full control over his imagination and he did not let it run wild with fantasy, but instead, conjured up the image of his father, and according to some sources, of both parents, at will *(Yerushalmi, Horiyos, 2; 5)*. And in this way, through an act of creative visualization, Yoseph was thus able to overcome the immediate temptation.

Personal and collective redemption begins with the redemption of our imagination. When a healthy imagination, founded on an accurate assessment from within of what is going on in reality, can envision and dream, it enables one to then hope, desire, and pray for that envisioned reality to manifest.

For this reason, as mentioned, the Hebrew word for Snake/ *Nachash* has the same *Gematria*/Numeric Equivalent as the word *Mashiach*, the redeemer: 358. This is a hint that the ultimate redemption of the world requires the transformation of the *Nachash*/Snake into the *Mashiach*/Redeemer — turning false fantasy into holy *Dimyon*/Imagination.

The name *Chavah*/Eve is from the word *Chaya*/Life, as she is the mother of all life *(Bereishis, 3; 20)*. Yet, her name is not *Chaya*, which would be spelled *Ches, Yud, Hei*, but rather *Chavah* — *Ches, Vav, Hei*. Why?

In the un-redeemed world, the world of negative fantasy represented by the Snake and the Tree of Knowledge and Duality, she is called Chavah - with a *Vav* - so that the name should sound similar to the Aramaic word *Chaviyah*, which means Snake *(Teshuas Chein, and the Ohev Yisrael, Bereishis ad loc.)*. But there will come a time when the *Vav* will become a *Yud*. There will be a total transformation of the *Chaviyah* and she will be, as she should have been, called *Chaya (Shaloh Ha'Kadosh, Meseches Pesachim, p. 199)*. This is a time when we will be able to transform the reign of the snake into the Messianic era, transforming false fantasy into holy, positive imagination.

EGYPT AND THE CRISIS & ENSLAVEMENT OF IMAGINATION:

Our collective exile began as slaves in Egypt/*Mitzrayim*. Based on the root letters of the Hebrew word for Constriction/*Metzar*, Egypt is understood as a place of suffocating limitation.

The ancient Egyptians were sun worshipers. The sun represents predictability, inevitability, and routine — in other words, a stuck or fixed reality. As the book of *Koheles* says, *"Ein Chadash Tachas Ha'shemesh*/there is nothing new under the sun" *(1; 9)*. According to the steady shine and circuit of the sun, there is no "new". The solar system is rigid and unchanging. The sun rises and sets in the same way each day. The stars stay in their same circuit, year in and year out. This is similar to the reality of a slave. A slave is a slave and there is no room for freedom or change. It is ontological, innate — at least that is what the ancient Egyptians believed.

In a "sun" universe — which Egypt was, as hinted at by its worship of the sun "deity" Ra — there is rigid order, with no room to break out of the pre-set order of things. In this way, there is no room for a slave to become a free person.

Essentially, this makes for a world without any hope of a dream ever coming true. And without dreams, a world of deep existential alienation and stupefaction sets in.

The ancient Egyptian society was based on a strict and unmovable hierarchy of order. There were slaves, masters, priests, first-born sons, demigods and gods incarnate. Most early civilizations were founded on hierarchies of power believed to be in alignment with the very form and nature of the cosmos. As there were ranks among the heavenly bodies, this was reflected in the earthly "constellations" so to speak. The religious rituals and great monuments erected in Egypt were there to mirror these hierarchies. This was a type of 'order' or caste system, and no one was able to change his or her rank or class. You were either first-born or not, you were either master or slave.

The very first instruction the Israelites received as a nation was the Mitzvah to sanctify the new moon as a marker of their calendrical cycles *(Shemos, 12; 1-2)*. The Hebrew months are therefore defined by the movement of the moon, the lunar cycle.

The moon waxes and wanes, changing its shape as it moves through its cycle. In contrast, the sun is always 'full', so to speak; its shape does not change. While there may be nothing new under the sun, the Zohar appropriately points out that it is specifically beneath the moon that we should look for novelty and innovation, as the moon is constantly changing and new *(Zohar 1, p. 123b)*. A Hebrew month, which is determined from the lunar cycle, is called a *Chodesh*. *Chodesh* comes from the word *Chidush* or 'novelty'.

Lunar time gives us the possibility to imagine, to dream, to hope, to pray for an alternative reality. The moon waxes and wanes, comes and goes. It represents the power of seeing the potential of something that is not immediately visible.

To become a free people we first needed, at the very least, to imagine the possibility of freedom. We were slaves for such a long time that we started believing that it was the only possible reality, that this was just our lot, that slavery was ontological and inevitable. At that point, slavery was no longer just a physical condition. Rather, we had begun to think of ourselves as slaves. We claimed ownership of the narrative that was forced upon us. The external voice became our internal narrative.

To become redeemed we needed to first redeem our imagination. Hashem wanted us to start believing in the seemingly miraculous, in the unnatural and non-predictable. To liberate our internal *Da'as*/Awareness and begin imagining and dreaming that it was indeed possible for us to be free.

Hashem wanted us to deeply understand that, in truth, nothing is really routine, predictable, or even natural. "All things and occurrences are miracles and have no nature, per se" *(Ramban, Shemos 13; 16)*. Every moment is a completely renewed creation, a miracle, a novelty. Nature is nothing but a continuously renewed miracle.

During the night, in the "moon" reality, we can dream and imagine for ourselves that we are no longer slaves. We can believe in the dream of the possibility of freedom, of letting go of the strict hierarchy and class system.

To move from slavery to freedom we first need to believe that it is even possible. We must first imagine a new reality, and only then does that reality become a possibility. Before the Mitzvah to sanctify the new moon, before we were empowered by the "Living G-d" to connect with the power of *Hischadshus*/Renewal, our *Koach Ha'M'damah*/Power of Imagination was itself in exile.

Our collective and individual exile in Egypt was so deep and invasive that we sunk to the "forty-ninth level of impurity", a level of existential debasement almost entirely devoid of any vitality or hope for improvement. As a result of being oppressed and beaten down for such a long period of time, not only did we act like slaves and go about our slave labor in silent compliance; what is even more devastating is that we began to imagine and believe that this was actually who we really were. Our *Da'as*/Awareness and *Dimyon*/Imagination were enslaved along with our physical bodies.

A person can be physically in exile and yet feel entirely free, and yet a person can be physically free and feel like they are in utter exile. This is due to the exile of the imagination and inability to dream and pray.

THE BIRTH OF AN-OTHER BEGINS WITH DREAMING – IMAGINING THE POSSIBILITY:

Every true development or creative novelty begins with a dream. Take the first creative act in which humanity was somewhat involved in the Torah — the creation of *Chavah/* Eve. The Torah narrates that Adam needed to fall asleep, initiating a dream/night/moon reality, and only then could Chavah, his potential-other and eventual wife, be "created". "And Hashem caused the Adam to fall into a *Tardeima/* Deep Sleep; and while he was sleeping, he took one of his *Tzela/*Sides…" (Bereishis, 2; 21).

This narrative of the creation of Chavah, cited above, is the second version of the story. The Torah, in chapter 1, tells a similar but slightly different story. In an earlier verse the Torah says, "Let us make mankind in our image (the Hebrew root word *Tzel*) and in our likeness (the Hebrew root word *D'mus*)…male and female He created them" *(Bereishis, 1; 26-27).* Besides the fact that in this version of the story

Adam and Chavah are both created simultaneously, they are also both created in the *Tzel*/Image and *Demus*/Likeness of their Creator. Mankind is called Adam from the Hebrew root *Demus*/Likeness, which is connected to the word *Dimyon*/Imagination, as mankind is created in the likeness of the Divine imagination, so to speak.

But returning to the second narrative, which represents a deeper and further evolved (or devolved) state of creation, it is now the human beings' turn to imagine and create each other. "And Hashem caused the Adam to fall into a *Tardeima*/Deep Sleep (*Tardeima* also has the root letters of *Domeh*, likeness), and he took one of his *Tzela*/Sides..." *(Bereishis, 2; 21).*

Chavah was created in Adam's dream, in his imagination first, and only then in actuality. The same is also true in reverse. Adam was created in Chavah's dream. Because when it says, "and Hashem put 'the Adam' to sleep", this Adam was both male and female, as the Torah said, "Male and Female He created them" *(Bereishis, 1; 27. Eiruvin, 18b).* Hashem put this 'androgynous', male/female human to sleep and then both 'sides' dreamed of each other, resulting in the 'creation' of two separate beings.

At this point in the story Adam imagines Chavah as a separate and unattached reality. The same words of *Demus* and *Tzel* are used in both the Divinely created Adam/Chavah as well as in the second story of Adam/Chavah creating themselves as separate entities. In all relationships we first need to create the space for another person by actively imagining this reality before such a possibility is even feasible.

We are created through and with the Divine imagination and we in turn are able to create and innovate with our own Divine-like power of imagination. A realized person, a true Adam and *Tzadik*, is one who is in full control over themselves and can actively use their power of imagination at will, as explained earlier.

DEPTH OF EXILE IS THE EXILE OF IMAGINATION:

The exile of imagination occurs from the outside–in, as in the previously mentioned example of Egypt where the slaves were fed the information from 'without' that they were born slaves and were meant to die as slaves. The redemption of the imagination, on the other hand, occurs from the inside-out, such as when Hashem guided the Israelite slaves to the realization that nothing is predictable and that there is always the potential for a new reality. This is something that every person knows intuitively deeply within. No person today is considered an ontological slave or master, although, through our choices we can live as if we were enslaved to our passions, our surrounding cultures, or our circumstances.

Redemption occurs when you gain control of your imagination, not the other way around. Fantasy functions from the outside-in, healthy imagination is from the inside-out.

We first envision a truth or desired reality, and only then does that reality occur.

TO BE HUMAN IS TO DREAM:

The Hebrew word Adam/Human is rooted in the word *Dimyon*/Imagination. We are created in the Divine imagination, as it were, and we create our fluid reality through our imagination.

We are not Homo Sapiens. More accurately, according to the Torah, we are Homo Imaginus.

What makes us human, what distinguishes us as an Adam/Human, is our ability to reimagine our lives, and life in general, differently than the way it appears in the moment.

The opposite of healthy imagination is idolatry, which occurs when we become stuck on one image. When this happens we mistake a part for the whole and we end up worshiping a frozen and graven image, a single snapshot of reality.

The saddest thing in the world is when we lose touch with our *Dimyon*/Imagination.

We become stuck in our lives when we do not have the ability or courage to reimagine our circumstances to be different than they are now.

We cling desperately to our status quo, as miserable or as unsatisfying as it may be, because our imagination is in exile. We cannot even imagine an alternative reality for ourselves.

////////////////////////////////////

» A Simple Creative Visual:

There are many suggestions of creative visualizations that have been taught by the great teachers, mystics and rabbis throughout the ages. Over the course of this book many of these will be explored. Yet, before this is done, let us begin with a very simple form of visualization that most people will be able to accomplish, even those who have difficulties holding an image in their mind's eye.

This meditation is a creative visualization designed to help a person let go of their negative baggage and ideas that hold them back. The goal is to release yourself from the repressive self-images that say: "You cannot do this or that. You are unworthy, not capable. You are a failure, a hypocrite. Who are you fooling?" This is the *Kelipa*/Concealment of "Egypt" that says: "You are who you are, and you can never change." Egypt is a reality of stuckness, stiffness, rigidity, and constriction.

Every time a person wants to make a change in their life for the better — whether they want to start being a better person, or start accepting upon him or herself a new Mitzvah, spiritual practice, or diet — there is the inner voice of doubt and negativity that says: "You can never do it. You always start but never persevere. You are a hypocrite. Who are you fooling? You're a slave to your past choices or mistakes and you will never become free in the present."

In order to break free of this way of thinking, you need to imagine the possibility of a radical new you. Take five minutes and envision what or how this new you could look, feel, move, or speak like. Where are you? What have you accomplished? How does it feel to be successful at achieving your dreams? In order for this to be a real possibility you must remember that every month/*Chodesh*, every day, every moment is a *Chidush*, a new moment with an infinite array of fresh and new possibilities.

» FOUR IMPORTANT INGREDIENTS TO SUCCESSFUL VISUALIZATIONS:

There are a few fundamental principles regarding the practice of creative visualization. These will provide basic guidance and context before delving into the more experiential work.

As with anything in life, if you want to achieve something you need to first ensure that you truly desire to achieve it. Following that, you must determine if you firmly believe that it is indeed possible to achieve such an accomplishment.

Take a mundane achievement like making money. If you really want to make money the only way you will be successful is if you truly desire it — living and breathing your ambition to make money. In addition, you also need to have the resolute faith that you are capable — with G-d's help — to make money.

This is true with everything, both physical and spiritual. In order for a desire to materialize this desire cannot be a fleeting or weak craving, but it must burn with passion, filling every waking moment with enthusiasm and motivation to achieve the goal. Ultimately, together with such desire and zeal, there needs to be the faith that you can in fact achieve your ambition.

Visualization works the same way. It is not enough to visualize in the mind's eye what one desires. One must be filled with a burning passion — dreaming, working, scheming and planning at every moment how this vision can be realized. And again, coupled with this strong desire must be the absolute faith that this dream is a real possibility.

Sometimes a person, no matter how hard he tries, cannot visualize a certain 'image' that he thinks he desires to achieve. He feels a resistance. He feels that he is forcing himself. It does not feel organic and natural. The truth is that we have to learn from everything. The fact that one attempts at visualizing a goal and feels forced can also indicate to the person that perhaps the desire is not strong enough, or that on a deeper level you really do not want or desire such a thing; or, ultimately, that you do not really think it is possible. Either way, one needs to reexamine his desires and faith in the midst of the experience.

Desire and faith are requisites to the success or lack thereof of any visual practice. We must desire what we are visualizing and have deep faith and trust that it is possible to achieve.

Now that we have established the most functional perspective for success, here are four basic ingredients that are integral to the crystallization of any visualization practice:

1) Success Depends on Detail.

We need to ensure that when we visualize an image it is as detailed as possible. Do not spare any detail, elaborate on them as much as possible, down to the minutia of the image. If you are visualizing a wall, notice the colors, the patterns, the cracks, the texture.

Also, one needs to visualize the totality of the experience completely from A-to-Z. For example, when a person is visualizing an image of healing one should imagine the entire process all the way up to the post-healing cleanup. One may visualize putting away the medical utensils or whatever tools or props were used during the healing. This is necessary in order for one to create a full sense of closure, moving from sickness to healing.

Closing is very important. It puts the "seal" on the experience. If, for example, you imagine yourself crossing a bridge on your way into a new reality, you can look back, burn the bridge behind you, and then look forward to see the new shore ahead. Or if you are leaving a room, make sure you close the door behind you before you end your visualization.

2) Practice as Often as Possible.

To have success in visual forms of meditation one needs to practice them as frequently as possible. They do not need to be long sessions. Ideally twenty minutes is a good time frame. But even just a few minutes — even two or three — can be very beneficial.

Visualizations are like any other thing in life — the more one practices the more positive results one will get. Frequency matters tremendously. As you become better at it, the consequences are also heightened. Choose a visual and its details, practice at least once a day for an extended period of time. Forty days is a good number, as forty is the number that represents transformation.

Reb Mendel of Rimanov teaches in the name of the Arizal that in order to undo negative patterns of behavior a person should assert a positive pattern for forty consecutive days, corresponding to the time of *Yetziras Ha-v'lad*/the Formation of a Viable Fetus *(Ilanah D'chaya, Ohr Ha'ner, Os 40. R.*

Elimelech of Lizensk. Tzetel Katan ,16). To undo a set of patterns we need forty days. To create a new pattern we also need forty days. So set aside forty consecutive days that you are dedicating to this practice.

The best time to practice any one of the visualizations that will be explored further in this book is either early in the morning, before the "morning prayers", or late in the evening, before one retires for the night. Some of the practices that will be explored come in tandem with the formal prayers so as to induce a state of higher consciousness before reciting the Amidah, for example; and other practices are worthwhile for any time of day. Yet, there is something about the early morning and late at night that is more conducive for inward practices, as the Kabbalists explain.

The early morning has immense potential for spiritual work and practice, both as a time to lay the foundation for the upcoming day ahead, as well as being a pristine time of day before the energy of your environment has become soiled with the hustle and bustle of commerce and circumstance. The same is true with late in the evening, which serves as both a foundation for your upcoming dreams, as well as being a more open time when the dust of the day has settled and the air is a little more clear, so to speak. Along these lines our sages tell us that, "most of a person's wisdom is learned at night" *(Rambam, Hilchos Talmud Torah, 3; 15).* The day is good for acquiring knowledge and information, while wisdom is gained at night.

3) ENGAGE YOUR OTHER SENSES.

If you find that you have a hard time conjuring up images than use your other senses to help conjure up the visual. For example, imagine hearing a conversation that is occurring at your new job, or hearing yourself speak as if you were a *Tzadik*, or smelling freshly baked goods. Think of the smells and sounds that come up in this new reality. Try to feel and sense it. In this way, if you cannot 'see' the image, you can create the image with your other senses.

This is very important as not everyone has the same capacity to visualize. Some people are not very visually oriented, they are more auditory or kinesthetic. Therefore, use whatever sense you normally use when you imagine something. When it is time to visualize something, if images do not come up just use another sense to create the 'visual'.

Even if you are someone that can visualize easily, for the visual to truly create a shift in consciousness we need to engage the others senses as fully as possible. In other words, not only should we conjure up an image to see what we are trying to achieve, but we also need to strive to hear, smell, taste and touch the experience. Ideally, it should be a full-body immersive experience. If, for example, you are visualizing yourself standing at the Western Wall you need to imagine the feeling of the cool Jerusalem breeze brushing up against your face, the smell and aroma of the Jerusalem air, the feel of your feet and fingers touching the cold stones and a particular taste in your mouth.

Also keep in mind that even if you normally do have trouble visualizing, it will, like any art, get easier with practice and patience. To assist in learning how to effectively visualize you may look at an image such as a picture or aspect of nature, for example, for a period of ten-twenty seconds. Then, immediately close your eyes and continue seeing that image in your mind's eye. This is a good simple training exercise to develop the visionary capacity.

You can do this repeatedly. Open your eyes and look at the image once it has faded from your mind's eye. Close your eyes and try to hold the image again. Open your eyes to see it, then close and hold it. Do this over and over again.

Another effective way to train yourself in the art of visualization is to recall a particular scene using the sense that is most prominent. If you are an auditory person, for example, try to recall a powerful auditory experience, like when you were sitting and singing *Nigunim*/Spiritual Melodies, or the surround sounds of a walk through the forest. Focus your attention on the sounds that you are recalling and audibly sensing. You will notice that in due time this auditory experience will morph into other sensory experiences and you will begin to actually "see" the experience that you are recalling through another sense.

4) The Power of Affirmations

The linguistic technique of repetitive affirmations is another effective method of influencing one's consciousness on deep structural levels, beyond the surface of the ego and intellect.

The celebrated Chassidic Rebbe, Reb Arele Roth *(1894-1947),* speaks of telling yourself truths you know to be true over and over again, actively affirming and reaffirming them, so that the ideas of the mind penetrate deeper into one's consciousness.

On a very basic level this is the pedagogic principle at play in our repetitive liturgy. By saying the same statements, which are the fundamental truths of reality, over and over again we are effectively engaging in a practice of prolonged neuro-linguistic programming. The ancient Rabbis understood the power of repetitive affirmations thousands of years ago and put it into practice in the form of our daily liturgy.

Creative visualizations and positive affirmations both reach the same place within our deeper subconscious. Therefore, combining them makes them even more powerful.

Just like there is an internal image of self, there is also a continuous dialogue or narrative that is expressing itself within us. We are continuously taking in stimulus from the outside world and then inwardly dialoging about it. We are telling ourselves things like, "this thing is really nice." Then another voice says, "but it is bad for you." And then another voice says, "but from another angle it is actually temporarily beneficial," and so on ad infinitum. We are constantly analyzing, assessing, arguing with, and affirming the plethora of ideas and instincts that arise within our stream of consciousness.

An affirmation is used to reinforce to yourself that the positive imagery you have consciously created and the ideas you have developed are true and real.

An affirmation is meant to render a concept or image firmly in one's deeper consciousness. It is a declaration that what we desire to be or achieve is already true in reality. Once the visual is secured and the affirmation penetrates, our actions will automatically follow.

» PREPARATION FOR EACH MEDITATION

> Meditation begins with the commitment to show up to this present moment.

> Put aside expectations of how the experience should be.

> It is preferable to carve out a time that can be fully allocated to your meditation practice, free from other commitments and distractions.

> Clear a space that is welcoming, clean, and comfortable for you to sit for a set amount of time.

> Regarding the duration of the sit, start out small and stay consistent, rather than aiming high and eventually feeling overwhelmed. Take it step by step and keep the motivation burning.

> Meditation is a practice of being present, of showing up and honoring that nothing else need be done in this moment, so set up your meditation time in such a way that you can be fully available. It might mean waking up a few minutes early before everyone else's day begins and your responsibilities to others ensue, or maybe, for you, it means taking some time away from the computer screen. Treat yourself to this experience

of needing to do nothing else but be where you are.

> We need to enter into meditation with intention and with a sense of being present.

> Distractions are one of the main reasons we are not present, either our mind is reminiscing about the past or worried about the future.

> We need to clear the clutter from our mind and reduce the potential distracting forces in order to open the space for presence. In "Breathing and Quieting the Mind", a book previously published, there was in depth exploration of ways to quiet the mind and become more present. Suffice it to say that by taking 3-5 breaths with the awareness that we are releasing toxins with every exhalation, we can more smoothly and quickly let go and enter into a relaxed space.

> Turn off your ringer. Sit comfortably in your designated meditation spot, yet not so overly relaxed that you may want to fall asleep. Take a few shoulder rolls and stretches. This light stretching will release tension in the muscles specifically around the spine as well as prepare the lung tissue for fuller respiration.

> It appears that the most effective body position to practice visualization would be to sit upright, at the

edge of your chair, allowing for the expression of the natural curvature of the spine. This enables you to sit up tall and remain alert. A straight spine is the most conducive posture for alertness and awareness. Rest your arms by your sides, hands in your lap. Your feet should be resting flat on the floor. Do not cross your legs.

> When you prepare the body in this way, you minimize the power of external stimuli, allowing your focus to be inwardly-directed.

SAMPLE MEDITATION
A CREATIVE VISUAL

....

Set a soft timer (or have someone else observe you) in order to fully enter this meditation without any worry of what needs to be done afterwards. This time is for being present. Allow yourself the gift of this experience.

For those new to meditation practice, it is recommended to start with anywhere from 10-20 minutes. This is not a competitive practice, so if that amount of time feels overwhelming to you, best to start slowly, and steadily build on a strong foundation.

Invite all of yourself into this space here and now. In a comfortable seat, preferably with your eyes closed, take a moment to let go of all the noise, chaos and movement in your life; simply be.

....

Just as we need to minimize external stimuli via the sense of touch, the same is true with the other senses. To help with visualization, it is beneficial to gently close your eyes, shutting out the external world in order to move more inward to your inner field of vision.[1]

....

You may notice various sounds, sensations, thoughts or feelings crossing your mind. Sense everything without manipulating it; accept what is and relax from the urge to act.

....

With a deep exhalation, focus on the breath leaving your body, naturally and without force. Inhalation is the body's instinctive response to exhalation, effortlessly being drawn into the lungs from the power of the pressure created by exhaling.

....

Visualize yourself standing in front of a gigantic wall that stretches up to the highest heights, as far as your eyes can see, as well as out to the furthest ends of left and right.

....

As you focus on this wall, notice a tiny door appear in the center.

....

---

1 When Rabbi Chayim Vital —the primary disciple of the Arizal - writes about doing any type of inner visualization or awareness he writes that one needs to close the eyes *(Shaarei Kedusha, 4; 2;1. Shar Ruach HaKodesh, Hakdamah 5, Yichud 10).* Living a short time before R. Chayim in the city of *Yerushalyim*/Jerusalem, the Kabbalist Rabbi Yehuda Albotini (1453- 1519) speaks about intense visualizations, where one imagines oneself above in Heaven, and writes that one should, not only shut one's eyes, but actually "Shut his eyes very tightly, and clench his hands tightly...take very long breaths" *(Sulam Ha'aliyah, 10, p. 102).*

Open the door and squeeze through it.

As you are squeezing yourself through the door, all that which is attached to you needs to be shed. Only that which is core and essential comes with you.

Feelings of expansiveness rise as you cross into this unexplored terrain. Openness, the awareness of new opportunities and the freedom of unbounded potential come to the surface.

Imagine yourself dressed in new clothes. Your name is called, it sounds new, fresh. In this space, everything that previously was has been left behind on the other side of the wall. You are a new you, with all of the best possibilities in the world available. Turn around to face the wall again.

Walk back through the door, back into the reality that you had left behind, but completely transformed and refreshed with a renewed sense of vitality and optimism.

Gently open your eyes.

CHAPTER 2

··

THE POWER OF THOUGHT

THE PRACTICE CITED ABOVE IS A MORE GENERIC FORM OF CREATIVE VISUALIZATION, ALTHOUGH IT IS OF COURSE CONSISTENT WITH THE TORAH'S OUTLOOK. NOW LET US MOVE INTO SOME MORE INDIGENOUS, CLASSICALLY TORAH-SOURCED VISUAL MEDITATIONS.

The power of our thoughts is magnificent and immeasurable. In fact, everything essentially exists within our thoughts and imagination. We do not see things the way they are, but rather the way we are. What is more, we are continually projecting our thoughts outward and seeing what is external through the prism of our internal programs and perspectives.

Indeed, we can never know with our logical mind a thing-in-itself. In fact, in relation to us, any external object we observe does not truly exist independently of the mind that perceives it. Things are real for us because we see them, whether literally or within our mind's eye.

The way we see and imagine things to be is actually the way they are, at least to us. Such is the power of our thoughts and imagination.

Our thoughts and imaginations create our reality. For this reason, the totality of who we are is present wherever our thoughts are. In the words of the Baal Shem Tov: "In the place where a person's thoughts are, that is where they truly are." When we can imagine something or somewhere in our mind's eye, we are not simply 'here', wondering about 'there'; rather, we are actually 'there'. This is an important principle when it comes to inner visualizations. If done correctly, with the entire strength of our being, we are able to actually be in the 'place' of our visualizations.

///////////////////////////////////////

VISUAL ONE: IDEA

» VISUALIZING BEING WITHIN
   THE TEMPLE

We will now explore our first visualization, first from a theoretical perspective, and then from a place of practice. The
first creative visualization comes from the teachings of the
saintly Chassidic Rebbe, Reb Elimelech of Lizensk *(1717-
1786)*.

Overall, during *Tefilah*/Liturgical Prayer, our bodies are
positioned to face in the direction of the Holy of Holies
in Jerusalem *(Shulchan Aruch, Orach Chayim, Siman 94; 1)*. Not
only are we positioning our bodies in the direction of the
Holy of Holies, but, when we recite the peak and essence of
the prayers, the *Amidah*/Standing Prayer, we should imagine ourselves as if we were standing in the actual rebuilt and
rectified Temple in Jerusalem *(Shulchan Aruch, Ibid, 95; 2)*, and
more specifically, in the Holy of Holies within the Temple
(Mishna Berura, 94; 2).

Reb Elimelech speaks of a person creatively visualizing him or herself praying in the *Beis Hamikdash*/The Holy Temple.

To quote:

"A person should visualize in his mind when he is praying that he is standing in the land of Israel and within the *Beis HaMikdash*/Holy Temple. He should visualize that he is actually seeing this vision (with his own eyes)…Through this practice one will experience true clarity in prayer."

(Noam Elimelech, Lech Lecha, p. 19)

While Reb Elimelech seems to have popularized this method, this actual visual practice seems to have been utilized a few hundred years earlier by previous pietists, and there are even sources for this practice in non-Chassidic texts *(See also: R. Yoseph Yitzchak of Chabad Igros Kodesh Vol. 8, p 200. R. Klunimus Kalmish of Peasetzna Hachsharas Ha'Avreichim, Chap 4).* The Lithuanian moralist and kabbalist R. Alexander Zisskind *(? – 1793)* writes that when people are praying they should imagine themselves literally standing in the Holy of Holies. According to R. Zisskind this visual should be maintained throughout the entire duration of the prayers, or at least it should be recalled a number of times during one's prayers.

To quote:

"Before one begins the *Amidah*, the peak of the dai-

ly prayers, one should visualize that they are actually standing within the *Beis HaMikdash* and they should exercise their desire to be there. How beneficial it is to call to mind this visual throughout your prayers."
(Yesod Shoresh Ha'Avodah, Shar Ha'karbon, p. 82)

The point of this visualization is to imagine that you are literally standing in the Temple and that you are praying in that most sacred of all spaces. If possible, try to imagine yourself present within the Holy of Holies, the inner most chamber of the sanctuary. Rabbi Yaakov Emdin, in his *Siddur*/Prayer Book, calls the *Amidah* the "court of the Holy of Holies" *(See also Tikunei Zohar, Hakdamah 3b)*. According to this teaching, when one recites the Amidah they are metaphorically standing within the "court of the Holy of Holies." The active visualization of this image just makes one more acutely aware of this truth.

In the times of the Temple the only time one was allowed to enter the Holy of Holies was on the holiest day of the year, Yom Kippur; and even then it was only the High Priest that was allowed to enter. This is the most private, intimate time and space of the entire yearly cycle.

Regarding the entry of the High Priest into the Holy of Holies on Yom Kippur the Torah says, "And there shall be no man in the Tent of Meeting when he goes in to make atonement in the holy place..." *(Vayikra, 16; 17)*. The Medrash *(Medrash Rabba, Vayikra, 21; 12)* asks, "Is not the High Priest a man?" The verse says "no man", and yet the *Cohen Gadol* is a man who enters. The *Medrash* goes on to explain that when the High Priest entered into the Holy of Holies he was transformed and his face would burn as flames, and he would take on the appearance of an angel. He was no longer a 'man' as it were. Once one enters into the Holy of Holies, the deepest inward place within, he loses his defining external features and he surrenders his *Tzuras Adam/ Human Image.*

Regarding this same verse, "And there shall be no man in the Tent of Meeting when he goes in to make atonement in the holy place," another Medrash states that not even angels were present. Even those whose image appears as human (i.e., angels) were not allowed entry *(Yerushalmi, Yumah, 8; 2).* At this most resonant moment the *Cohen Gadol* had elevated himself beyond his normative human faculties and even beyond the level of angels. He was, at that moment, beyond angelic. There was nothing in between him and his Creator. This was the most exalted and intimate unity. His very essence, above and beyond all his definitions and manifestations, his very core, was, at that moment unified with the essence, as it were, of the Infinite One.

Every day when we reach the peak of prayer, the *Amidah*, we reach out, we yearn, we aspire, and we seek to reveal our intrinsic connection with our Creator. At that moment, we are the *Cohen Gadol* entering into the holiest space at the holiest time.

This visualization makes this reality tangible, vivid and embodied.

According to the Peasetzna Rebbe, the visualization of oneself praying within the *Beis HaMikdash* is, indeed, factual. With one's power of concentration and controlled imagination, "one in fact elevates and experiences an ascent of the soul and he sees, even if he does not rationally comprehend, what his inner soul is seeing..." *(Derech HaMelech, Parshas Tzav)*.

For someone deeply steeped within the wellsprings of Torah, the visualization of standing in Jerusalem on the Temple Mount in the rebuilt holy Temple within the Holy of Holies has a particularly evocative and profound resonance. The image stimulates and inspires feelings of awe, trepidation, love and humility. For many, however, this image does very little to arouse them. In fact, the image perhaps conjures up complicated political issues and all other types of mundane reality. The Holy of Holies represents the holiest place on earth. There is the literal space, but there is also the Holy of Holies within the dimension of consciousness.

Everything in life exists on three dimensions — Time, Space, and Consciousness. Whatever exists on one level exists on the other two. What exists in *Olam*/Space exists also in *Shana*/Time, and also in *Nefesh*/Consciousness. The Holy of Holies in space exists within the inner most sanctum of the Holy Temple in Jerusalem. The Holy of Holies in Time is Yom Kippur, our deepest day of the year. A day we let go of all physical attachments, food, drink, and intimacy in an honest attempt to discover or rediscover who we really are and what we truly want out of life. And the Holy of Holies within Consciousness is our deepest level of soul, our core, our essence.

Internally, the Holy of Holies within us is the deepest place of self, the deepest level of our *Neshamah*/Soul, which we alone have access to. Before we enter into prayer we should seek to enter into this deepest place within ourselves, and attempt to communicate with Hashem from that place.

When we enter the Holy of Holies we are entering into the ground of our very beingness, or better yet, our non-beingness. We are accessing a place within us that is beyond doing or manifesting. Imagine yourself there, in the deepest place in the world, and the deepest place in your soul — now pray from that place.

When it says that, "no man was present when he entered the Holy of Holies," this means that he was so at one with himself that he was completely unified; there was no 'other' part of himself observing himself. If you live in a state of inner conflict, then even when you are alone, you are there with 'an-other.' That 'other' person is the part of yourself that is observing and judging you. Being fully alone is when one is alone with no inner dialogue or dichotomy, no self-judgment, just pure being. In each of our lives we all have memories of this 'place' — whether it was a physical place in our childhood home, or a time of the year, whether years back, or even a day ago — where we felt really safe and alone, totally protected within our personal Holy of Holies.

Take a few moments before you begin to pray to create this mental image and literally walk into the Beis HaMikdash, simultaneously journeying into your own inner sanctuary. It may also help at this time to recall a safe time or place where you have personally been truly alone, with no judgment or critique. Now visualize yourself entering that space — the deepest, quietest, safest space within, a place that is beyond emotion or expression.

That's it. There's nothing else. No externalities. No feelings. No awe, no love, no angels, nothing but pure Divine space, beyond expression — a place of pure Being.

VISUAL ONE: PRACTICE

» ENTERING THE HOLY OF HOLIES – THE INNER OF INNERS

Set a soft timer (or have someone else observe you) in order to fully enter this meditation without any worry of what needs to be done afterwards. This time is for being present. Allow yourself the gift of this experience.

For those new to meditation practice, it is recommended to start with anywhere from 10-20 minutes. This is not a competitive practice, so if that amount of time feels overwhelming to you, best to start slowly, and steadily build on a strong foundation.

Invite all of yourself into this space here and now. In a comfortable seat, preferably with your eyes closed, take a moment to let go of all the noise, chaos and movement in your life; simply be. Just as we need to minimize external stimuli via the sense of touch, the same is true with the

other senses. To help with visualization, it is beneficial to gently close your eyes, shutting out the external world in order to move more inward to your inner field of vision.

You may notice various sounds, sensations, thoughts or feelings crossing your mind.
Sense everything without manipulating it; accept what is and relax from the urge to act.

With a deep exhalation, focus on the breath leaving your body, naturally and effortlessly. Inhalation is the body's instinctive response to exhalation, effortlessly being drawn into the lungs from the power of the pressure created by exhaling.

Visualize yourself standing wherever you are. Say you are living in New York, close your eyes and see yourself standing in your room in New York.

Imagine yourself being able to fly. See yourself as you lift off.

As you are flying ever upwards, you are becoming lighter, both physically and also mentally, as more and more baggage is dropped.

The higher you fly, the lighter you become.

From a bird's eye view you can see the entire globe. Emanating from the Holy Land, you notice a brilliant light that draws you to it.

Landing in Jerusalem, you arrive in the courtyard facing the Kosel, the Western Wall.

. . . .

Standing at the Western Wall, the cool Jerusalem breeze blows up against you. You smell the aroma and feel your feet touching the cold stones.

. . . .

Invite all of your senses to be present.

. . . .

Standing at the Western Wall, your prayers ascend from a place of deep Kavanah/Intention.

. . . .

A small crack in the wall calls your attention. It suggests the presence of a secret door.

. . . .

As you push hard against the stone, the passage way slowly opens up and you are able to squeeze through.

. . . .

You come out on the other side into a magical world, alive and brimming with lights and illumination. The feeling of salvation gushes forth. This is it: A redeemed world, the World to Come, Paradise on Earth.

. . . .

You are standing at the base of the mountain. Peering up, you see the most splendid edifice you have ever seen, the Beis HaMikdash/the Holy Temple, bathed in sacred fire and light.

. . . .

You slowly and consciously begin your ascent up the mountain, drawing closer and closer to the Holy Temple.

. . . .

The nearer you draw to this most sanctified of spaces, the more baggage, armor, and masks are being shed.

Upon arriving at the top of the mountain, with great awe you enter into the outer courtyard of the Temple. There is a lot of hustling about, people are moving, bringing offerings, singing and playing music. You cannot make out the faces of these people, but you feel enveloped by their sacred activity. The Divine presence is very palpable in this place.

You walk deeper into the Temple, entering the Holy space. There is a tangible quiet in this chamber. The gentle light of the Menorah is burning, the pleasant smell of freshly baked bread, from the showbread, wafts through the air along with the incense from the inner altar. Everything is done in silence, there are no words being spoken. There is just a great overwhelming air of palpable peace. You feel very at ease, very serene, very holy.

Your attention is drawn towards the curtain in the back of the room that separates the Holy from the Holy of Holies.

Like a moth to a flame you are beckoned to the Holy of Holies, the inner most chamber. You walk towards the curtain with trepidation and unmistakable excitement. You are filled with reverence, awe and deep love. One foot in front of the other, you arrive at the curtain separating the outer chamber from the inner chamber, The Holy of Holies.

Your hands part the curtain, you enter.

. . . .

Here you are in the most sacred space there is. All your external baggage was released at the entry way and you are totally free, alone, and in perfect stillness. There is no chaos, noise, or external excitement. Even your body, the externality of your soul, is unrecognizable.

. . . .

You are in the safest, holiest, most real place in the world, and this is felt deeply in all of your limbs and sinews. It is just you all alone with your Creator, in unity, in oneness.

. . . .

Stay here as long as you like, there is nowhere else to be.

. . . .

When you feel the sensation of the breeze drifting along the skin of your face, you are awakening to the presence of your body in space again. Begin to step away from The Holy of Holies, walking backwards towards the curtain, still facing forward. Slowly turn and delicately part the curtain as you walk out.

. . . .

Exit the Temple, descend the mountain, and squeeze yourself through the crevice in the Wall from where you came. You are now in the courtyard by the Western Wall again. Face-to-face with the Wall, your soul on fire with love for this connection, you are being drawn backwards, and up, up, up, and away, all the way back to the place from where you had originally traveled.

. . . .

You are transformed and the ride back is full of ease and inner peace.

Slowly open your eyes.

VISUAL TWO: IDEA

» DIVESTING ONESELF FROM THE PHYSICAL

The next visual we will explore is the practice of divesting oneself from one's physical form.

This is a very important practice where we are learning to separate the mind from the body, and the spirit from any sense of corporality, as it were. Rabbi Chayim Vital writes *(Kesavim Chadashim. Sha'arei Kedusha, 4; 2)* that the first requirement to be able to practice any of the meditations that he suggests is this ability to "divest oneself from physicality." This is a fundamental meditation practice. There are various mental and spiritual preparations required for meditation, but in terms of the actual practice, the divestment of materiality is essential.

To quote:

"A person needs to be able to isolate his thoughts to the extreme, divesting his body from his soul until he does not feel as if he is within the material world at all, but rather he is only spirit. And the more that he divests himself from the material world the more his awareness will increase. If he senses a sound or movement that distracts his thoughts, or if he voluntarily brings up a material (oriented) thought, immediately his spiritual thoughts will cease to cleave to the Above. And he will not attain anything. Because high holiness does not rest upon a man when he cleaves to the material, even a hair's breadth...The point is that even though a person is inwardly worthy for the Holy Spirit/Ruach Ha'kodesh to rest upon him, if he has not accustomed himself to completely divest his spirit from his body, the Spirit will not rest upon him."

(Sha'arei Kedusha, 4; 2)

A little further on he writes:

"...Close your eyes and divest yourself from the material. (Imagine) as if your soul has left your body and is floating upwards into the sky...(He then outlines a detailed meditative practice, which involves repeating a particular text over and over again...eventually entering into a trance state of automatic speaking...or a semi-conscious dream state...he then writes that if you followed the outline of the practice and 'nothing happened,' know that)

either it is because you were not worthy (i.e., you have not refined yourself) or because you were not able to properly divest yourself from the material."
(Sha'arei Kedusha, 4; 2:1)

As we can see, this is a fundamental practice to master before moving on to any more complex meditations or visualizations.

DIVESTING FROM THE PHYSICAL BEFORE AND DURING PRAYER:

Our sages tell us *(Berachos, 32b)* that the Early Pious ones, the *Chassidim Ha'Rishonim*, would sit for an hour before each prayer, at which time they would experience a *Hispashtus HaGashmiyus*/A Divestment from Materiality. Only then would they begin to pray *(Tur, Orach Chayim, Siman, 98. Mechaber, ibid. Shaloh, Asarah Hilulim, 9.93. Nefesh HaChayim, Shar 2; 14)*. They would thereby reach a mental/spiritual state wherein they were detached from all bodily sensation. They experienced themselves as being removed from any physical form and as a result were able to enter a placeless place beyond physicality.

Furthermore, our sages tell us that we should walk into the room in which we mean to pray a measure of two doors before beginning our prayers *(Berachos, 8a)*. Besides the literal meaning of not standing near the exit when we pray, this means, metaphorically, that as we prepare ourselves for prayer we need to exit one reality/door as well as enter into a new reality/door *(Maharal, Nesivos Olam, Avodah 5. See also: Sefas Emes, Vayerah, p. 77).* The two doors represent the physical and spiritual realms respectively. We need to take leave of the physical plane and meditatively enter into a higher world of spirit. We are thus leaving behind one door, one room, one reality, and entering into a completely different, higher and deeper one.

Similarly, we are told that it is preferable to pray in a *Shul* that is further from your home than in one that is close by, for then there is reward for every step taken to get there *(Sotah, 22a).* Besides the literal meaning of this teaching, which is that we should exert energy in the performance of a Mitzvah, the inner meaning is meant to express the idea that in order to properly pray we need to distance ourselves from our centers of personal necessity (i.e., our "homes" and our egos). This will allow us to more readily shift our perspective from being focused on our physical self to focusing instead on our inner reality, from being self-centered to being G-d-centered.

"Praiseworthy are the righteous," says the Zohar, "who know how to set their prayers correctly. The words uttered in prayer ascend on High and as the words ascend from chamber to chamber the righteous ascend with them, until they are presented before the King. In this way, both the words of prayer, as well as the one who utters them, appear before the King" *(Zohar 2, p. 250a)*.

But how does one divest oneself from his physicality? How does one practice this technique before or during prayer? And furthermore how does one practice this technique throughout their day? For this practice is not only beneficial during prayer, but allows one to become less attached to their ego narrative and thereby frees one from their personal worries and doubts in general.

Cleary, the real hard work is to actually experience a sense of *Hispashtus HaGashmiyus*, which results in a quieting of the body and mind, as well as a humbling and silencing of one's *Yesh*/Ego self. But although this state is the ultimate aspiration, this experience is quite advanced and difficult to attain. To begin, we will start with a visualization of *Hispashtus HaGashmiyus*, and from there, we may attempt to reach a more integral experience.

Visualize taking leave of your body, feeling weightless and drifting Above:

Essentially, the goal of this visualization is for a person to utilize his imagination and envision himself hovering above the sky cap *(Tzeva'as HaRivash, p. 17b. Ohr Ha'emes, p. 101. Note. Rambam, Hilchos Tefilah. 5; 4)*. One needs to feel themselves removed from their physical form as they attempt to experience an internal separation from the density of the body and its desires. While at the same time, with one's full array of mental capabilities, one needs to vividly envision this separation.

At first, we begin by becoming aware of our body, its sensations and limitations. Then we imagine our consciousness slowly rising upward from the body, thus enabling us to observe the body from above.

Start by focusing your awareness on the place where your feet/shoes are touching the ground. Then gently move your awareness upwards, towards your legs and backside resting on the seat or floor. Stay with this awareness for a few moments. Then slowly move your consciousness further up the body to your torso, neck, mouth, nose, eyes, and forehead, and stay with this awareness for a few moments. Next, allow your consciousness to fill your entire top of the head and gently guide your consciousness to leave your head. It is easier for consciousness to leaves the body via the third eye, or through the (front) soft part of a baby's head, which is called the "anterior fontanelle", this is the spot where the head *Tefillin*, similar to a crown, is placed.

As your consciousness exits the body and allow it to rest just above your head. Now, let your consciousness to start rising even further upward, first hovering above the room and observing your body in its seat, and then moving onward completely beyond the room. Slowly, but picking up speed, allow your consciousness to rise above the building, further and further away from the town or city, into the clouds, above the clouds, and on and on into the vast expanse of the cosmos.

As your awareness is gradually moving upward it is becoming lighter and lighter and floating higher and higher. As you feel yourself moving higher and higher you are able to escape the reign of gravity and feel yourself floating within a vast empty space. At some point you bump up against the sky-cap. At this time you sense a dense blockage. You move towards its center and push it open. A flood of magnificent, brilliant light comes pouring forth. You are moving faster and faster towards the light, becoming ever lighter and less encumbered. There is another vast expanse, but again you bump up against another skycap, and again you manage to push forth beyond it. But this time, the light that gushes forth is unfathomable. Everything seems to be shimmering and sparkling like a crystal held up to the sun. At the center of it all is a great Light. You are moving faster and faster towards this infinite, brilliant light, so warm and welcoming.

But just as you are getting closer and closer you are suddenly thrust down and forcefully pushed all the way back to your body.

Early Chassidic Rebbes teach *(Likutei Yekarim, p. 3. Baal Shem*

Tov Torah, Parshas Ekev, 46) that during meditation, when we feel we have entered a vast empty space, we should attempt to feel the full expansiveness of such a space. In order to do this it helps to expand one's visual field to include the entire abyss that surrounds them and to make sure not to remain narrowly focused on the most immediate surroundings. As soon as we feel secure in "that place" we have to move even further upward, and then higher, always making sure not to "fall back down," constantly moving upward and inward. In order to do this we need to overcome any fear, or perhaps frightening images, that stand in our way or hold us back as they are the *Kelipos*/Concealments of each successive world that wish to hold us back. The goal of the visualization is to consistently move forward, inward, upward until we are able to feel the closeness and cleaving between the mind and Hashem.

To quote:
> "A person has to go from level to level when he wants to rise upward. At first he needs to think about rising to the level of *Rakiah*/Atmosphere (skycap or heavens), which takes "five hundred years." And with his mind he should then broaden the skycap (heavens) in all directions so that it does not appear narrow and small, but rather expansive in all directions.
> And as he stands there he must call to mind that he needs to rise even higher, and then even higher than that. But he cannot rise instantaneously and reach all "seven

heavens" in one movement. Rather, he needs to move from one heaven to the next…

When he comes to the first skycap (heaven) he needs to ensure two things: A) that he does not fall down, B) and also that he is continuously moving upwards.

Since he is literally, in his thoughts, at the first skycap he can therefore progress to the next skycap until he rises to the world of angels (Yetzirah), and then onward to the world of the Throne (Beriah).

After that he will arrive and enter into the world of *Atzilus*/Unity.

And there he should cleave with his mind to the Creator.

When he begins this inward journey he will see the image of a man as well as the image of wild dogs – which represent the *Kelipos* (hindrances) that exist in the world of Asiyah. One needs to be strong and unafraid.

(In the above visualization one sheds their materiality slowly, dropping the body incrementally. As one enters more and more into the vastness of heaven, slowly the body disappears, as it were. The body/form becomes smaller and smaller as the vastness of the cosmos becomes larger and larger.)

But sometimes one can rise above without the body, just with his soul/awareness, as he divests himself from his body. This is called *Hispashtus HaGashmiyus* –where one does not feel the sensations of one's body or the image of this world. Rather, one only sees (with his mind's eye) the upper worlds, including all forms of angels.

And then when he comes into the world of Atzilus he has very little (bodily) sensation, and is therefore able to sense more subtly the Divine closeness.

At this point he becomes aware of the future."

(Likutei Yekarim, p. 3. Baal Shem Tov Torah. Parshas Ekev, 46)

Indeed the floating upward is part of visualizing the lightness of the body. As the person is drifting higher and higher into the greater vastness of empty space, they are becoming lighter and lighter and thus sensing a lessening of the heaviness of the body. This is what is known as a divestment from the physical form.

When you look at someone head on they appear to be 6 feet tall. Stand a bit higher than them and they look to be 4 feet tall. Stand on top of the roof and look down and they appear to be 2 feet tall; from a plane, maybe only 2 inches. So what is the real height? Well, that depends on the perspective of the observer.

As we move higher and higher into vaster and emptier space, our body becomes less and less perceivable.

From the perspective of Asiyah — we are our bodies, physical beings; from Yetzirah — we are our feelings, emotional beings; from Beriah — we are our thoughts or minds, mental beings.

We let go of more of ourselves the higher/deeper we move. We can lose ourselves in music (Yetzirah), or in subtle thoughts (Beriah). In Atzilus there is only pure awareness, there is no 'self'. We cannot imagine ourselves into that reality, as by definition, if we are thinking, then we exist. But we are able to slip into that reality from Beriah. This is similar to the experience in meditation of realizing all of a sudden that you are actually meditating. The moment you have this thought, you are not there anymore; the spell has been broken. You are thinking, not being.

This is a very subtle and delicate awareness characterized by the lessening of the sensations and weight of the body. It is very quiet and deep. Any external noise, such as birds chirping or even the 'thoughts' of another person present, as the Baal Shem Tov teaches *(Baal Shem Tov Torah, Parshas Ekev, 47-48)*, can distract one and draw them back down into the material world of Asiyah.

Visualizing oneself as a being of light can help a person lessen their connection to or dependence on the emotional and mental gravity of their coarser bodies.

We can either think of ourselves as a body that has a soul, or as a soul that is expressed through the medium of the body.

The principle is: the more light (soul), the less vessel (body); and the more pronounced the vessel, the less intense the light. The more we identify with our soul, our purpose, and our connection with the Creator, the less dense our body becomes, and, as a result, the less demanding our bodily needs are in relation to the needs of our soul. The body, and all that the material world represents, becomes more transparent the more we identify with our soul.

The Torah provides a good example of this dynamic in the character of Moshe. Over time, the face of Moshe became radiant *(Shemos, 34; 29)*, which means that his skin was transparent to the light of his soul, much like the body of Adam and Chavah in the Garden of Eden *(Rabbeinu Bachya, Bereishis, 3; 21)*. Think of this in terms of a shade and a lamp. The lamp is the soul, the life force, and energy of the body. The lamp-shade is the body itself. When the shade is properly secured upon the lamp it too seems luminescent, transparent and illuminated. When, however, the shade separates from the lamp it loses all its light and luster. When we understand that our bodies need to be attached to our soul and that our real light and life is our soul, our bodies too become luminescent.

Rabbi Chayim Vital writes of a meditative practice with light as its focus.
To quote:
   "If you are praying, or simply desire to have proper in-

tention, imagine that you are light and that you are sitting in light shining from all sides and directions, and within this light there is a throne of life..."
(Kesavim Chadashim. Shaarei Kedusha 4, Shar 2; 12)

Much of the conversation above is about divestment and untangling oneself from the body and materiality, which seems to suggest that the point or goal is to get away from the body in order to identify with the soul, but this needs further clarification.

Three Levels of Attachment:

This practice of "removing oneself from the physical" does not mean that a person completely forgets about the body or the needs of the body, although it can mean that as well. But on a deeper level it means that a person begins to function from a place of detachment or non-attachment, and then only later learns to integrate their body and soul from a place of positive re-attachment.

There are three levels of attachment or non–attachment. The first level is our natural innate level of ego and self-ishness. On this level there is a tenacious bond between our sense of self and our physical needs. There is a strong reluctance to surrender anything. This is our *animal consciousness.*

Then, with mental and spiritual maturity comes the second stage where a person learns to be less or not completely attached to the needs of the ego and the body. A person becomes transcendent of self and assumes an attitude that whatever happens is OK. One is then able to relinquish any form of ambition or desire. This can be called *angelic consciousness.*

But we are not meant to be angels. If we were meant to be angels why would our souls descend to this earthly plane and not simply exist in the realm of spirit, why become embodied at all if the purpose is to be dis-embodied? Rather, the purpose of human incarnation is to have an ego/ambition/desire while at the same time making the ego transparent to the higher, selfless, transcendent self. The Divine purpose of humanity is realized in the transformation of our physical/animal selves. This can be called *soul consciousness.*

The practice of divesting yourself from the physical means to divest yourself from the egotistical self-centered relationship with the physical (where you need this or that and cannot survive without it) in order to develop an integral relationship between body and soul (level three) that comes from passing through the portal of non-attachment (level two). From a place of detachment you re-attach your body and soul knowing full well that the Divine purpose is fulfilled within the realm of the physical. You must enter level three through level two. When you do so you are then connected to the body, the physical, but from a Divine perspective, as it were.

This is the purpose of the practice of Hishpashtus Ha-Gashmiyus, the divestment of the materiality of level one in order to reinvest your soul into the holistic materiality of level three.

THE ESSENCE:

This subtle balance between being both attached and detached from the body requires us to tap into and reveal our essence, that aspect of us which is connected to the Essence of all Reality. This is an awareness of both the paradoxical fullness and emptiness of everything of this world.

There is *Yesh*/Being, manifestation, fullness, form, and physicality; and there is *Ayin*/Non-Being, un-manifest, empty, unformed, spirit, which the *Yesh* ultimately comes from and is always heading back towards. And then there is the Essence, which transcends and includes them both. The Essence is the context that maintains both the fullness and emptiness, the *Yesh* and the *Ayin*, simultaneously.

When we approach life from an egotistical *Yesh* perspective there often arise unhealthy attachments: "I need this or that, and if I don't get it I am not a complete, whole, or happy person." This is the inner monologue of *Yesh* consciousness.

When we empty ourselves of *Yesh* as much as humanly possible and enter into *Ayin*, we feel no attachments, we are free of all 'things.'

Yet, the highest and deepest level is integrating the two states of *Yesh* and *Ayin*, but from a more expansive and inclusive perspective. In order to accomplish this unification one must divest oneself from coarse unconscious physicality through a divestment of all attachments in order to reenter a more conscious and creative state of physicality that is aware of and responsive to spiritual reality. One must evolve past stage one and grow into stage three, but only through stage two. In this way one is able to reconnect to the physical in a conscious and healthy way, which is in fact the Divine purpose.

From this perspective the body still exists. We do indeed have a vessel. But the vessel is made transparent in order to be unified with the soul. In this way our vessel becomes integral to our light, our purpose and our Divine mission.

As mentioned, *Hispashtus HaGashmiyus* is a practice that is relevant to any form of mental or visual meditation. It is a first initiatory step leading up to any internal mental practice. It is the first ingredient to be able to practice most methods of meditation. That is not to say that divestment from the physical is the only preparatory exercise. There are in fact numerous mental and spiritual preparations available for practitioners. But in terms of this actual practice, divestment from the material is an essential foundation.

Astral Projection & Autoscopic Vision:

In the practice of *Hispashtus HaGashmiyus* a person's sense of awareness, the seat of consciousness is removed from and elevated 'outside' the body. One lifts oneself out of the body, and from this perspective the actual body appears lifeless. One sees the body lying below as if from another location unrelated to the body.

Within the realm of *Hispashtus HaGashmiyus* there is also a form of autoscopic vision, which is an opposite phenomenon. An autoscopic hallucination is where one sees a reflected image of themselves as an external entity, and therefore perceives a projected image of one's body. In this case, the seat of their awareness is still rooted in their actual body, but they observe an external body-double in front of them. In an autoscopic vision the person sees the other body as alive and vibrant, perhaps even talking back to him.

Autoscopic vision is a form of self-seeing hallucination, as it were. The truth is that this can come about when a person suffers from a brain tumor, stroke, migraine, or epilepsy. Psychologically there is also a similar disorder referred to as derealization, and there are many clinical and psychological reasons provided for its occurrence.

If, however, it is an authentic mystical experience then this phenomenon occurs because one has become capable of perceiving their ethereal body. According to the teachings of the Kabbalah there is what is referred to as a *Guf Dak/* Ethereal Body in addition to a person's *Guf Gas/*Coarse Tangible Body. The *Guf Gas* is the physical body that we can all see and feel. The *Guf Dak* is a kind of mentally projected energy field or light-body *(Avodas Hakodesh 2; 26. Rabbeinu Bachya, Toras HaNefesh, 4. There are numerous names for this body double: Chaluka D'rabanan / garment of the sages. Zohar 1, p. 66a. Shaarei Kedushah 1; 1. Malbush / garb. Seforno, Kavanas HaTorah. Tzelem / shadow, or aura. Nishmas Chayim, 1; 13).*

A person's relationship with his energy-body is symbiotic and reciprocal. It is the means through which the physical body expands and develops *(R. Shem Tov ben Shem Tov, Sefer Ha'emunos, 6; 4).* Conversely, it is also sustained by the physical body throughout one's life by the person's very own behavior and mindset *(The Mabit, Beis Elokim, Shar Hayesodos, 53).*

There are pious and integrated individuals who are able to project their *Guf Dak* into a distant location, even while they are vested within their *Guf Gas*. Physically they can be in one locality, while spiritually they can project a manifestation of themselves into another, perhaps even distant place. This phenomenon is referred to as astral projection, or out-of-body traveling. The celebrated Chassidic Rebbe, R. Zusha, once remarked that he saw the face of his revered brother R. Elimelech in his home, even while R. Elimelech was not physically present *(Menoras Zahav, Miketz)*.

Those who are realized masters and are in total control of their internal and external reality have the power to detach their 'substance' (their ethereal body), from their 'form' (their material body), and dispatch it at will. The sending out of this energy-body to another place allows the 'person' to be in two different places simultaneously, existing in a non-localized state. In this type of projection consciousness resides both in the projecting self, the *Guf Gas* and within image that is being projected and guided, the *Guf Dak*. In a way, this projection is similar to *Hispashtus HaGashmiyus* in that the seat of consciousness is (also) outside the *Guf Gas* and resides within the *Guf Dak*, the ethereal body, but dissimilar in that the experience occurs within the physical/vibrational plane of reality; whereas *Hishpashtus HaGashmiyus* is entirely "beyond" this realm of existence.

Yet, as mentioned, there is also autoscopic vision where the seat of awareness is within the coarse body (the *Guf Gas)* while it is observing the *Guf Dak* (the ethereal body), and the *Guf Dak* is vibrant, animated and even audible, so to speak.

Chemical imbalance is indeed the grounds for many such cases as found in those who suffer from brain tumors, strokes, and migraines. And in these cases such imbalance may often be its root cause. However, in some situations the physical symptom is merely the effect, while the cause may be an authentic interaction with the meta-physical and super-natural plane, as in a prophetic–like experience *(Shoshan Sodos, p. 69b. Ramak, Ohr Yakar, Shir HaShirim, Derisha 2; 2. The Ramah, Torahs Ha'olah, 14. R. Tzadok HaKohen, Dover Tzedek, p. 96a).* Occasionally, the ethereal image can communicate and transmit wisdom to the person having such an experience. In the prophetic experience the prophet's coarse body goes into a state of suspended animation. The prophet may fall to the ground and behold a mirror-like image of his own body that is vibrant, alive, pulsating, and transmitting prophetic insight *(Shushan Sodos, p. 171-172. See also Safer HaGilgulim, 64. Emek HaMelech, Hakdamah 3; 1. Sheivet HaMusar, 35).*

This experience is not reserved for the prophets alone, for "some of the pious attain an observation of their own image" *(Pardes Rimonim, 31; 4).* Indeed, it is a most extraordinary phenomenon and certainly one that demands a mastery over one's power of imagination. It demands that one be a "ruler over his spirit" *(Mishlei 16; 32),* as it were. To experience this type of 'talk-back' one needs self-control on all levels of his being — physical, emotional, mental and spiritual. Still, with effort, toil and perseverance this too is attainable.

ATZILUS WITHIN ASIYAH VS. ATZILUS WITHIN ATZILUS:

An important point must be made about the entire concept of *Hispashtus HaGashmiyus*/Divestment from the Physical, wherein a person meditatively experiences a state of *Ayin/*

No-thing-ness. At first glance one may speculate that the ultimate experience of *Ayin* is easily accessible and readily available; all one needs to do is meditate and visualize oneself in a state of *Ayin* and one therefore achieves the level of *Ayin*. According to this perspective, no matter how coarse a person may be or how attached and connected he is to his ego-based narrative, so long as he can meditatively practice *Hishpashtus*/Divestment from the material world he is in fact transcendent. In other words, even a person who is ego-driven, and perhaps even evil, can, through a quick meditative session reach Atzilus, the innermost world of Transcendence.

But can that really be true? What then would be the difference between a *Tzadik* and a *Rasha*? A *Tzadik* being a wholly integrated and impeccably ethical individual both in relation to other people as well as to his Creator, and a *Rasha* being a totally debased and immoral person.

Sadly, the truth is that many people who "indulge" in such spiritual practices do so for spiritual "entertainment" and are often even more ego-driven and obsessed with themselves than are other people. There seems to be a narcissistic vein that runs through many so-called spiritual seekers. But is not the practice of *Hispashtus* meant to distance a person from such a debased state? Does the practice itself not elevate a person beyond their *Yesh*/Ego existence and into a state of *Bitul HaYesh*/Self-Nullification and *Ayin*/No-Thingness?

To better understand this phenomenon a holographic paradigm needs to be employed. Every macro-stage and state
includes all other states and stages in micro-form. *Atzilus/*
Transcendence is the highest/deepest reality. In contrast,
Asiyah/Physicality is the lowest and densest. In between
Asiyah and Atzilus is *Yetzirah*/the Emotional world, and
Beriah/the Mental realm. These are the four macro-worlds/
stages/states and each one of these four includes all four
levels in micro-form. There is Atzilus on its own (i.e., as a
world), and there is also the level of Atzilus within the world
of Asiyah. There is Asiyah on its own (i.e., as a world) and
there is also the level of Asiyah within the world of Atzilus.

A person who is stuck in the world of Asiyah is utterly attached to the needs of their body, totally engulfed in the
desires of their ego, and is only able to sense their separate "I". Therefore such a person can only attain elevation
within the world of Asiyah. There is a low-ceiling, so to
speak, on their ability to evolve and transcend themselves
and their current reality. And when such a person experiences *Hispashtus*, even when they can conceptually meditate
and divest themselves from materiality to a degree in order
to enter into a more Atzilus-like reality, they are still only
able to attain, at most, the level of Atzilus within the world
of Asiyah.

When a person elevates himself and his way of life beyond
the world of Asiyah by breaking the limitations of his body

or going out of his physical comfort zone to help another person or to do a Mitzvah, then he reaches beyond the level of Asiyah through his very actions.

Now if he meditates and experiences *Hispashtus* he will experience the level of Atzilus within the world of Yetzirah. Since he is, by virtue of the very way he is living, already at the level of Atzilus (*Ayin*, non-attachment) within Asiyah (the nullification or elevation from physicality), the meditation practice then serves to propel him beyond that level into the world of Yetzirah. The level of Atzilus that he is then able to attain through the practice of *Hispashtus* is of Atzilus within Yetzirah.

An even higher and deeper way of living is when a person works on refining his emotions and therefore attains a degree of Atzilus within the world of Yetzirah by virtue of his internal wellbeing and balance. Practically this means that he lives from a place of *Ayin*/Non-attachment on an emotional level, without any trace of (negative) anger or lust. As a result he is neither affected by praise nor hurt by denigration. Therefore when he meditates and experiences *Hispashtus* he is able to attain a degree of Atzilus within the world of Beriah.

Beyond the emotions, an even deeper and higher way of living is the path of transforming the very way one thinks and perceives. This occurs when one's inner world of mind is filled with only holy and transcendent thoughts such as words of Torah and deeper meaning. Then when this pure and holy person practices Hispashtus he is actually able to attain the level of Atzilus within the world of Atzilus.

The practice of this meditation always elevates one to the next level of Atzilus beyond where they are starting from.

This is all to say that a person's actions and ethics in this world affect the heights of consciousness he is able to reach in meditation. That is why authentic Kabbalah never proscribes spiritual practices or exercises through which to attain higher levels of consciousness in a behavioral vacuum. *Torah, Halacha, Mitzvos,* and *Derech Eretz* (common sense and conviviality) are essential ingredients in one's spiritual development, and in fact create the greater context of one's character within which any personal transformation can occur. Physical, emotional, and mental maturity, purity and discipline provide the foundation upon which any further spiritual elevation is predicated.

This is a very important principle that needs to be considered and pondered. To live our lives at our maximum potential we need to do the real deep and hard work of refining ourselves on all levels of our being — physical, emotional and mental — so that when we do practice *Hispashtus* it is a genuine spiritual experience and not merely another form of debased "elevation."

GOOD TIMES FOR HISPASHTUS: LYING IN BED:

One more point about *Hispashtus HaGashmiyus* worth mentioning, although a fuller exploration of *Hispashtus* will be expounded upon in a future book, G-d willing. We should keep in mind that throughout the day there are more opportune times to practice than others. There are certain times during the day, for example, before falling asleep, when there is an almost built-in mechanism that can assist a person to achieve *Hispashtus*.

When a person is lying in bed and the body is lethargic, weak and tired it can be an opportune time to practice *Hispashtus*.

The way to do this would be as follows; as you are dragging your tired body into bed imagine that your "body" is so exhausted that it does not have the strength to climb into bed, and as you are getting into the bed, your "body" literally "falls" and remains stuck on the floor.

Another method is to lie in bed exhausted and drained from the day's work and while fully aware of the body's tiredness, you imagine the body, the "garment" of your soul, falling off the bed and unto the ground.

This type of *Hispashtus* comes with ease and is effortless, because of the natural tiredness of the body, the body allows itself to drop more easily and your consciousness can thus rise more smoothly, as it does during a dream state.

Good Times for Hispashtus: The Mikvah:

Many have the custom to immerse themselves in a *Mikvah* (a ritual bath of water) daily or before Shabbos. Going to the *Mikvah* is another fitting time to achieve *Hispashtus*. There are various elements why this is true. For one, the very act of immersing in water is a form of *Hispashtus* and a *Hispashtus* that is palpably felt.

In Hebrew to immerse is to *Tovel*. *Tovel* contain the same letters as the word *Bitul*, to nullify. Going under water is an act of self-nullification. We are land based creatures, our existence is dependent on oxygen and when we go under water we enter a non-being reality. When we hold our breath under water, we cease being as we know it. If land is where we exist, under water is the place where we cease to exist. The mere act of being under water is conducive for *Hispashtus* as you are practicing *Hispashtus* by the very act of being under the water. Additionally, there is also the element of not wearing any garments while immersing.

Not only is being under water a shedding of the material and physical body, the entire process of going into the *Mikvah* as an exercise of *Hispashtus*. Slowly undressing, garment by garment there is a visceral sensation of letting go, a sense of peeling away the layers, stripping away the garments of your being.

Before you are about to undress notice what you are wearing, feel the weight of your clothing, the soiled quality of the fabric pressing against your body. Imagine each piece of clothing as an extraneous layer, inhibiting an inauthentic expression of who you are, and how you are living your life. Allow each piece to drop to the ground, one after the other, until you are unclothed, free of all unnecessary covering.

Now that you have gone through a *Hispashtus* of your literal garments, as you slowly go down the steps into the Mikvah notice how the water is receiving you completely, and the lower you step the more enveloped you become. At this point, not only did you drop your external garments, but now under the water you have let go of your entire body and all your external and physical limitations.

Mikvah, as the time just before bed, is a "natural" time to practice *Hispashtus*, and in many ways, it is the most powerful and potent time to attain *Hispashtus* and experience true soul elevation.

VISUAL TWO: PRACTICE

» DIVESTING ONESELF FROM PHYSICAL FORM

This visualization is best practiced during the evening, after sunset.

Set a soft timer (or have someone else observe you) in order to fully enter this meditation without any worry of what needs to be done afterwards. This time is for being present. Allow yourself the gift of this experience.

For those new to meditation practice, it is recommended to start with anywhere from 10-20 minutes. This is not a competitive practice, so if that amount of time feels overwhelming for you, best to start slowly, and steadily build on a strong foundation.

Invite all of yourself into this space here and now. In a comfortable seat, preferably with your eyes closed, take a moment to let go of all the noise, chaos and movement in your life; simply be. Just as we need to minimize external stimuli via the sense of touch, the same is true with the

other senses. To aid visualization, it is beneficial to gently close your eyes, shutting out the external world in order to move more inward to your inner field of vision.

You may notice various sounds, sensations, thoughts or feelings crossing your mind. Sense everything without manipulating it; accept what is and relax from the urge to act.

With a deep exhalation, focus on the breath leaving your body, naturally and effortlessly. Inhalation is the body's instinctive response to exhalation, effortlessly being drawn into the lungs from the power of the pressure created by exhaling.

From a comfortable position, preferably outdoors, turn your gaze up to the sky. If, for any reason, you are unable to be outdoors or to turn your head upwards, simply turn your inner gaze upwards with eyes closed. Travel with your gaze up into the expanse of the sky.

The higher you go, the lighter you become as the weight of your body and gravity's pull gradually lessen, unburdening you. Admiring the vastness and beauty of the night sky, offer praise to the One Who created such beauty. In the vastness of the cosmos observe how grand each individual star is, as well as how much distance there is from one star to the next. The more keen your attention, the more overwhelmed you may feel by the sheer magnitude of existence.

Embrace this opportunity to be humbled like a small speck of dust in the vastness of the cosmos.

Hold this inner space of awe within the greatness of all that is outside of you.

And when you have reached a plateau here, ascend yet again, rising higher and higher, becoming lighter and lighter.

The higher you climb, the lighter you become until you experience freedom from your materiality.

In this ethereal–like existence, return all the way back into your body.

Secure the conjoining of body and soul by taking a few deep breaths.

Gently open your eyes.

On the following page is an alternative version of the above practice.

VISUAL TWO: PRACTICE

» Alternative Method: Expanding Oneness with All

Set a soft timer (or have someone else observe you) in order to fully enter this meditation without any worry of what needs to be done afterwards. This time is for being present. Allow yourself the gift of this experience.

For those new to meditation practice, it is recommended to start with anywhere from 10–20 minutes. This is not a competitive practice, so if that amount of time feels overwhelming for you, best to start slowly, and steadily build on a strong foundation.

Invite all of yourself into this space here and now. In a comfortable seat, preferably with your eyes closed, take a moment to let go of all the noise, chaos and movement in your life; simply be. Just as we need to minimize external stimuli via the sense of touch, the same is true with the other senses. To aid visualization, it is beneficial to gently close your eyes, shutting out the external world in order to move more inward to your inner field of vision.

You may notice various sounds, sensations, thoughts or feelings crossing your mind.

Sense everything without manipulating it; accept what is and relax from the urge to act.

With a deep exhalation, focus on the breath leaving your body, naturally and effortlessly. Inhalation is the body's instinctive response to exhalation, effortlessly being drawn into the lungs from the power of the pressure created by exhaling.

From a seated or standing position, bring your awareness to your toes. Guide your awareness up your body: feet, legs, torso, arms, hands, neck, mouth, nose, eyes, forehead, all the way to the crown of the head.

Rest your full presence of mind just above your head.

Expand out and up until you can observe your body from above. Continue traveling upward, rising above the roof of your home or wherever you are at, until you are able to see the building below.

Rise above your city, then beyond your country.

Keep rising above the globe of the earth into outer space.

Traveling into the vastness of the cosmos, observe how grand each individual star is and how great the distance is from one star to the next. The more keen your attention, the more overwhelmed you may feel. Embrace this opportunity to be humbled.

Hold this inner space of awe within the greatness of all that is outside of you.

And when you have reached a plateau here, ascend yet again, rising higher and higher, becoming lighter and lighter.

The higher you climb the lighter you become, until you experience freedom from your body-mass.

In this ethereal—like existence, return all the way back into your body.

Secure the conjoining of body and soul by taking a few deep breaths.

Gently open your eyes.

VISUAL THREE: IDEA

» Visualizing being in Gan Eden, Paradise, World of Souls

In the previous methods of visualization one is either becoming aware of being in the most sacred space (inwardly and outwardly), or even divesting oneself from the material body altogether as they travel up and out into the cosmos. In the following method one aspires to go 'beyond' the world as it were. In this manner, the goal of this visualization if to enter, via one's mental capacity, into the world of souls — a world of disembodied consciousness. One thereby journeys beyond the vastness of the cosmos and swims into a world of pure spirit.

Following a divestment from the physical, which places one's awareness beyond the body, one is then able to move into the world of *Gan Eden*/Paradise.

In *Halacha*/Jewish law, we are encouraged during our prayers to direct our minds and hearts upward, as if we were literally standing in the presence of the Shechinah *(Sanhedrin, 22a)*. We should thus imagine ourselves as if "we are [standing] in heaven" *(Rambam, Hilchas Tefilah, 5; 4. Rabbeinu Yonah, Berachos, 25a)*.

And where in Heaven exactly should we picture ourselves to be? Specifically, we should envision ourselves being in *Gan Eden*/The Garden of Eden, the world of souls. Rabbi Eliyahu De Vidas *(16th century, Tzfas, Israel)* suggests that one should imagine oneself while praying or studying Torah — or any time for that matter — as if he is not present in this world, but rather that he is standing in *Gan Eden* in the presence of the Shechinah.

To quote:
> "Therefore it is very good for man at the times that he is involved in prayer or study to picture himself as not standing in this physical world, but rather standing in *Gan Eden*, in front of the Shechinah."
> *(Reishis Chochmah, Shar Hakedusah, Chap 4)*

To augment this practice you may also want to imagine yourself in *Gan Eden* praying or studying in the presence of *Tzadikim* of the past such as Moshe *Rabbeinu*, Rabbi Akiva, Rashi or the Baal Shem Tov.

In this practice that is being suggested you are not only setting a mental *Kavanah* to connect yourself with the souls of
the *Tzadikim*, as many teachers have encouraged *(Meor Einayim (Chernobyl) Parshas Beshalach. See also The Chasam Sofer, D'rashos, Parshas Nitzavim, regarding the prayers on Rosh Hashanah and
Yom Kippur)*, but you are actively conjuring up a visual image
of yourself praying amidst the *Tzadikim* and thereby creating an even stronger sense of *Yichud*/Unity between your
soul and theirs. The very act of visualizing this *Kavanah*,
rather than just intellectually thinking about it, brings it to
life and involves more of your whole being in its resonance
and repercussions.

When a person is praying or studying Torah, says Reb Levi
Yitzchak of Berditchev *(Kedushas Levi, Shir Hashirim)*, he
should have a thought that he is now in *Gan Eden* and all
of his ancestors and the lofty souls of the past are all listening to his voice and gaining immense spiritual delight *(Shir
Hashirim, 8; 13. Medrash Rabbah Ibid, 8. Pri Eitz Chayim, Sha'ar
Tikkun Chatzos 2)*.

In this way, one visualizes oneself learning or praying in the
presence of the holy and noble souls of the past and these
souls are, in turn, also listening to his or her words of prayer
and study. When a person can truly visualize and perceive
himself as being in *Gan Eden* while studying or praying he
will then also be able to pray, study or meditate from an
Edenic place within himself. This is an inner reality free of

jealously, desire, haughtiness, arrogance and ego. Therefore his prayers will be more pure, focused and well-intentioned *(Maggid Devarav L'Yaakov, 262. Darchei Tzedek, 1; 81).*

As previously mentioned, our sages suggest that, "a person should walk in the measure of two doors before prayer" *(Berachos, 8a).* Meaning that in prayer we are exiting out of one door (this world), and entering through another door into the spiritual world of souls. We should therefore leave this earthly realm and enter into a higher world, effectively leaving one reality behind and entering in to another. When we pray, study, or, by extension, do anything with mindfulness, awareness, and deep intention we are at that moment within *Gan Eden*, in the presence of *Tzadikim* of the past who are not only passively present but are actively listening and paying attention to our actions and intentions. In this way we are actually nourishing the souls of the *Tzadikim*.

VISUALIZE AN IMAGE OF A *Tzadik* THAT YOU KNOW:

To make this visual even more tangible, beyond simply imagining yourself standing and praying in the presence of the *Tzadikim* of yesteryear, you may also want to imagine a *Tzadik* or *Tzadikim* that you have actually known or physically seen as you are learning or praying *(Yosher Divrei Emes, Os 33. Likutei Yekarim, 129a).* This is in fact an effective preparation for deep transformative prayer or study. Picture yourself praying with *Tzadikim* that you have met with or seen with your own eyes. Imagine standing next to your Rebbe and praying with all your heart.

In addition, *Gan Eden* is not just a 'perfected location' or a 'safe place', but along with its 'image' comes a sense of transformed consciousness. It is, ultimately, a higher and deeper reality. When a person imagines himself in *Gan Eden* he envisions himself being in a *Gan Eden* reality, which is a world empty of all jealousy, lust, pride and ego. Imagine that the guiding principles or driving forces in your life have nothing to do with how much honor you will have, or how rich, famous, powerful, or respected you will be for doing the right thing or succeeding in your endeavors. In this reality you are just pursuing and performing the truth because it is true. By imagining oneself being "there" in *Gan Eden*, in the reality of paradise, you will create this reality for yourself and, according to the Magid of Mezritch *(Maggid Devarav L'Yaakov, p. 325)*, you will be able to pray without ulterior motives and vain thoughts as if you were already in *Gan Eden* devoid of all anger, lust, jealousy, pride, power and greed.

Although there is no *Mitzvah*/Obligation to fool yourself, and the person praying knows full well that he is most likely not on such an elevated level as he is probably still full of jealousy, anger, arrogance, greed and ego, nonetheless this visualization is still a powerful and effective practice. As the Maggid explains, when a person studies or prays with love and awe, thereby attaching his mind and heart to the Creator and to the ultimate reality of how "there is no place devoid of Him" and also that "the whole world is filled with Hashem's glory," then the end effect will be that within everything that person sees he will begin to see the life force of the Creator. In other words, through the mere act of 'imagining' this state of consciousness and praying with sincerity as if already 'there,' a person will be catapulted, at least for the time spent in prayer and meditation, into such an elevated state.

Often, one will find that a visual on its own is hard to hold in one's attention and he may therefore want to add other senses into the practice. For this reason many *Tzadikim* suggested that to make the image more real and easier to conjure up, it might also be beneficial to verbally declare before praying, "I hereby bind myself to all the *Tzadikim* of the generations" *(Likutei Moharan I. 2; 6, 9; 4. See also: Yosher Divrei Emes, (Zabarazh) 2. 33. Be'er Mayim Chayim (Chernowitz), Parshas Vayetzei).* This way you are both using your visual power of imagination coupled with the auditory power of speaking something into being, and, in effect, making it more real.

As it is with sound, the same is true for the other senses as well. For example, if one is using this *Gan Eden* visualization before or during prayer a corresponding bodily shift can also help maintain the focus. In the words of the *Shul-*

chan Aruch, the Code of Jewish Law, you may want to "lift your eyes upwards, towards heaven, to awaken intention" *(Shulchan Aruch Ha'Rav, 95; 3)*. Simply effecting a shift and tilt of the head towards the "Above" can refocus your intention upwards. Often a physical, external movement facilitates a more inward, mental movement. Shifting your head or your gaze upward stimulates and directs one's thoughts "Upwards" towards the Heavens.

The point is that in order to help focus your awareness in the visual sense one can use all the senses at their disposal including the tactile (tilting the head upwards), the auditory (verbally stating that, "I hereby bind myself to all the *Tzadikim* of the past"), or for that matter the olfactory (one can actually attempt to smell the *Reiach*/Scent of Gan Eden). Even if you are not privy to that heavenly scent, certainly there is a particular scent that reminds you of a state of perfection, ease, peace and harmony.

VISUAL THREE: PRACTICE

» EXISTING WITHIN GAN EDEN

Set a soft timer (or have someone else observe you) in order to fully enter this meditation without any worry of what needs to be done afterwards. This time is for being present. Allow yourself the gift of this experience.

For those new to meditation practice, it is recommended to start with anywhere from 10-20 minutes. This is not a competitive practice, so if that amount of time feels overwhelming for you, best to start slowly, and steadily build on a strong foundation.

Invite all of yourself into this space here and now. In a comfortable seat, preferably with your eyes closed, take a moment to let go of all the noise, chaos and movement in your life; simply be. Just as we need to minimize external stimuli via the sense of touch, the same is true with the other senses. To aid visualization, it is beneficial to gently close your eyes, shutting out the external world in order to move more inward to your inner field of vision.

You may notice various sounds, sensations, thoughts or feelings crossing your mind.

Sense everything without manipulating it; accept what is and relax from the urge to act.

With a deep exhalation, focus on the breath leaving your body, naturally and effortlessly. Inhalation is the body's instinctive response to exhalation, effortlessly being drawn into the lungs from the power of the pressure created by exhaling.

From a seated or standing position, bring your awareness to your toes. Guide your awareness up your body: feet, legs, torso, arms, hands, neck, mouth, nose, eyes, forehead, all the way to the crown of the head.

Rest your full presence of mind just above your head.

Expand out and up until you can observe your body from above. Continue traveling upwards, moving above the roof until you are able to see the building below.

Rise above your city, then your country.

Rise above the globe of the earth into outer space.

As you travel further into the infinite cosmos, every time you reach a skycap or sense that you have reached an insurmountable border, push through it and go even higher.

And then when you have reached a new plateau, ascend yet again, rising higher and higher, becoming lighter and lighter.

The higher you climb, the more brilliant and filled with light reality becomes.

Every time a new ceiling, skycap is passed through a new reality is revealed that is even more brilliant and brighter than before.

Finally, you pass through another gap in the skycap and the most brilliant light you have ever experienced comes gushing forth. In this sparkling new reality, you begin to make out the outlines of beings of beautiful light, radiating holiness and purity.

You are now in the realm of Gan Eden/The World of Souls.

Some souls you may recognize, as they are Tzadikim that you may have seen, or maybe you have encountered them through their teachings that you may have studied.

You are embraced by an overwhelming feeling of joy, holiness and purity.

Everything in your personal life comes into crystal clear focus.

. . . .

There are no longer any illusions, uncertainties or doubts as to what is your Divine purpose in being created. You are a soul enclothed in a body and are in this world for a mission and purpose that only you can accomplish.

. . . .

In this spirit of elation and clear-mindedness, gently open your eyes.

. . . .

///////////////////////////////

VISUAL FOUR: IDEA

» Visualizing Being at Sinai

Sinai is the source of all revelation. At Mount Sinai, following the exodus from Egypt, we collectively experienced and received the revelation of the Torah. In this way Divine Wisdom and Truth were revealed for us to wrestle with and unpack for all subsequent generations.

At Sinai we experienced a collective mystical experience. The earth shook as fire and smoke poured forth from the mountain. The entire Community of Israel stood together in awe at the foot of Sinai as the Divine Presence thrust them into profound revelation. The thunder of awakening surged through each heart and mind as a transcendent voice spoke out: *Anochi Hashem Elokecha*. The literal translation of this phrase is, "I am Hashem (The Name), your G-d."

At that moment we all knew that indeed the only true existence is "*Anochi*/I am Hashem." Nothing else is independently real. All manifest existence is empty and literally non-existent without the continued sustenance from the One Ultimate Existence.

While the event at Sinai occurred in the past and will never be repeated, the echoes of Sinai are still felt today. There is forever a *Bas Kol*, a faint echo resonating from Sinai *(Avos, 6; 2)* that registers within our deepest selves.

Beyond the 'echo' of Sinai, which is heard deep within the souls of the entire nation of Israel that stood at the foot of the mountain, we are instructed by the Torah to remember this archetypal revelatory event every day of our lives. There is in fact a continuous Mitzvah to remember this experience. It is one of the six constant Mitzvos that inform and direct our consciousness at every moment.

We can take up this obligation and remember Sinai by reading over the events as described in the Torah, or we can even visualize the actual event in our mind's eye, complete with all the attendant sights and sounds of such an experience — the fire, the smoke, the trembling earth, and the synesthetic sound of Hashem's speech uttering, *"Anochi Hashem."*

The *Kav Ha'Yashar*/The Just Measure, which is a classic work of *Mussar*/Religious Ethics, was written by the Kabbalist and moralist Rabbi Tzvi Hirsch Kaidanover and is one of the most prominent texts of ethical and moral guidance published in the last 300 years. This was and is a popular text even among followers of the Baal Shem Tov. The Tzemach Tzedek (third Chabad Rebbe) instructed his disciples to study the *Kav Ha'Yashar (Likkutei Dibburim I, p.54)* as part of their spiritual regimen. Incidentally, part of the reason for its popularity is that it was published in both Hebrew and in Yiddish, the common spoken language of Eastern European Jewry. Interestingly enough the word *Yashar* that appears in the title has the same letters as the author's Yiddish name, *Hirsch*.

The *Kav Ha'Yashar* strongly encourages people to envision the giving of the Torah at Sinai complete with all its details — the fire, the smoke, and the sounds —immediately upon awakening *(Kav Ha'Yashar, Chap 1)*.

Sometime later, the *Sheim M'shmuel (Parshas Yisro)* explained that since, "A person is where their thoughts are, by creating a visual image in the mind's eye of the actual giving of the Torah we are once again there, at Sinai receiving the Torah."

Upon awaking one should visualize the giving of the Torah on Mount Sinai. Imagine standing in a state of purity, awe and trembling, literally perspiring in exaltation. The mountain is bellowing with flames, the Shofar sounds are blasting, and amidst the sounds of thunder and lightning a profound life- and history-altering prophetic revelation is taking place. The world is aflame with Divine light and you are actually standing at the foot of the smoking mountain receiving the Torah.

You just woke up and here you are at the peak of the greatest collective mystical experience of all time. What a way to start your day and wake up from your physical and spiritual slumber.

This concept of visualizing the giving of the Torah on Mount Sinai is also cited in *Halachic*/Legal texts. Although in those texts it is mostly concerned with one's focus during the weekly public Torah reading. Concerning this it is taught that when the Torah portion of the week is read on Shabbos, one should visualize and attempt to feel that the Torah that is being read in Shul is the very Torah that was received on Mt. Sinai *(Bach, Hilchos Kerias HaTorah, Siman 141)*.

Whether we practice this once a week, as the Torah is being read, or every day upon awaking, the objective is that we take an idea that we generally hold to be true on an intellectual level and attempt to integrate it on a more visceral level through the act of creative visualization. Using the power of inner visualization we can further this process of transforming what we know to be true into something that we actually experience. Through a visual we ingrain what we know in the mind into the deeper levels of our psyche. The fact that we did receive and are in fact continually receiving the Torah from on High is a fundamental principle of Torah. Yet, this is an intellectual truth that, when re-experienced within the mind's eye, becomes that much more acute, vivid and real.

VISUAL FOUR: PRACTICE:

» Re- experiencing Matan Torah/ Receiving of the Torah

Set a soft timer (or have someone else observe you) in order to fully enter this meditation without any worry of what needs to be done afterwards. This time is for being present. Allow yourself the gift of this experience.

For those new to meditation practice, it is recommended to start with anywhere from 10-20 minutes. This is not a competitive practice, so if that amount of time feels overwhelming for you, best to start slowly, and steadily build on a strong foundation.

Invite all of yourself into this space here and now. In a comfortable seat, preferably with your eyes closed, take a moment to let go of all the noise, chaos and movement in your life; simply be. Just as we need to minimize external stimuli via the sense of touch, the same is true with the other senses. To aid visualization, it is beneficial to gently close your eyes, shutting out the external world in order to move more inward to your inner field of vision.

You may notice various sounds, sensations, thoughts or feelings crossing your mind.

Sense everything without manipulating it; accept what is and relax from the urge to act.

With a deep exhalation, focus on the breath leaving your body, naturally and effortlessly. Inhalation is the body's instinctive response to exhalation, effortlessly being drawn into the lungs from the power of the pressure created by exhaling.

Now visualize your mind being emptied upon each exhalation in preparation for receiving an imaginable gift. Count at least five exhalations that fully empty you from within. You may take as many as you need until you physically feel the sacred hollow space revealed within you.

Imagine having prepared and purified yourself for days, and that you are now standing in the desert at the foot of Mount Sinai.

You can feel the heat of the desert sun. You can sense the texture of the sand beneath your feet. Everything seems very real and visceral.

Slowly move towards the bellowing mountain, roaring with loud thunder and lighting, in great awe, excitement and trepidation.

As you slowly inch yourself closer and closer to the mountain, the Shofar sounds become louder, the smoke becomes thicker and the fire hotter.

You stand at the foot of the mountain in an awe-inspired state of purity, trembling with exaltation. Amidst the sounds of thunder and lightning you sense the world is aflame with Divine light as you are literally standing at the smoking mountain receiving the Divine revelation of Torah.

The Divine Presence thrusts a great and profound flow of abundance upon you. The thunder of awakening surges through your mind, heart and being, and you hear a Transcendent voice ring out: Anochi Hashem/I am Hashem.

At this moment, it is absolutely clear to you that indeed the only true existence is, "I am Hashem." Nothing else has any true independent existence. All manifestation is empty and literally non-existent without the continued sustaining life-force emanating from the Ultimate Existence.

This is the essence of the Torah and it is a gift you receive anew at every moment.

Allow the truth of this realty to vibrate throughout your entire being. Feel empowered, charged, and infused with purpose and mission. Gently open your eyes.

VISUAL FIVE: IDEA

» Visualizing that YOU are the Tzadik

In the previous methods of visualization one imagined themselves as being in *Gan Eden* or in the Holy of Holies, at the foot of Mount Sinai, or in the presence of *Tzadikim*. As one engages in these types of visualizations he is, essentially, still separate from his imagined reality. One is visualizing or observing 'perfection,' but it is not his reality. There is a deeper level where one aspires to visualize oneself as the *Tzadik*, at this very moment, in this very place. In this method Paradise is recognized as being within you, as it were.

On a simple level this is accurate in that there are *Nekudos Tovos*/Points of Goodness within each one of us. As Reb Nachman of Breslov elaborates, no matter what a person has or has not done in their life there are always 'points of goodness' within each and every one of us and it is our

Avodah/Spiritual Work to acknowledge, articulate, and amplify them.

Or, as Reb Tzadok writes *(Tzidkas Ha'Tzadik, 58)*, each one of us is a *Tzadik* in relation to at least one particular issue in life. We all have an area or two in which we excel and have little struggle. For some people it could be that they are in possession of an even-tempered nature and they are therefore not prone to anger. For others it may be a natural yearning to pray or meditate. And yet for others, it may manifest as a natural inclination to pursue justice.

On an even deeper level, there are sources that speak of a person imagining himself as a *Malach*/Angel during his prayers *(Safer Hayashar, Shar 13; Tur, Beis Yoseph, 95; 1. Mishnah Berurah ibid)*. But the truth is that our "souls" are rooted within an even deeper inner space than angels or any otherworldly creature.

There are "worlds," "angels," and "souls." Worlds are the outer manifestation, the place of apparent duality and separation. They are thus related to speech, as in: "Hashem spoke and said 'let there be light,' and there was light." Angels occupy a more subtle realm and are therefore connected to the *Ruach*/Wind within the mouth, before it manifests as speech. Souls are the most inner reality and are therefore connected to the breath itself, as in, "He blew into his (Adam's) nostrils a breath of life."

Indeed, when we try to visualize ourselves as angels, and even beyond that, as souls or perfected beings, this is not a fantasy or foolish mental projection. On the contrary, it is rather a materialization of a profound truth. This is who we are at our core. Our revealed, often damaged, flawed, imperfect self is the external level of self. But deep down, in essence, we are perfect.

This perfection is not a destination or a location, but something residing deep within.

At the deepest root of our soul, at our *Shoresh Ha'Neshama*, we are all *Tzadikim* at one with our Source and rooted within the Infinite Light of Hashem. R. Chayim Vital *(Shaarei Kedusha, 3; 5)* writes that, "a person should turn his attention away from all physicality and conjure up an image as if he is ascending into the upper/inner worlds, and he should have intention to receive the light from the source of his soul, where his soul comes from..."

Some years later the Baal Shem Tov taught *(Baal Shem Tov Torah, Ekev 31)* that a person should continuously visualize in his mind's eye that he is literally enclothed within the Light of Hashem, sitting peacefully within this Infinite Light *(Ohr Haganuz L'Tzadikim, Bereishis)*. Indeed, your deepest self is light, completely connected and perennially perfect. This is your point of origin. This is who you really are. You originate from the unified light of Hashem and you are thus able to conjure up an image of your soul ascending into ever more refined levels of Light.

There is our original nature, our primordial state, which we all are at our core; and there is our more revealed self. There is the "perfect self" and there is the "imperfect self." We are a composite of both, neither completely one nor the other. There is a part of the self that is still imperfect and we are working towards perfection, and there is a part of the self that is always and forever perfect. We are both perfect and imperfect at all times.

The imperfect self is our self as manifest in this world, a composite of our imperfect actions or inactions, our imperfect speech, and certainly our imperfect, even negative thoughts. Our 'lower' self is constantly evolving and hopefully progressing (not regressing) as it moves from the lower level of *Nefesh* (base ego instincts) to the ascending levels of *Ruach* and *Neshamah*. This is the part of the self that is constantly striving, aspiring and moving.

Then there is a part of the self, our *Yechidah*/Unique Oneness, which is always perfect, whole, and unified with the Ultimate Perfection.

There is a part of us that struggles, has ups and downs, sometimes falls or slips, and gets back up and fights. Life on this level is a continuous battle, either we are moving

up or down. This is the striving self — the part of self that
is born into lack and always in search for fulfillment. But
we ought not to forget that there is also a part of us that is
always pure, whole and perfect. There is a part of us that is
above all struggle, striving and ambition. This part of the
self is unified and therefore there is no reason to struggle,
because there is no 'where' to 'go.'

There is inevitably a time for *Gevurah*/Strength, where one
constructively criticizes oneself and demands more of oneself in order to grow and move forward. But we also need
to make sure we balance this out with Chesed, wherein we
acknowledge our achievements and accomplishments. On
the deepest level there is a part of us that is always perfect
and can never become sullied, and the more we live from
that place the more our imperfections are in fact perfected.

Our unsullied portion of perfection is our inner, perhaps
even concealed, *Tzadik*-Point. We need to learn to teach
ourselves to imagine ourselves as a *Tzadik* and live from
that place of perfection *(Tzav Ve'Ziruz 24, p.340)*. Regarding
this, the Rebbe Maharash, the fourth Chabad Rebbe, says
that every person should imagine themselves as a *Tzadik*
for at least fifteen minutes a day.

This is not simply an illusion or mere fantasy, but something that is essentially true. Maybe it is not true in the way
a person lives and manifests himself in this world, but in

essence it is true. There is a small sliver of Infinity, of Hashem, within each one of us — a small measure of perfection and unity.

Throughout our lives we can live from either one of these two aspects of self. Clearly it is mentally, emotionally and spiritually more productive and healthy to see yourself from the perspective of your true potential and aspire to live up to that image than to see yourself as a negative person and struggle with that image. We become what we imagine ourselves to be. Arguing and defending one's limitations will ensure that one will remain forever limited.

Every person has an inner-image in their subconscious that informs their life. If you believe deeply that you are a failure, you will continually fail. And if you believe deeply that you deserve goodness and blessings, you will open yourself up to goodness and blessings. People who argue on behalf of their limitations, whether they feel themselves powerless because of their past actions, low IQ, negative upbringing, or lack of education, are sure to keep them. The reverse is also true.

In life you can either view yourself as a *Rasha*/Wicked Person and struggle with and through that self-image, or you can realize that there is a small Tzadik within you, a small measure of perfection and goodness, and aspire to live up to that image. Instead of subscribing to your negative "fantasy," which is not true (i.e., that you are a *Rasha*), use your

Dimyon/Power of Imagination to tap into who you truly are, a *Tzadik*.

Life is best served when we can envision ourselves at our best, to imagine ourselves as a *Tzadik*, which potentially we really are.

The mindset of a *Tzadik* is worthwhile as a general mindset, but it is especially useful in relation to specific issues in life. Say, for instance, a person is working on and refining a particular attribute — they wish, for example, to overcome their instinct to flare up in anger. One should imagine oneself as if he or she has already perfected that very attribute that they are working on refining *(Michtav M'eliyahu 5, p. 38)*. In essence, they should imagine that the negative trait has already been perfected, and work from that paradigm.

This is an example of how such a practice may work regarding specific issues or struggles. But, as stated, to see oneself as a *Tzadik* should be a general outlook on life. You are a *Tzadik* (in potential) and you are transcending your issues and struggles with ease.

This *Tzadik* visualization is an appropriate practice for all times of the day, especially when we are temped into something that we know on an intellectual level is not good for us, or when we feel like we are struggling with various inner voices vying for control of our actions and energies. In these conflicted cases the ego often says one thing while our moral compass says something else, or our instincts tell us one thing and our Divine self says another. These are exceptionally good times to practice this visual. It can give one strength to clarify and act upon that which they know to be good and true in the midst of a moral struggle.

Another good suggestion is to begin the day this way. Set the foundation of the day on this premise. Secure a template or principle upon which all the details of the day can unfold in a positive manner. Set up the context in which the day's content will be perceived and processed.

Every day, before we officially start the day, this is a good visualization, especially when it is coupled with the *Modeh Ani* prayer, which thanks Hashem for returning our soul to our body after sleep. As we are recognizing that, "the soul You have given me is pure" (meaning perfect, untarnished, undamaged), we marry this verbal declaration to a visualization as we imagine our perfected self.

R. Chayim Vital speaks about visualizing oneself as "light" coming from "Light"; yet, there is also a simpler and more straightforward image that can help facilitate this awareness of perfection and wholeness. It may help if a person were to recollect moments in their life that they may have felt very connected and in tune with their deepest self.

For example, visualize yourself intensely praying the *Neila* prayer, the final prayer of Yom Kippur. For many this is the most moving, riveting and awe inspiring prayer of the year. As the "Days of Awe" are coming to a close many of us feel the overwhelming intensity and holiness of the day and, at those final moments, truly open ourselves up to the Divine Beyond.

The day of Yom Kippur unfolds like the peeling of an onion. You peel away layer by layer of your surface identity, going deeper and deeper. And as you do, maybe you tear up and begin to cry. As you are getting deeper and deeper more and more of you is being revealed. You are, in this way, making a connection with your deeper self and allowing yourself to reveal the unbroken but hidden connection you have with the Creator of the universe. This is an appropriate image of oneself to visualize as they are seeking to connect with their inner *Tzadik*.

There is also an even simpler, mundane image that one can use to conjure this image of his perfected self. The *Tzadik* is the 'big' self, the higher/deeper self that is not disturbed by pettiness, the self that lives from within the big picture and does not get caught up in the distractions of life, but remains focused on and committed to his or her spiritual goal or destiny. We all have this *Tzadik* within us and throughout life this higher/deeper self does indeed manifest. Think of a time that you were exceptionally grateful or happy, your wedding day for instance, when, by accident someone stepped on your toes, but because of the deep joy you were feeling, such a small disturbance did not matter in the slightest; you remained focused on your joy. This is another image of the type of person you can truly be, so happy and holy that you are immune to the trivial nuisances that constantly arise from within the midst of life.

VISUAL FIVE: PRACTICE:

» You are a Tzadik!

Set a soft timer (or have someone else observe you) in order to fully enter this meditation without any worry of what needs to be done afterwards. This time is for being present. Allow yourself the gift of this experience.

For those new to meditation practice, it is recommended to start with anywhere from 10-20 minutes. This is not a competitive practice, so if that amount of time feels overwhelming for you, best to start slowly, and steadily build on a strong foundation.

Invite all of yourself into this space here and now. In a comfortable seat, preferably with your eyes closed, take a moment to let go of all the noise, chaos and movement in your life; simply be. Just as we need to minimize external stimuli via the sense of touch, the same is true with the other senses. To aid visualization, it is beneficial to gently close your eyes, shutting out the external world in order to move more inward to your inner field of vision.

You may notice various sounds, sensations, thoughts or feelings crossing your mind.

Sense everything without manipulating it; accept what is and relax from the urge to act.

With a deep exhalation, focus on the breath leaving your body, naturally and effortlessly. Inhalation is the body's instinctive response to exhalation, effortlessly being drawn into the lungs from the power of the pressure created by exhaling.

Begin by slowly breathing in and out. Bring awareness to your external body, focus on your inhalation, and begin moving your awareness inwards.

Think about all your labels and self-definitions: I am the son or daughter of so and so. I do this or that professionally. I am short, tall, thin, heavy, light-skinned, dark-skinned. I am learned, skilled, talented, etc.

Think about all the things you have and all the things you do.

With every inhalation, dig a little deeper: Who am I? I am not my possessions, my feelings or even my thoughts, as "I" am the thinker and feeler. So then, who am I?

With each inhalation go deeper, and with every exhalation shed the layers and labels of your personality.

With each new exhalation, release every single label you identify with in all of its familiarity, safety, comfort and habit.

With each inhalation, go deeper and deeper, shedding layer upon layer of identity, until you experience a sense of pure consciousness.

....

As the external identities are shed, affirm: I am not my body, nor what I do or have, nor my thoughts or feelings. I am at the threshold of my deepest core. This inner core, the soul, the Light of the Creator, is my true identity. This is my point of origin.

....

I am a soul within a body, not a body that has a soul.

....

This soul resides in the deep place within that is always pure and perfect. Your authentic self is light, meaning, connection, unity, perfection. This is you! As the inhalations continue, go deeper and deeper, consent to allow your exhalations to radiate this light outwards.

....

As you exhale, ground your feet, rooting down physically and spiritually as you illuminate your surroundings from within. Grounding down on your exhalations provides more freedom of movement and flexibility to your upper body, especially around your heart. Allow the exhalation to shine outward, to the front and back.

....

Continue with this breathing pattern for a few more relaxed moments.

....

Gently open your eyes.

....

» TAKING ANY IDEA & PUTTING IT TO AN IMAGE

The visualization practices detailed above are a sampling of some of the exercises that are suggested and written about in classic texts, with minimal variations to make them more accessible — but there are many more. In fact, every abstract idea or concept can be connected to a visualization in order to bring it to life, so to speak.

Here is an example of the most 'imageless' of all notions — the Infinite Creator, the essence and root of all reality, the "be-er" of all beingness, about whom it is considered heresy to even attempt to describe, let alone visualize. Not only is it beyond our finite capacity to conceive of or capture Infinity, but also it is logically impossible to contain the "everything" in the form of "something." And yet, in certain cases even the Creator can be 'put' into an image in order to help the novice and initiated alike in their focus on prayer.

It is extremely difficult to pray 'to' Hashem, to reach out and open up to the Source of all Life without some type of image, even if only an image of light. It is nearly impossible to 'visualize' Infinite formless perfection. But a pious person wants to pray and to have a personal relationship with Hashem. They want to feel intimacy with Hashem, and yet, how can one try to conceptualize that with which they seek to connect with without some type of image. There are wise sages that suggest *(see; Bnei Machshava Tova, 7)* that one can begin to visualize an image while attempting to pray, while holding in their mind that there is no substance to the image whatsoever. In this way, the novice may be able to connect more tangibly with the 'imageless' Infinite One during prayer. And from there they may move from the image to the imageless, from the 'thing' to the 'no-thing.'

So, as you begin to pray, imagine that you are speaking to the most powerful omnipotent and yet loving person — exponentially more powerful and more loving than anyone you have ever encountered. Either before or in the midst of praying, visualize that you are standing in front of a majestic ruler, all-powerful and benevolent. In addition, this royal figure that evokes awe and trembling also happens to be your parent, which further evokes a sense of limitless and unconditional love. Furthermore, this figure is your friend, which then evokes a paradoxical feeling of familiarity and intimacy.

This image will help your mind and heart grasp onto a 'something,' allowing you to sharpen your focus and hone your attention and awareness as you direct it towards Hashem. The subtlety of this movement emerges as you progress deeper and deeper into your prayers, feeling closer and closer, experiencing less separation and more unity, until your mind and heart begin to expand and your awareness becomes more transparent and subtle. Perhaps even a spark of prophetic insight will become revealed to you and you will sense, albeit not in a conventional way, the imageless, ineffable and unimaginable Infinite One.

The nature of the mind is such that it needs to hold on to something before letting go of everything. This is a visually stimulating method with which to begin your prayers, so that even while you know intellectually that there is 'no-thing,' you are still attached to a 'some-thing,' whether the image is of a royal, benevolent, loving and familiar figure or of brilliant light. But as you deepen and soften your aware-ness the image becomes more vague and elusive, slowly evaporating and revealing your mind naked without the veil. The image of the figure or the light implodes and dis-appears and you are left with pure pulsing awareness. The image is the veil, but as you are looking at the veil you are acutely aware that it is only a veil, concealing and revealing that which is hidden beneath, behind and beyond it.

VISUAL SIX: IDEA

» DEATH PRACTICE

One final creative visual worth noting that is brought down in many authentic sources is a very intense, harsh and vivid practice where one visualizes jumping into a raging fire.

The early Chassidic master, Reb Elimelech of Lizensk, writes:

> At any time, when one is free from studying Torah, especially when one is idle with nothing productive to do, sitting alone in his room, or lying in bed unable to sleep, (instead of sitting or lying there daydreaming) one should have in mind the *Mitzvah*/Commandment/Divine Invitation of, "And I shall be sanctified among the children of Israel." This is the *Mitzvah* of *Kiddush Hashem*/Sanctifying Hashem's Name and Presence. This is often understood as being willing to sacrifice one's very life for the sake of Hashem.

One should sense within his soul and imagine with his mind's eye that a great blistering fire is burning right in front of him, with the flames reaching up to Heaven. And because of one's deep desire to sanctify Hashem's name he breaks his natural inclination (for life) and throws himself into the fire to sanctify Hashem's name. From this good thought, Hashem will consider it as if he had physically done such an act. This way he is not lying awake or sitting there idle.

He is fulfilling a Mitzvah.

(Tzetal Katan 1)

Essentially Reb Elimelekh is offering this visualization of self-sacrifice as an alternative to just sitting there or idly lying in bed. In this way one can make spiritual use of every moment, including their 'down-time.' This teaching is part of the *Tzetel Katan*/The Small Note, which presents a complete program and approach to living a spiritual and elevated life. Similarly the famed reclusive Kabbalist R. Alexander Zisskind (a contemporary of R. Elimelech) teaches that when one envisions oneself giving up their lives, literally imagining being killed performing a sanctification of Hashem's name, it creates immense delight on High. Furthermore, this type of meditation can be practiced at all times of the day *(Yesod V'Shoresh Ha'Avodah, Avodas Halev, Chap. 11.)* The Zohar *(Parshas Balak)* writes that when one says the *Shema* with deep intention it is as if he has given over his life to sanctify Hashem's name. The Shaloh writes that one should actually have this intention of giving over one's very life when saying the Shema.

In a similar vein, and apparently a source for R. Zisskind, the Arizal *(Derushei Kriyas Shema She'al HaMita)* recommends that before one goes to sleep one should imagine himself going through all four forms of death penalty described in the Torah, thereby erasing all accumulated negativity and spiritual blemishes.

These two teachings, the one from R. Elimelech and the other from R. Ziskind and the Arizal, both seem to advocate a similar 'death' visualization, yet upon deeper analysis they are quite different from each other. The imagery of death can either catapult one towards a sense of ultimate existential release and transcendence or towards an utter neglect of and general disgust for the flesh and any bodily temptation or sensation.

In the image of R. Zisskind one is encouraged to conceptualize and visualize death in all its gruesome details. One visualizes experiencing his own death with all the attendant pain, hurt and suffering. The debasement of corporeality is the objective. None of this is found in the teaching of R. Elimelech. There are no gory details, but rather a sense of transcendence. The fire can be viewed as a fire of Divine love wherein one experiences a burning passion for Hashem, and for that reason alone wants to surrender all of his silly attachments to the material world and throw himself into the holy fire of Divine Love where "the flames reach up to Heaven." The fire itself becomes a vehicle of transport and uplift through which the person 'rises' up to Heaven.

There are, however, other Chassidic sources that speak of imagery fairly similar to R. Zisskind. An early Chassidic Rebbe teaches that to break any (negative) desire or lust one should imagine that he has already died and been buried in the earth and that now his skin is rotting and bones are disintegrating. This type of stark, existential visualization is sure to quell and dissipate any and all negative desires and lusts *(Arvei Nachal, Parshas Ki Tetze. Note, Zohar 1, p. 201b. Sheim M'shmuel, Parshas Tzav).*

In general, there can be a positive take-away from these types of visualization, so long as they do not bring one to depression and despair. Sometimes, it is not such a terrible idea to visualize your own death and think about how people and the world at large would react. What would they say about you? What is the mark you left on this world? How will you be remembered? *(Bnei Machshava Tova, p. 22).* This type of visualization can help a person to achieve greater focus on the things that really matter in life, and to more easily let go of the things that do not really matter.

Often when a person bumps up against his own mortality, through an illness or accident for example, he may emerge from such a trauma more focused and inspired to actualize that which his soul and higher self truly yearn to accomplish and experience.

These types of visualizations are helpful so long as they are not morbid and do not lead to despair. Our sages say a person should embark upon the path of *Teshuvah*/Self-Transformation a day before he dies. But the obvious question arises: How does one know when that will be? To which the Sages reply: "Let man do *Teshuvah* today lest he die tomorrow" *(Shabbos, 153a)*. The question, however, is why say "a day before," and not phrase it this way, "Do *Teshuvah* now because perhaps you will die today?" The answer is that our sages had no intention of telling a person that they should think that death is immanent or looming. That thought, constantly replaying in one's head, would only create more anxiety and apprehension. So, to paraphrase, they said, 'Sure you will live today, but think about tomorrow. And if you really think about it deeply, you may want to reassess and realign your life today' *(Maor Vashemesh, Vayigash)*.

Taking these considerations into account, for the contemporary and especially immature spiritual seeker it would be better to avoid the more gruesome visualizations suggested by the earlier Kabbalists. For our purposes we will focus on the *Tzetal Katan*/The Small Note of R. Elimelech and what is suggested therein.

There are multiple ways of looking at this practice advocated by R. Elimelech. The most apparent purpose of such a practice is to elevate every moment of life and transform it into something meaningful. In other words: Nothing should be trivial. Even lying in bed can become a profound, albeit, intense opportunity to perform a Mitzvah and 're-veal' one's intimate connection to Hashem. Every moment is either a Mitzvah or the opposite. There is no such thing as impartial or neutral time. There is only positive or negative. Either we are in a Mitzvah reality or we are in the opposite. The word *Mitzvah* comes from the grammatical root meaning 'Connection.' Every action or exchange is an opportunity for a Mitzvah. It is therefore a chance to connect — with our deeper selves, with others, with all of creation, and with the Creator.

The opposite is also true. The inherent system of free choice opens the possibility of *Aveira*. While commonly translated as "sin," *Aveira* is connected to the grammatical root *Avar*, meaning — "other side." This has the connotation of separation.

As *Mitzvah* is conceived of as connection, Aveira can then be understood as separation. In life all of our thoughts, words, and actions bring about either connection or separation. This visual suggested by R. Elimelech creates the opportunity for a Mitzvah while one is in the midst of its opposite. In fact, *Kiddush Hashem* is a very profound Mitzvah and one that most people do not ever have the actual merit to fulfill in a literal sense. (R. Yoseph Caro desired the opportunity to perform the Mitzvah of *Kiddush Hashem*, as his teacher R. Shlomo Malco did, but was denied.)

In addition, but perhaps from the opposite vantage point, through such a creative visualization of the total surrender of one's ego there are also numerous spiritual, mental and developmental benefits that can serve one's inner evolution.

Our ego, which is predicated on the natural desire for survival, is innate and universal. We share this characteristic with all of creation. Selfishness, the desire to receive for the self alone, is dominant. The ultimate altruistic and selfless act is the sanctification of Hashem's name, a total surrender of one's body and ego. But this act, even though it is a Mitzvah, goes against the Divine intention for creation, which is for us to be embodied.

By extension, once a person is ready, at least inwardly, to give up all their attachments (including even his own body), all of life's trivial pursuits — all the pettiness, hurt, jealousy, and grudges one holds against others — slowly begin to dissipate. All small-mindedness is rendered tedious, uneventful, and not worthy of paying attention to. Slowly, one comes to live a deeper/higher life because of the sacrificial willingness itself. If you can really let go so dramatically, even if only in a moment of visual meditation, this allows you to be lighter and freer in relation to all the many things you do, have, or desire. It gives you an expanded perspective and proper focus.

From another vantage point, this visual meditation can also be viewed as a kind of preparatory death practice of sorts. People who encounter death — either in battle, through illness, or by accident — tend to come out of the experience a little more awake and aware. Often people are just floating through their daily life, mindlessly flowing downstream like a leaf in the water. When they are suddenly faced with their own mortality, they tend to wake up. They begin to ask the real questions of life. Not how can I make more money, but rather, what is the root of my desire for money? Not how can I procure this or that pleasure, but rather, what is the purpose of pleasure? And finally, the vexing existential questions set in: Who am I? Is there a purpose to my life? Why am I here?

This inward creative visualization, accomplished while lying in bed for example, if done correctly and with detail, can be the closest thing many people (thank G-d) come to actually encountering their mortality before the inevitable decline of life. The goal is to visualize yourself dying and then to 'come back' and open your eyes, allowing for a clearer, sharper, more focused outlook to come into focus. Ultimately, it allows you to appreciate and value the true meaning of life moment to moment without actually having to go through (Heaven forbid) an actual tragedy.

In fact, in a very deep way, as the *Sefas Emes* points out *(Parshas Emor)*, a person who is able to break his natural desires and surrender his ego with patience, clarity and a settled mind is even greater than a person who hurriedly surrenders his life (or appetites) in a moment of haste.

A person who faces a pistol and jumps into the fire does so in haste. It is much harder to sit calmly and contemplate your choices and then with a settled mind leap into the fire like a moth to the flame. This approach from R. Elimelech demands mindfulness and patience and therefore the effects are more lasting, integrated and real.

In this way meditatively practicing *Mesiras Nefesh*/Self-Sacrifice by jumping into the fire in one's mind while lying in bed has a double advantage: 1) A total self surrender is performed in 2) a gradual, relaxed, and well thought out process. Emerging from this meditation can certainly provide one the proper focus needed to persevere and overcome any negative inclination or temptation that distracts him from his true purpose and path.

VISUAL SIX: PRACTICE

» DEATH PRACTICE

Set a soft timer (or have someone else observe you) in order to fully enter this meditation without any worry of what needs to be done afterwards.

For those new to meditation practice, it is recommended to start with anywhere from 10–20 minutes.

Invite all of yourself into this space here and now.

Whether lying in bed, or sitting upright in a chair, close your eyes for a moment. Visualize yourself holding a lit candle in front of a fireplace that has not yet been lit.

Extend an outstretched arm, with candle in hand, and light the fireplace.

The flame catches. The fire begins small, concentrated, bright, but is growing stronger. With each passing moment the flame jumps higher and higher and grows more and more intense.

Allow the image of the fire to fill your entire vision. Its heat is growing stronger and spreading out into the air, reaching you where you sit.

Allow the fire, which is the source of Divine reality, to represent all that is true and everlasting in this life. Anything that is momentary or false has no place in this holy fire of truth.

As you connect more and more with the flame and the eternality that it represents, allow the inner flame of your heart to burn brighter and brighter. The flame on the outside beckons the flame within.

Have the Kavanah/Intention that you are about to throw yourself into the fire to Sanctify the Name of Hashem.

In a moment of unity, draw closer to the fire until you are standing on the edge of the pit and all that is left to do is jump. Jump into the flame! Jump into the flame immersing yourself in all that is true and forever alive, the Eternal Reality.

In allowing yourself to be consumed by the flame of Divinity, your essence only strengthens and burns brighter.

Dance in and with the flames.

Gently open your eyes.

PART TWO

IMAGERY

CHAPTER ONE

....

USING PHYSICAL OBJECTS AS FOCAL POINTS

WHAT WE SEE HAS JUST AS MUCH, IF NOT MORE, OF A PROFOUND EFFECT ON US THAN WHAT WE HEAR OR UNDERSTAND INTELLECTUALLY. An image can lodge itself deep into our psyche and then subliminally inform and guide all of our choices, often without us even being aware of how these images are affecting our decisions.

To live a spiritually healthy and productive life one needs to ensure that he surrounds himself, as much as is under his control, with only positive and holy images.

The images we surround ourselves with evoke certain reactions or behaviors accordingly. Even the colors we wear and surround ourselves with elicit certain psychic responses. If one wears black, for instance, one is reminded of mourning or mystery; and conversely, white evokes a sense of purity or sterility. This is true of both colors and images.

PROTECTING THE EYES:

Imagery has a profound effect on our psyche. The things we see, whether consciously or unconsciously enter into our psyche and inform our thoughts, emotions and behavior. As much as we can, we need to protect our eyes. We must ensure that we look at objects and events that enhance and inform good and noble thoughts, feelings and actions.

One way to do that is to surround yourself with positive and expansive imagery. When you are walking down the street it is important to make sure that your eyes only attach themselves to images that you know are good for you, spiritually, mentally and emotionally.

This protection of the eyes can of course be more easily enforced in the comfort of our own home. This means simply that the coloring of your home, the images you hang on the walls, and the overall environmental ambiance should be conducive for spiritual growth. This also means that one should not intentionally surround oneself with violent or profane imagery.

A home should be a safe space, a secure place. We need to make sure that we do not bring the turmoil or chaos of the outside world into the home. There is no reason for every war and murder to be known in all its gruesome details. A home is a sacred space. Many great Torah teachers suggested that a home should be filled with or at least have some windows so one can gaze up to the heavens, the stars, and the expansive universe. Rabbi Chayim Vital quotes his teacher, the Arizal, as saying: "My master, of blessed memory used to tell me, 'it is good for man to live in a home that has windows open to Heaven so that he can look there at all times and lift his eyes to the Above in order to contemplate the wonders of the Creator in creating the heavens and earth *(Sha'ar Ruach HaKodesh, p, 35).* The vast sky above opens you up and fills you with awe and wonder.

"Anything disgusting that is seen will create that same negativity in one's own soul" *(Even Ezra, Devarim, 23; 14).* The opposite of course is also true —anything positive that is seen will create that very positivity within one's own soul and psyche.

In simple words, we need to create an environment that is, as much as possible, surrounded with positive imagery. The amazing thing is that, according to our sages *(Kesuvos,*

5a), we have natural blinders or shutters, as it were, on our bodies. The eyelids serve to protect the eyes from sights not meant to be seen, and the earlobes can serve as covers to shield one from sounds not meant to be heard — such as Lashon Harah/Negative Speech. The point of this teaching, beyond the appreciation of our natural physiology, is that we do in deed have control over what we let in to our consciousness. It is, to a great extent, our choice to determine what we hear and see.

PROTECTING THE OPENINGS OF THE BODY:

The Torah says, "You shall set up judges and law enforcement officials for yourself within all your gates" (Shemos, 16; 18). This can be, and is, read literally, as in — the gates of the cities we live in need to be protected by judges and law enforcement. And yet, implicit in the very words, "for yourself," is the possibility for the directive to also be related to each individual person, and at all times. Inwardly speaking, the Torah is telling us to set up judges and law enforcement at the entrances of our own 'gates', i.e., our openings to the world around us — our eyes, ears, mouth, and nose. These are known as the seven gates of awareness.

The body is our soul's home and we need to protect and guard it from hazardous and potentially destructive influences. Of course we need to open our mouths to eat the proper kosher foods, but, equally as important, we also need to make sure that the sights and sounds that enter our body are also kosher and spiritually uplifting.

Four of our five normative senses are located in the head, with the sense of touch being distributed throughout the entire body — although it too is ultimately connected to the brain as the epidermis is filled with nerve endings that send signals through the spinal column to the brain where the feeling is then registered. But the actual intake of the other four senses are in the 'head' — the two ears and the sense of hearing, the two eyes and the sense of sight, the two nostrils and the sense of smell, and the mouth and the sense of taste. All in all, there are actually seven openings in the head — two ears, two eyes, two nostrils and the mouth. These seven orifices correspond to the seven branches of the Menorah, the Candelabra of the Temple. Much like the Menorah that can only be fed "pure oil" to illuminate the Temple, the same is true with our own inner Menorah. In order for us to shine brightly, illuminating our own path and giving light and warmth to others, we need to ensure that the 'oil' we intake and use to illuminate our countenance is pure and refined.

As mentioned, we have been given natural, biological gates to protect ourselves such as eyelids to protect our vision, lips and teeth to protect our speech, earlobes to allow us to filter the sounds that reach us, and nostrils to close against unwanted smells. It is up to us to devise a system of judgment and law enforcement, to use our naturally provided 'gates' to guard the senses from negative input that can potentially harm us spiritually, emotionally, and/or mentally.

Throughout the day we are continually being bombarded with sensory input — imagery, sounds, smells, and countless other stimuli. Most of these are subliminal and their impressions are lodged deeply into our subconscious.

While we may aspire to turn away or avert our attention when we see or hear something negative, in order to fully protect ourselves from things that can harm us even subliminally, we must consciously put up barriers to protect our senses.

An example of this would be the choice to not watch television at all, rather than just looking away from negative imagery that appears on the screen. Once we put ourselves in a situation in which we can be exposed to negative and harmful imagery, it may end up seeping in even through the subconscious. To guard ourselves we must choose to create or decide to only enter into situations that will provide us with positive sensory input.

We thus gain clear vision and an unprejudiced ability to choose a path for ourselves that is aligned with our deeper purpose. We cease to be a mere extension of whatever advertisements or propaganda we may have encountered and unconsciously integrated, and instead create our own reality based on our internal compass and soul purpose.

We also need to be attuned to what would be considered negative. Even subtle negativities can have a corrosive impact. The eyes are very delicate and powerful instruments. They have a spiritual quality, as it were, and even the slightest dust of intrusion causes harm *(Ohr Hachayim, Devarim, 32; 10)*. We therefore need to protect them from even the slightest negative influence. It is obvious that obscenities or violence are harmful to us as they are detrimental to our emotional, mental and spiritual well-being and we ought to stay away from seeing them, if possible.

But to live a truly well-adjusted life we need to be more attuned to more subtle negativities, for example, not even looking at a person who is in the midst of an angry outburst. Our sages *(Megilah, 28a)* speak about the practice of not looking at the face of a *Rasha*/Wicked Person, for example, a murderer, because it can weaken one's eyes and spiritual sensitivity. Looking at a *Rasha* has a negative effect on the consciousness of the observer *(Maharsha, ad loc. Maharal, Nesivas Olam, Nasiv HaTzedek, 3)*.

Early Kabbalists also speak about not looking at the face of a person who is enraged with anger *(Safer Chassidim, 1126. Maamor Yavak, Maamor 2; 13)*. In fact, to do so is considered a *Kasha Le'shichah*/Cause of Forgetfulness. An angry person exudes negativity. Forgetfulness is at times considered a sign of *Kelipa*/Negativity or Concealment, as it conceals one's learning and commitments in the moment. This negative forgetfulness extends outward from the person who is angry. Looking at that person can therefore have a negative effect on the observer, as one allows their influence to impact them through the 'gates' of the eyes.

Furthermore, besides a serious *Rasha* (such as the example used above of a murderer) or one who is in a fit of anger, we should generally try to not look at anyone who we know harbors negative thoughts, words, or actions, as it can have a detrimental effect on our awareness *(Turei Even, Megilah, 28a)*.

It must be pointed out that the converse is certainly true as well. Looking at your teacher while teaching Torah, for example, has a profoundly positive effect on you. Not only will you understand the lesson better *(Eiruvin, 13b)* and tune in to the deeper wisdom that flows to and from the teacher as he is teaching *(D'rashos Ha'Ran, Derush 8)*, but the very act of looking at the teacher draws down goodness and blessings *(Ya'aros D'Vash 1, Derush 12)*. One receives goodness and blessings from merely looking at one who embodies goodness and blessings.

THE SUBTLE PROTECTION
OF THE EYES:

All of the above is related to protecting oneself against negative imagery in order to not allow these images to enter
your consciousness in the first place. Yet, many times it is
quite impossible for various reasons to turn one's head or
avert one's eyes in an obvious manner. Often, it might just
be considered rude or disrespectful to 'put up one's blinders'
while in public or engaged in some sort of social encounter.
This kind of behavior, while arguably beneficial for one's
own spiritual state, can be off-putting to others, creating a
damaging social barrier. It is therefore not beneficial for the
spiritual state of others beside oneself. Therefore, at times a
more subtle and fine-tuned approach may be needed. The
idea is to have one's eyes (or ears) wide open and yet to not
be susceptible to the effects of negative imagery. To have
one's eyes wide shut, so to speak.

Ultimately, it is not enough to restrict or determine "what"
we look at (this is only the first stage of spiritual development); we also need to learn "how" to see - this is a more
mature developmental level where we are able to take more
responsibility for the ways in which we process what we
come into contact with. When our minds and eyes are
trained, like any muscle in the body, they become more
strengthened. And the more we train ourselves in the art
of "how" to see, the actual "what" of what we see will have

a less corrosive and, in turn, more positive effect upon us. This is predicated on developing a strong and adaptive spiritual immune system, so to speak. In order to engage this level of practice, one's faith should be strong, and one's consciousness should be securely rooted in the foundation of the soul.

This is not as simple as training oneself to look away when they encounter negative visual stimulus - although, looking away does demand a lot of will power. This practice is much more complicated and requires rigorous inner training to learn to 'see' the Divine goodness and manifest goodness within everything and everyone. This way of seeing is a type of "raising the sparks," and a way of finding the *Nekuda Tova*/Point of Goodness within all that exists.

TRAIN YOURSELF TO SEE THE GOOD:

When a thief who picks pockets sees a holy *Tzadik* walking down the street, all he sees is pockets. This is just like when you are hungry and you walk down the street, all you see is food. This just goes to show that ultimately you observe on the outside what is on your mind on the inside.

The author of the *Chovas Ha'Levavos*/Duties of the Heart, a classic 10th century work of moral and spiritual philosophy, tells the story of a wise sage who was walking along the streets with his disciples, when all of a sudden they happened upon a dead animal, the carcass of a donkey. The students were appalled in disgust. But the teacher gently noted, "Well, did you notice such white teeth on the animal?" *(Chovas HaLevavos, Sha'ar HaKeniya, Chap 6).* The students all saw just a dead carcass, and yet the sage was able to immediately find a sliver of redemptive beauty within the apparent ugliness. What jumped out to him were the beautiful white teeth of the animal, not the overall state of its decay.

This story is very simple, yet profound. Everything and everyone has some sort of beauty. The teacher was able to notice this beauty over and above everything else. He was trained in the "how" of seeing. The students all saw the "what", the dead carcass, but the sage's "how" had been transformed; his "how" was trained to always notice the good, the beautiful.

This is the true challenge. Not simply to cover our eyes or to look away from what we consider negative imagery, although most of the time this is the best solution, but to really learn 'how' to see, which means how to interpret, process, contextualize, and refine what we see. This is the art of seeing.

THE OBSERVER AFFECTS THE OBSERVED:

On a deep level the way we see things (the "how") actually effects "what" we see. Not only do we see things the way we are, not the way they are, but, even deeper, our seeing actually affects what is seen.

The Torah says: "Do not stray, following after your heart (mind) and eyes" *(Bamidbar 15; 39)*. But do not the eyes come before the heart? Normally, one sees something and then desires it. So why is the order reversed, listing the heart/mind first and then the eyes? This is because we do not see things the way they are, but rather the way we are.

Who we are, what we think, and how we feel determines how we see the things around us, and even deeper, actually affects the things around us.

The ancient philosophers and physicians argued about how we see things. There were two general theories regarding exactly how seeing works: A) In order to see something, the light from the object comes towards and we receive it; or, B) Our eyes emit the 'light' of vision, which goes out to meet objects. In other words — is the trajectory of sight from object to subject, or from subject to object? *(R. Meir Aldavia Shevilei Emuna, Nosiv 4, p. 154.*

Rabbi Gershon Ben Shlomo, Shaar HaShamaim, Maamor 9, p. 53.
Rabbi Tzadok, Komtez HaMincha, 2).

Today, empirical scientific evidence proves that sense-objects are received in our brain. As you look at something, the words on this page for example, rays of light pass from the page to your eyes, these then register as an inverted image of the page in your retina. Light-sensitive cells then cause impulses to pass through your optic nerve leading to complex electrochemical patterns in your brain, which you finally interpret as a page with words on it. This is a one-way path, from the object to the subject.

But one thing still remains a mystery in this process. Why do we see the image of the page in front of us as 'outside' of us, when the image is actually appearing within us, or within our brain?

If one were perceiving accurately perhaps it would be more natural to say, "I am seeing a page in my mind," rather than saying, "I am seeing a page two feet away from my face." It is only our projection of the image outward onto an assumed 'external' world that makes objects appear independently outside of our own mind.

Therefore, while light is received by our eyes and nervous system, we can also argue, to a degree, that we project or 'emit' the light of vision outward. Our minds extend to the outside world, so-to-speak *(Likutei Moharan, 1; 76).*

Taking this idea further, we enter the realm of basic quantum theory in which the observer is understood to affect the observed. This is the premise of the famous Wave/Particle Duality in which light appears to be both a wave and a particle depending on how one observes it, i.e. through which instrument.

Biologists and theorists also discuss another mystery: Some people can accurately sense when an unseen person is staring at them. Here, not only does a 'seer' affect the physical properties of the seen, but an external 'seer' can actually seem to affect our internal qualitative state. This is the amazing power of 'seeing.'

According to the deep teachings of Torah this works both ways — what we look at also affects us, even on a physical level. The Medrash mentions the story of a dark skinned king and dark skinned queen who gave birth to a lighter skinned child. Rabbi Akiva suggested that during conception the queen was gazing upon a lighter skinned statue that was in the room *(Tanchuma, Naso. See also Avodah Zarah, 24, with regards to the red heifer)*. If this is to be taken literally, this means that the visual image of the light skinned sculpture imprinted itself upon the imagination of the queen and it became so powerfully ingrained that it affected the actual physical makeup of her eggs and eventually the child that was conceived at that very moment. We "receive" from what we see.

In the world of *Halacha* this idea is also present, but with a bit more nuance. In Torah law, seeing or looking is not actually considered a form of 'receiving pleasure,' resulting in *Meilah*, the misappropriation of sacred objects. We can see this in the laws pertaining to sacred objects in the Temple. Such Sacred objects, dedicated to the Temple in Jerusalem of old, were not allowed to be used for mundane activities or personal pleasure outside of their ritual usage. If someone were merely looking at a sacred object, this was not considered Halachically as actually receiving mundane pleasure from the object *(Kerisus, 6a)*. And yet, there is still a prohibition from idly looking at such an object *(Pesachim, 26a)*. Furthermore, it is forbidden to receive optical pleasure from something that is prohibited *(Tosefos, Sukkah, 53a. Note: Pri Chadash, Orach Chayim, 467; 9 with regards to the prohibition to receive pleasure from observing Chametz)*. This implies that according to *Halacha* there is in fact something that is transferrable from the seen to the seer, although the Halachic literature does not go as far as the Kabbalistic literature in ascribing such power and influence to the act of seeing. The emphasis in the Halachic literature seems to be on avoiding the influence of that which is negative. While it does seem to discount the internal impact of looking at a positive or holy object, it is still nevertheless prohibited to idly gaze upon it.

To summarize: What we see and the way we see it affects both us and the things we are viewing *(Berachos, 58a. Shab-*

bos, 33a. Magen Avos (The Tashbatz) Avos, 2; 16). We not only "receive" from what we see, but we also "give" to what is being seen. For example, someone with pure intention emits a positive energy when looking at something, and the opposite holds true as well. An impure person looking at something projects their image upon the surface of that which they are looking at. Their internal impurity is externally projected upon that which they perceive *(Ramban. Vayikra, 18; 19. Shevilei Emuna, Nosiv HaShelishi, p. 114. Tzeida LaDerech, Maamor 2, Klaal 1; 2. Sichos HaRan, Chap. 242. See also: Nishmas Chayim, Maamor 3; 4. Kav Ha'Yashar, Chap 2).* Our vision transmits subtle vibrations out into the universe and towards the object/person we are viewing.

A pure-intentioned person of good-will looking at something emanates goodness and blessing, whereas a bad-intentioned person (one who acts, thinks and speaks negatively) emanates negative vibrations and they can – if one is not protected – be harmful and damaging *(Agrah DePerkah, Chap. 160; Ya'aros D'Vash 1, Derush 12. Malbim, Mishlei, 23; 7).*

Our eyes are truly powerful tools. They are indeed a reflection of the ultimate Creative ability. This is reflected in an ingenious Kabbalistic correspondence drawn between the four-letter name of Hashem and the human eye. The four-letter name of Hashem, *Yud-Hei-Vav-Hei*, represents the Ultimate Source of creation. The four letters are superimposed on the basic four personas/levels of the Sefiros. The *Yud* is Keser (or Chochmah), the upper *Hei* is Binah, the *Vav* is the emotional Sefiros, and the final *Hei* is Malchus. According to Kabbalah the four colors of the eye correspond to the four letters in the Name of Hashem. The outer 'white' of the eye is Keser (or Chochmah). The streaks of red and a gold like color correspond to the upper *Hei* (Binah). The actual coloring of the eyes — which for some people is brown, blue or green — corresponds to the *Vav*, the emotional Sefiros. And the final *Hei* is Malchus, the almost black color of the pupil of the eye *(Zohar Chadash, Yisro. Kav HaYashar, Chap. 2. The pupil is connected with the mother - Niddah, 31a- which is Malchus)*.

To reiterate the point one more time in order to drive home the message: Looking and seeing are not passive or non-invasive actions. Rather, they are very powerful and creative, effecting and transforming what is being observed. The 'who' that is looking affects the 'what' that is seen by virtue of the 'how' with which they perceive.

The more the 'how' of seeing positively transforms the 'who' that sees, the more the 'what' that is seen will be positively transformed as well; thus creating a feedback loop of positive influence, from the 'how' to the 'who' to the 'what' and back again.

CHAPTER TWO

....

THE SPIRITUAL DANGER OF A VISUAL

THE SPIRITUAL PERIL OF OBJECT-BASED VISUALIZATIONS:
....

WHENEVER WE USE AN ACTUAL OBJECT AS A FOCAL POINT FOR VISUAL MEDITATION THERE IS ALWAYS THE DANGER THAT THE OBJECT CAN LEAD TO A FORM OF WORSHIP, MUCH LIKE AVODAH ZARAH/IDOLATRY.

In truth, everything — whether subject or object, person or idea — can be a form of Avodah Zarah. The moment a 'something' becomes an 'everything,' it is idolatry. When a person confuses any one 'part' (whether it is an idea, an object, or a person) for the whole of which it is merely a part, this is the essence of idolatry. Hashem is the Creator of every-thing and everything is included within the One. When we take something or someone and place it or them outside of the All that is One, that is idolatry.

While this is true for all things and ideas, even when used merely as focal points for meditation or contemplation, it is especially relevant with regard to actual objects. If one uses an actual object as a focal point, certainly if there is some mystery or majesty to the object, admiration can easily turn into worship. Objects of contemplation can become objects of devotion, reverence and even deification. This is the reason that, for the most part, objects are not employed for meditation practices.

The Rambam, otherwise known as Maimonides, writes that the source of all idol worship was the original reverence mankind displayed towards the Creator's wonderful awe-inspiring creation. From admiration, the feeling became devotion, and ultimately turned into deification *(Hilchos Avodei Zora, 1; 1. Derashos HaRan, Derush 9)*. In other words, at its root idol worship was an honest expression of an authentically spiritual and monotheistic sentiment, a reverence for Hashem's creation. But over time, when there emerged a state of spiritual immaturity or regressive devolution, people began to see the trees at the expense of the forest, so to speak.

Take *Kiddush Levenah*, for example, the wonderful practice of looking up into the sky at the beginning of each month to take notice of the new moon and recite a blessing. When we bless the moon, special caution is taken so that the moon should not become the object of our devotion. We observe the new moon and begin the blessing, but throughout the entire recitation of the blessing we do not gaze at the moon until we have completed the attached verses *(Shaloh HaKadosh, Sha'ar Ha'osyos, p. 334. Quoted also by the Magen Avraham, Orach Chayim, 426; 8. Be'er Heitiv 6, ad loc.).* Beyond appearances - i.e. so as not to be assumed by the casual passersby that we are moon worshipers, the resistance to gazing at the moon while reciting a blessing insures that we too do not actually mistake our practice as that of moon worshipers.

When a person does wish to use an actual image, as opposed to a mental image in the mind, as a meditative focal point, he should not become completely fixated on the object itself. To guard against this it would be preferable to look at the object, fix the image in his mind's eye, look away from the object or close his eyes, and then focus on the image of the object as it is imprinted within his imagination. He should hold his inner gaze on the image of the object in his mind's eye as long as possible. Only when the image fades should he open his eyes or turn back towards the actual object in order to look at it again and re-imprint the image in his mind for further contemplation.

Optimally, it would be best to begin with an image that is elusive, dynamic, or non-stationary, such as a jumping flame, a flash of lightning, or the sun/moon light rippling on a body of water. Each of these images are continually in flux, perpetually disappearing and reappearing. The moment you try to grasp the image, the image dissolves. The images are radically elusive.

In the Torah's primary description of a personal mystical experience, found in the beginning of the book of Yechez-kel/Ezekiel, the prophet "sees" with his mind's eye a series of mystical, mythical creatures along with "[an] appearance that was like burning coals or torches. Fire moved back and forth among the creatures; it was bright, and lightning flashed out of it. The creatures sped back and forth like flashes of lightning" *(1; 13-14)*. These 'entities' are dynamic images, moving to and fro in rapid succession.

Deeper in his vision when he beholds the *Kavod Hash-em*/the Glory of G-d, again he "sees" an image that had "the appearance of a rainbow in the clouds on a rainy day" *(1; 28)*. This is another image of something transient and ephemeral.

In addition, the most prominent collective mystical experience was experienced at Mt. Sinai during the giving of the Torah. This was the meditative 'visual' experience par excellence. The entire nation 'saw' the inner workings of the

Merkava/Chariot, which is considered to be the ultimate 'structure' or 'vehicle' of supernal reality and transcendent consciousness. Indeed, there was great danger that the very image of the chariot itself would become an item of worship or object of devotion, which, in fact, it did during the events of the Golden Calf. Because of this danger inherent in the visual encounter with spiritual reality, the entire episode was experienced in the manner of, what the Kabbalists call, *Ratzu v'Shuv*/Running and Returning *(Megala Amukos, Shemos, Derush 1; 4)*. The visual image was revealed to them, but as they were overwhelmed from its immensity and majesty they retracted and retreated from the mountain *(Shabbos, 88b)*, only to be brought closer again *(Tehilim, 68; 13)*. In this way the people were continuously moving back and forth in relation to the image, repetitively coming into and going out of the immediacy of the experience.

In the book of Exodus, following the episode of the Golden Calf, *Moshe*/Moses re-ascends up to the Divine Presence to seek atonement for the people. In the midst of his pleading for forgiveness he requests a vision of the Divine glory, "Show me Your glory," he asks *(Shemos, 33; 18)*. But he is told, "You cannot see my face and live" *(33; 19)*. And then he is told, "There is a place near me where you may stand on a rock. When My glory passes by, I will put you in the cleft of a rock and cover you with my hand until I have passed by. Then I will remove my hand and you will see my back, but my face must not be seen" *(33; 20-23)*. Perhaps the idea of

Hashem "passing by" and revealing only the "back" suggests a vision that appears so rapidly and instantaneously that what one sees appears to him to have already "passed." All he gets is a glimpse of the "back" of that which has already gone.

There is a delicate and dialectical tension that needs to be acknowledged and respected when using an object as a focus for meditation. One must strike a balance between observing the object and not becoming fixated solely on its image to the exclusion of what that image represents and points towards. At best, we need to use images that imply their own self-transcendence. In visual meditation one must seek to move beyond the object itself to reach that which it alludes to. Take the practice of using a flame as a focal point, for example.

When a person focuses on a flame they observe an image that is constantly leaping upwards in perpetual motion. The image itself intimates that which is beyond the flame. When gazing upon the flame of a candle, a flood of concepts rushes into the mind of the meditator such as the quest to constantly reach higher, the connection between the ephemeral flame and the body of the wick and candle, the little bit of light that gently dispels so much darkness, and so forth.

The goal of a visual meditation is not the image or object itself, but that which it represents and reminds one of in relation to his soul's journey and spiritual development. The same is true regarding the practice of observing one's *Tzitzis*. The purpose of the visual focus, as stated explicitly in the Torah, is to be reminded of the entire structure of all 613 Mitzvos. Thus, the strings hint to something spiritual beyond themselves. The image or object itself serves as a bridge to another reality of perspectival clarity and poetic inspiration.

This is perhaps the deeper reason why we bless the new moon each month, in contrast to the sun. The sun represents predictability and constancy *(Koheles, 1; 9)*. The sun is called *Shemesh* in Hebrew, from the word *Mash*, which means something that is touchable or tangible *(Shemos, 10; 21)*. The moon on the other hand is elusive. One day it is full, then it is empty, one day you can see it, then suddenly it is gone, like a dancing flame. Its very nature intimates motion, process, development, and dissolution. It is not static. It is constantly becoming and undoing itself. This is a physical manifestation in nature of the very psycho-spiritual characteristics and perspectives one needs to acquire and develop in the context of visually oriented meditation.

To drive this point home even more forcefully the very last verse of the Torah speaks of the greatness of Moshe in relation to the wonders he performed with a mighty hand "before the eyes of all Israel." Rashi asks, "What wonder and great act did he perform 'before the eyes of all Israel?" Strangely enough, the act that Rashi singles out is the breaking of the *Luchos*/Tablets at the time of the Golden Calf. These are the final words inscribed in the Torah, Hashem applauding Moshe for smashing the very Tablets of the Law written by Hashem Himself *(Rashi, Devarim, 34; 12)*. Upon seeing that the people of Israel had erected a visual image (the Golden Calf) once they thought that he (Moshe, who to the people was also an "image") would no longer be amongst them, he realized that this image (the Tablets) would also potentially be turned into an object of worship, and so he broke them. Before the "eyes" of the people Moshe shatters the one and only visual image/object that he has brought down from the invisible, imageless world.

This is a most powerful and iconoclastic message stated at the most climactic moment in the Torah. It is an exclamation point of sorts, a stern and surprising warning to be hyper-conscious and careful not to turn even the *Luchos* into just another idol. Rashi is stating a most revolutionary idea: That in fact it would be better to destroy the *Luchos* themselves than to turn it into an object of idol/idle worship. The very last teaching in the Torah is therefore more concerned with "how" we see than "what" we see, "how" we think as opposed to "what" we think. For even the most holy positive objects or images can be turned into a negative influence depending upon how we relate to it.

THE VISUALS

We will now explore a series of actual objects or images recommended for use in visual meditation practices. Some of them are based on Mitzvos, while others are based in Nature. Either way, the same principles, as discussed above, apply to any and all visually-based meditations.

IMAGE ONE: IDEA & PRACTICE

» The Tzitzis

LOOKING AT THE TZITZIS:

There is a Mitzvah in the Torah that is directly related to seeing. The Torah says, "You shall make Tzitzis/Fringes out of strings to attach to your four-cornered garments, and you shall see them and remember all the *Mitzvos*/Commandments of the Torah in order to perform them, and you shall not wander after your Hearts and after your Eyes..." *(Bamidbar, 15; 39).*

Whether this means that we literally need to hang the Tzitzis outside our garments so that we can see them at all times, or whether it means that they at least need to be worn and available for us to see them if we pull them out, is debated *(The Arizal teaches that the garment of the Tzitzis should be under ones outer garments. Pri Eitz Chayim, Shar Tzitzis 1. Magen Avraham, Orach Chayim 8; 13. The question is also whether this applies to the Tzitzis, the strings as well. Likutei Sichos 33, pp. 95-104. Yichava Da'as 2, Siman 1).* Either way, there is clearly a Mitzvah to wear and look at the Tzitzis *(Sefer Charaidim, Chap 10; 1).* The seeing leads to remembering and the remembering then leads to doing.

Beyond the explicit purpose of remembering the Mitzvos, looking at the Tzitzis inspires awe, brings healing *(Likutei Moharan 7)*, and allows one to overcome anger, as will be explored.

In former times, in addition to the white strings that would be placed on the corner of one's four-cornered garments, some of these strings would also be dyed with *Techeiles* (a blue-like color) by all those who wore *Tzitzis*. This is in fact a Mitzvah directly from the Torah. The blue dye was made from the *Chilazon*, which is a marine creature. But over the years, as a result of the exile, the tradition was lost and many are uncertain today if this is a certain shellfish, cuttlefish, or something else. Therefore, most people today do not dye any of the *Tzitzis* blue.

But, it is clear from even a cursory glance over the traditional sources that gazing upon a particular color evokes particular sensations and responses. Our sages tell us that the blue-like color of the *Tzitzis* is similar to (the color of) the sea, and the sea resembles the sky, and the sky resembles the Heavenly Throne of Glory *(Sotah, 17a)*. This is a kind of color-coded associative symbolic chain that links one's awareness, from a simple observation of the color of one's clothes, to the depths of the blue oceans, to the heights of the blue sky, and all the way up to the sapphire throne, the *Kesei HaKavod*/the Throne of Glory.

The act of looking at the colored stings hanging down from the corner of one's garments is a continuous remind-er meant to evoke a sense of awe in the presence of the glory of Heaven. The blue of the Tzitzis was a very dark blue, like the color of the night sky *(Rashi, Bamidbar, 15; 41. The Rambam writes that the color of the Techieles is similar to the sky during the height of the day. Hilchos Tzitzis 2; 1. Zohar 2, p. 139a).* The blue colored Tzitzis provokes a sensation of awe, mag-nitude, and wonder, which leads a person to think about what is 'beyond the sky,' and even beyond the cosmos, i.e., to contemplate the Infinite Creator.

Rabbi Avraham Abulafia (1240- 1290c), the Spanish Kab-balist and meditation master, the father of what can be called modern "Prophetic Kabbalah," writes that the word Chila-zon can be subdivided into two words, *L'Chazon/*Towards a Vision. This ingenious wordplay implies that meditating on the blue dyed fringes hanging from one's garments can be a springboard to stimulate a higher and deeper vision and perception of reality. According to the Kabbalists *(Birchei Yoseph, Orach Chayim, 8; 4),* even today when most traditions maintain that the means and methods to dye the strings the proper color of blue has been lost and the strings of the Tzitzis should thus all be white, one should, when looking at some of the white strings, internally visualize them as if they were indeed colored blue.

LOOKING AT THE TZITZIS TO OVERCOME ANGER:

There is a Kabbalistic practice of taking hold of one's *Tzitzis* and looking at them in order to prevent and/or overcome one's anger or flaring temper *(Shaloh HaKadosh, Sha'ar Ruach HaKodesh, Tikkun 14. R. Yaakov Tzvi Yallish, Kehilas Yaakov, Ka'as, p. 755)*. In Hebrew the corners of the garments whereupon the Tzitzis hang is called a *Kanaf*. Numerically the word *Kanaf (Chaf/20, Nun/50, Pei/80)* equals one hundred and fifty. This is numerically equivalent to the Hebrew word for anger, *Ka'as (Chaf/20, Ayin/70, Samach/60)*. Therefore, to help prevent or even overcome anger one may want to gaze at the *Kanaf*/Corners where their Tzitzis are hanging.

Regarding Tzitzis the Torah says, "and you shall see them and remember all the Mitzvos… and you shall not wander after your Heart and after your Eyes…" *(Bamidbar, 15; 39)*. In other words, by meditating upon the Tzitzis a person will be reminded of not only the Mitzvos, what they must do, but also of their higher purpose in life, who they are. The mere looking upon them reminds a person of the life of the soul. The inner intention of the Tzitzis is to serve as a visual cue to remind us to not be tempted or fooled by what our eyes may see on the surface, but to see beyond the surface in order to get a glimpse of a thing's *Tachlis*/Purpose.

Anger is, for the most part, a reactive emotion. It mostly flares up when a person is functioning on autopilot or ego mode. The ego feels threatened or hurt, whether real or imagined, and the chemical and emotional reaction is anger. When we live this way our scope of vision is limited, we relegate ourselves only to what our eyes observe at any given moment. Looking at the Tzitzis can help us expand our horizons, broaden our doors of perception, and be more big-picture oriented.

There is a constant choice we all have to make at every moment: Do we re-act to life or do we behave pro-actively. Do we surrender ourselves to our external reality, for better or worse, by simply allowing it to further dictate our emotions? Or do we stand up and freely choose our own behavior based on deeply held beliefs, values, morals, and priorities? For instance, let's say you are walking down the street and someone bumps into you by 'mistake.' Do you immediately, without evaluating the situation, blow up and start a fight? Or do you take one quick moment to consider whether or not the person that bumped into you was an elder person with failing eyesight, or a medic running to help with an emergency? When you learn to take that one extra moment you will become the master of your emotions as opposed to the other way around. You will be in control of your life and your life (i.e., your external circumstances) will, therefore, not be in control of you.

Cultivating a moment of pause before acting allows you to make a levelheaded and proactive assessment of how to deal with any situation and act appropriately. For example, let's say, again, that you are walking down the street and you fall into a mud pit. Your first reaction may be anger. You get agitated, upset, and you lose your composure. This small obstacle becomes the biggest thing in your life in that moment, demanding all of your resources. But the angrier you get the harder it becomes for you to climb out of the pit. These emotions actually end up working against you. Suppose you are able to pause for a moment and reflect on the big picture of your life: Why am I here? What is my life's purpose? This small obstacle then becomes less pronounced, and now with a degree of level headedness you can work on devising and enacting a sensible strategy to get yourself out of whatever pit you have fallen into.

This is true with every single obstacle, temptation, or assumed instant gratification. One can either have a big picture vision of life in which they are less bothered by the small stuff, less tempted by the candy of life, or even, with a level of objectivity, more capable of extricating themselves from sticky situations; or, they can maintain a self-centered narrow tunnel vision in which the tiniest obstacles of temptation and instant gratification completely obscure their view of the big picture.

The moment you stop to look at the Tzitzis, you are: a) pausing and taking some control of your life, and b) you are being visually reminded of the big picture of your life, and of what is, in fact, your true purpose in this world.

The Tzitzis are an actual visual meditation device that is a genuine Mitzvah of the Torah, as the Torah itself tells us that, "you shall see them and not follow after your...wandering eyes."

IMAGE TWO: IDEA

» THE FLAME

THE FLAMES OF THE MENORAH:

There are many other Mitzvos that can be used as the visual focal point of a meditation practice such as the *S'chach/* Covering of the Sukkah, or the *Mezuzah*, the sacred object placed on the doorposts of one's home. But what is unique about the Mitzvah of Tzitzis is that the Torah tells us to actually "see them." This gives them a specifically visual character in relation to our own spiritual practice.

In addition to the Torah Mitzvos just named above that make for great visual meditation devices, there is a Rabbinic Mitzvah that seems to suggest that it too be used as a visual meditation device — that is the *Menorah*, the candelabrum that is lit for eight nights during the festival of Chanukah.

Following the lighting ceremony we recite a thanks-giving

prayer. In it we say, "These lights are holy. Permission is not granted to utilize them, but only to look at them." The flames of the Chanukah Menorah are not meant to be used for our personal or functional benefit, such as reading by their light. We may only look at them and appreciate them for what they are, not for what they can do for us. The phrase in the above quote is that "permission is not granted to utilize them, but only to look," which can be read as: we cannot use them, but we are meant to look at them.

For this reason, many sages throughout the centuries have suggested that we do indeed spend some time gazing at the flames of the Menorah. It is best to do this while we are introspecting, meditating, or offering praise. We can then receive the blessing of the lights of the candles as their image fills our visual field.

THE FLAME OF A CANDLE:

When looking at the flame of a candle what does one see? Noticeably there are three basic elements to the fire: the flame, the wick and the oil (or wax).

To quote the Zohar:
"The body is similar to the wick. The flame itself is analogous to the Divine presence that rests above the head. And the oil that fuses the two together, allowing the flame to join and remain connected with the wick, is our

Ma'asim Tovim/Good Deeds" *(Zohar, 3; 187a).*

"The wise man's eyes are in his head" *(Koheles, 2; 14).* According to the Zohar, this means that the wise are continuously aware of the divine presence that is above their heads. More importantly, this awareness informs their actions and insures their performance of good deeds and proper comportment. Meditating upon a candle's flame inspires us all to do the same.

In truth we are all like a flame, as the totality of who we are is reflected within the structure of the flame. Similar to the fire, the spiritual elements of self are perpetually reaching upward. Similar to the wick, our physical body gravitates downward towards the earth. And similar to the oil (or wax) our good deeds are what allow for a full integration between self, body and soul.

To live a balanced life we need to harmonize and synthesize spirit and body. Just as we instinctively tend to the needs of our body, we must also tend to the needs of our soul. Just as we seek spiritual wholeness, we must strive for physical wholeness. For, in truth, the two are totally interconnected and united making a single composite entity.

The Hebrew word *Nefesh*/Soul or Spirit is comprised of three letters: *Nun, Pei,* and *Shin.* These letters are an acronym for *Ner, Pesilah,* and *Shemen* —'flame', 'wick', and 'oil.' Just as a flame cannot manifest without wick and oil, our souls cannot manifest themselves within this world unless they are attached to physicality (i.e., our bodies and the world around us) by means of selfless and noble actions. Our actions are the clearest indicators of whether we are truly living what we believe.

IMAGE TWO: PRACTICE

» Visual Meditation on the Flame

Take a few minutes to sit near the lights of the Menorah.

Fix your gaze upon the flame and notice that the flame, wick and oil are all part of one seamless whole.

Turning inwards, become aware that you are both body and soul.

Does the oil of your actions strengthen the bond between the wick of your body and the flame of your soul?

Recognize that just like the candle, your body and soul are really parts of one seamless whole. Essentially there is no conflict between them.

Behold the depth of this harmony and allow it to dissolve all remnants of stress or inner strife. If unity is all there is within, there is no discord to be found.

IMAGE THREE: IDEA

» THE COLORS OF THE FLAME

Penetrating a bit deeper, if we begin to notice the fire itself we can become aware of the different shades of color within the flame. Essentially, there is the dark and intense blue light, and on the other extreme there is a white luminous, almost transparent light.

What do these colors represent?

The Zohar describes the following:
"Within the flame itself, there are two lights:
One white and luminous, the other black or blue.

The white light is the higher of the two, and it rises steadily.
The black or blue light is underneath the (white light),
Which rests on (the black or blue light) as on a pedestal.
The two are inseparably connected,
The white resting upon and enthroned upon the black...
The blue or black base is, in turn, attached to something

beneath it (the wick),
Which keeps it aflame and impels it to cling to the white light above.
This blue or black light sometimes turns red,
But the white light above it never changes color.

The lower light, which is sometimes black, sometimes blue, and sometimes red,
Is a connecting link between the white light to which it is attached above,
And to the concrete body (the wick) to which it is attached below,
Which keeps it alight.

The lower light always consumes anything under it,
Or anything brought in contact with it,
For such is its nature, to be a source of destruction and decay.

But the white light which is above it
Never consumes or destroys, and never changes."
(Zohar I, 51a)

To summarize, there are two main differences between the lower light and the higher light: a) the lower light continually fluctuates and changes colors, whereas the higher light is constant; b) the lower fire needs to consume and destroy another in order to exist, while the higher light does not.

The dark light, which is lower and denser, represents the natural, physical world. In this realm, organisms live by consuming and destroying other organisms, and everything is continually fluctuating and changing in appearance. After a living body has served its purpose it gradually rejoins the earth and becomes the soil upon which new life grows. Mineral becomes plant, plant becomes animal, animal becomes human, and human eventually returns to the minerals of the earth.

Soul and spirituality is represented by the higher, white fire, which does not need to overwhelm or negate an 'other' in order to exist. Deeper levels of soul are represented by more transparent shades of white. Near the peak of the flame it becomes so transparent that it is almost invisible, merging into the infinity of space. This is the unchanging, uninfluenced essence of the self that observes or registers the changing self 'below.'

The lower or outermost surface of the self could be called our 'storyline.' This part of us is in a constant state of change and movement. Every moment of our lives, and with every breath, we are constantly moving, shifting back and forth, expanding and contracting. Metaphysically speaking we are continually being re-created, becoming embodied, expiring and then re-embodying again. This is the 'lower light' that continuously moves and changes colors.

Ratzu V'Shuv/Running and Returning is the way the Divine light moves to animate creation. Divine life force pulsates, it is always running and retuning, touching and not touching, it is here and not here. The life force enters and immediately exits, and it is forever transient and elusive. This rapid back and forth movement defines our experience of this dimension. Every time we sense that we are experiencing some form of clarity, where we sense the Divine in our life, immediately this sensation disappears. This is similar to the experience of deep study, prayer or meditation. At the very moment you think to yourself, "I'm really doing it," the spell is broken, and you are back striving to reach that heightened state again. The moment we want to take hold of or appreciate the experience, it slips away and fades.

When we take a bowl of water and place it under sunlight the rays of the sun sparkle, in the manner of "running and retuning." The light does not settle in one place, and the moment we try to grasp it, as it were, it shifts. Rabbi Moshe De Leon *(Shekel HaKodesh, Sod Migdal Poreach B'Avir)* writes that this allusive image of the rays of the sun reflected via a bowl of water upon a wall is a good metaphor for the *Chayos*/Holy Creatures, which in the vision of *Yechezkel*/Ezekiel run and return as the overall life force enters and exits creation. This exercise of contemplating the sun's rays as they are reflected in a bowl of water can be used as a visual meditation device in order to gain experiential knowledge of the Divine process of continuous creation and constant flux.

But now back to the actual flame. Within the flickering and leaping of the lower light is a deep impulse to reach upward. This impulse is called *Ratzu*/Running. It corresponds to the yearning within us to expire in ecstasy or ascend from this world to a higher reality, like a moth to a flame. The steady higher light, which 'rests on the dark light as on a pedestal,' demonstrates a constant and quiet connectivity with the world below. This represents *Shuv*/Returning, an awareness that the purpose of life is in this world, here and now.

In the lower, less evolved levels of our psyche, 'running' is expressed as a desire to transcend the world while neglecting the body. Yet in the higher levels of our psyche, our 'running' energy is in total harmony with its divine purpose, which is to be within the world while inspiring transformation. There is a dynamic tension between 'running' and 'returning,' but they are meant to serve and enhance each other. 'Running' ensures an energetic lightness of being that prevents our involvement with world and body from devolving into self-centered pre-occupation or existential anxiety. 'Returning' ensures that we are grounded and that we do not neglect the body or slip fully into ecstasy and expire from the world.

On a deeper level the dark flickering light leaps up and down and therefore can be seen to contain both 'running and returning' within it. The motionless white light can be seen to be beyond 'running and returning' entirely. It doesn't even need to consume an 'other' in order to exist. Therefore, the white light can be seen to represent the greater context of life, the stillness and unity that is beyond the fluctuating 'storyline' of the world.

Breath is a physiological experience of the 'running and returning' dynamic. Each exhale represents the desire to 'run,' as we empty ourselves and expire. Each inhale represents the desire to 'return' to the body and fill ourselves with new energy. Between each inhale and exhale, as well as between each exhale and inhale, there is a moment of retention when we are neither inhaling nor exhaling. This motionless state of retention is beyond the 'running and returning' paradigm. And yet, in a sense, it contains both energies. This is the ethereal presence of the 'white fire' within our physiology. Both physical and spiritual wholeness and health depend on a balance of 'running and returning.'

In addition to the dark light and the white light, there is another element to the candle's flame. Just below the dark light there appears a tiny gap between flame and wick. Ultimately, if we wish to exude light, warmth, and wisdom we must first disappear like this void. When we attain a measure of self-nullification, the light that we project outwardly will be a warming, inspiring, and gentle brilliance.

THE COLORS OF THE FLAME:

Let us now go a little deeper into the above quoted passage from the Zohar. Looking more closely, the passage from the Zohar mentions several elements of a candle flame:

1) The FLAME ITSELF, in which the various manifestations of light appear;
2) The unchanging or steady aspect of the flame's WHITE light;
3) The fluctuating aspect of the BLUE or BLACK light;
4) The destructive aspect of the flame, symbolized by the RED color that sometimes appears within the blue or black light.

We will now add a fifth element that is not mentioned in the passage: If you look very carefully, below the blue or black light, there is a subtle, steady, white, almost transparent light where the flame is attached to the wick. So there are in fact "five lights" to a flame *(Note; Tikkunei Zohar, Tikkun, 21, p. 50a)*. Like the large, upper white light, this small white light does not change color. It is, in this sense, a diminished reflection of the upper white light. Because of their similarity, we could say that the first manifestation (the upper larger white light) is present within the final manifestation (the smaller lower white light). This is consistent with the principle, "The beginning is wedged in the end" *(Sefer Yetzirah)*.

The above five elements are then associated with different Divine names:

1) The FLAME ITSELF does not have a corresponding name for it is not an attribute of the flame, but is the silent totality or essence of the flame itself. Just as your name is irrelevant when you are thinking about yourself (since you are one with yourself). All names and descriptions are irrelevant to the total 'Self' or 'Essence' of Divinity.

2) The upper WHITE light corresponds to the Divine name, *Yud-Hei-Vav-Hei*. This is the main part of the flame that does not change color but "rises steadily upward," detached from the wick. It does not need to destroy or negate the wick in order to exist. This Name is called Hashem/The Name, or the Tetragrammaton. This Name connotes the changeless, transcendent attribute of Divinity. It often connotes an attribute of kindness since it transcends the world without destroying or negating anything. It is the Infinite 'beingness' that allows all things to be.

3) The light that constantly changes in appearance from BLUE, to BLACK, to RED corresponds to the Divine name *Eh'he'yeh*. This name means, "I will be." This is the name that G-d revealed to Moshe at the Burning Bush,

which indicates change or evolution. This is because the way G-d appears to us is always changing and evolving, according to our own fluctuating perspective and level of spiritual consciousness.

4) The RED light that appears within the blue or black light corresponds to the name *Elokim*. This name indicates the 'concealment' of the Divine in relation to the world. The letters of *Elokim* can be re-arranged to spell the phrase, *Ilam Yud-Hei*, 'the silencing of *Yud-Hei* (Hashem).' *Elokim* also alludes to the attribute of judgment or severity, such as the power of Divinity to consume worldly forces and negate what is not (apparently) Divine.

5) The SUBTLE WHITE light attached to the wick corresponds to the Divine name, *Ado-nai*. As this light is a reflection of the upper white light, the name *Ado-nai* is like a receptacle for the transcendent name Hashem. When, in the recitation of formal prayers, we come to the ineffable Tetragrammaton we recite instead this diminished, more tangible reflection, *Ado-nai*.

ALLUSIONS OF THE DIVINE NAMES:

Everything in the world reflects these five dimensions. Let us use a tree as an example:

1) The "Nameless Essence" of a tree is the entirety of the tree itself, without regard to its attributes.

2) The "Hashem" of a tree is its ineffable existence and boundless presence in the here and now. It is impossible to comprehensively describe a tree, or anything else for that matter.

3) The "*Eh'he'yeh*" of a tree is the fact that it is constantly changing, growing, and fluctuating with the seasons. A tree is always 'tree-ing,' or becoming.

4) The "*Elokim*" of a tree is that it is constantly revealing, through discernment and definition, only 'tree', and thus discarding or concealing everything else. It exerts its existence by negating all that is non-tree.

5) The "*Ado-nai*" of the tree is its name, 'tree.' We indicate a tree with this name, even though we know that what a tree really is transcends our linguistic comprehension or definition.

UNIFICATIONS OF THESE LIGHTS:

A *Yichud*/Unification is a contemplative method of drawing the power of transcendent Divinity into the manifest world. This method utilizes tools such as letters and their *Gematria*/Numerical value. Here, we will contemplate the three basic ways that the unchanging transcendent light of the Infinite One can unite with the changeable, manifest, finite reality.

- The *Yichud* of Hashem and *Eh'he'yeh*: When the numerical value of Hashem (26) is added to the numerical value of *Eh'he'yeh* (21), the sum is 47.
- The *Yichud* of Hashem and *Elokim*: When Hashem (26) is added to the numerical value of the name *Elokim* (86), the sum is 112.
- The *Yichud* of Hashem and *Ado-nai:* When Hashem (26) is added to the numerical value of the name *Ado-nai* (65), the sum is 91.

The total of these three sums (47 + 112+ 91) is 250. The Hebrew word *Ner*, 'candle' or 'light', is numerically 250 (*Nun*=50, *Reish*=200). Therefore, before we light a Chanukah *Ner*/Candle we should bring to mind these three Unifications. By doing so, we hope to invite the transcendent light of Hashem to shine within the world and its many manifestations.

There are twenty-five letters in the names used in the above Unification: Hashem has four letters and it appears three times in these Unifications, so we have 3 x 4 = 12. *Eh'he'yeh* also has four letters, *Elokim* has five, and *Ado-nai* has four, with a combined total of 13. Thus 12 + 13 = 25.

The number 25 in Hebrew is spelled as *Kof*/20 and *Hei*/5, spelling the syllable *Kah*. The word Chanu-kah can thus mean *Chanu*/Resting upon the *Kah*, 'the 25.' In other words, through the lighting of the Chanukah candles and

meditation upon their lights, the light of these three Unifications is meant to rest upon and settle into our lives. These
ideas are not just conceptual structures. Through the performance of the Mitzvah and meditation upon the image of
its light, they can actually be felt and absorbed.

IMAGE THREE: PRACTICE

» 1) Visual Meditation on the Various Colors of the Flame:

The FLAME itself represents what you are in essence, the totality of your you-ness prior to any mention of attributes.

Gaze at the flame and ask yourself, "Who am I in essence? Who am I at my core?" Now turn your gaze inward and enjoy a timeless moment of the irreducible you-ness of you.

The large upper WHITE part of the flame represents your inner "Hashem," your unchanging transcendent soul that is attached to the Infinite Creator. Gaze at the white light and ask, "What is the most stable aspect of my life, that which I hold onto, that which holds me?" Turn your gaze inwards, delighting in the awesome discovery that you are always held within the infinite light and loving kindness of Hashem.

The BLUE or BLACK light near the base of the flame represents your connection to Eh'he'yeh, the state of yearning that gives way to change, process, and becoming. Gaze at this light and ask, "What are my aspirations and dreams? What do I see myself becoming, and what can I do to begin that process?"

Then turn your gaze inward and recognize your yearning to embody more of your higher self, and to make room in this physical world for your transcendent soul.

The RED light that sometimes appears within the blue or black light represents your Elokim, the element of concealment or judgment in your life. Gaze at this area of the flame and ask, "What are the negative or destructive habits and thought patterns that I need to refine, reject, or release?" Turn your gaze inward and recognize any concealment of your soul's brilliance, freeing yourself from the grip of that which does not serve your highest purpose.

The subtle small WHITE light attached to the wick represents your connection to Ado-nai, the way you express your transcendent soul in the world. Perhaps the medium of this expression is your profession, your family role, or your social identity. Gaze at the small white light attached to the wick and ask, "How do I express my true identity in the world? How can I better reflect my soul in thought, word, and action?" Turn your gaze inward and recognize that your life and story are vehicles for your soul's purpose.

IMAGE THREE: PRACTICE

» 2) Simple and Direct Questions to Ask:

To amplify the five inwardly reflective meditations above, here are five simple and direct questions that you could ponder as you meditate on the Chanukah lights:

Five Direct Questions:

Take a few minutes to sit near the lights of the Menorah. Meditate on the five shades of light and ask these five questions to penetrate your core:

Who am I?

What is most precious to me?

What are my aspirations and dreams?

What do I need to release from my life?

Am I expressing my higher self in the world?

IMAGE FOUR: IDEA & PRACTICE

» LOOKING UP AT THE SKY

Besides the above Mitzvah-oriented visuals, such as looking at the Tzitzis or focusing on the lights of the Menorah,
there are many day-to-day visuals that can and have been
suggested for use in meditation. Take for example, the simple idea of gazing at a sunrise or sunset. This can be a very
profound and meaningful visual focus for one's meditation
and contemplation.

The 16th century Spanish born mystic and moralist Rabbi
Eliezer Azikri writes:
    "Since lifting one's eyes to Heaven adds *Da'as*/Proper
    Awareness, as it says, "I lifted up my eyes to heaven, and
    my understanding returned to me" *(Daniel, 4; 31)*, there-
    fore it is good to lift up our eyes to Heaven continuously,
    as it says, "My eyes were raised on high."
    (Yeshayahu, 38; 14. Sefer Chareidim, Chap 66 - 67)

During the same period of time when some of the great
Spanish mystics, philosophers, writers, poets, commenta-
tors, and Halachic codifiers found refuge in the holy city of

Tzfas, Israel (under Ottoman rule), the great Arizal, Rabbi Yitzchak Luria, was also there. As all great mystics of that time and place loved nature and the outdoors, the Arizal initiated a practice of going out into the fields to study, meditate or sing to greet the Shabbos Queen in the few hours leading up to Shabbos [1].

Being within the pristine life of nature and roaming through open meadows can do wonders for a person. The prophets of old would meditate alone in the fields and wander the countryside to ready themselves for prophecy *(R. Shimon Ben Tzemach Duran, Magen Avos, 2; 2. Kli Yakar, Bereishis, 4; 3. Rabbeinu Bachya, Bereishis, 47; 32).*

---

[1]   Although the Gemarah has harsh words for one who prays out in the open *(Berachos, 34b)*, this *(according to Tosefos ad loc., though Rashi disagrees, see also: Shulchan Aruch, Orach Chayim, 90; 5)* refers to a public space where there are distractions from other people. However, in the open and empty fields we can pray, as we find with the Patriarchs Yitzchak and Yaakov who prayed in the open fields. Certainly, we can do so when we do so temporarily and occasionally *(Orach Chayim, Taz 90; 2. Kaf HaChayim 90; 26.)* Note: The Medrash, on the words, "*VaYifga B'makom*/(Yaakov) encountered the space," says, "The whole world became like a wall in front of him" *(Medrash Rabbah)*. And so, indeed he was able to concentrate as if he was in front of a wall, which is the halachic preference for prayer as it blocks out all external distractions and focuses one inwards *(Tifferes Yonason, Vayetze, p, 68)*. Yaakov was thus able to focus inwards even as he was outdoors.

Unfortunately, this is not possible for everyone as many people live in urban areas where there is very little nature or open space. Even to get a glimpse of nature is a feat in such circumstances as the night sky is barely visible due to all the smog and pollution.

The wise Reb Bunim of Pshischah once told a group of his students to build homes on the banks of a river so that they could sit and meditate near the water and think about the wonders of Hashem's creation while sitting near the water. And so, they enthusiastically went ahead to gather the funds needed. Once they had the funds they came to their Rebbe and told him that they were ready and excited to build. Reb Bunim responded, "now that you are prepared to build, return the funds gathered for there is no reason to actually build." He then explained that what he wanted to do was create in them the "vessels" to be open to such a sensitivity and awareness - i.e., now, once they have been aroused towards such an experience, they can be open to have the same type of experience wherever they are. "In truth," he said, "one can sense the Creator's wonders on land or at sea." This is the deeper meaning of the verse that speaks about the wondrous act of the splitting of the sea, "And the people Israel went within the sea on dry ground" *(Shemos, 14; 29)*. This means that they traveled "on dry ground" with the same radical amazement and wonder as if they were within the sea. They felt and sensed the miraculous nature of the splitting of the sea even while walking on the dry land.

The very yearning and aspiration to be out in nature, to be radically amazed, opens a person up to create this same type of awareness at any and every moment, no matter whether they are sitting in the middle of the ocean or walking down a paved road in the downtown of a big city.

Yet, another, perhaps more direct and practical way to help circumvent this issue of living in an urban area is to create natural looking environments. This can be accomplished with warm and subtle colors in the home, or even painting your immediate environment to resemble nature. Clearly, this does not take the place of actually being in nature, but sometimes this is the only alternative. And, as we have learned, even an image of something can be effective in connecting us to its (and our) inner essence.

On the night of Yom Kippur, the holiest day of the year, the *Cohen Gadol*/High Priest spent the night in the Holy Temple of Jerusalem, the holiest place in the world, in preparation for his most important work the next day. He would stay up all night attuning himself — body, mind, and spirit — and readying himself for the holy service on Yom Kippur *(Yumah, 1; 1)*. The room that he sat in was decorated with pictures and images of a beautiful garden with rivers flowing out from the garden. In fact, the imagery on the walls was meant to evoke Adam in his pristine state prior to eating from the tree of knowledge, frolicking in the Garden of Eden in total bliss and spiritual harmony. The

High Priest was meant to sense that he himself was like Adam sitting in the Garden of Eden *(R. Moshe Isserlis, the Ramah (1520 1572) Torahs Ha'Olah, 3; 59).* This is a wonderful image. It demonstrates the power of a visual to create the ambience and set the tone, attuning one's consciousness to the task at hand.

LOOKING UPWARDS:

Of course, actually going out into nature, as opposed to a fabricated replication in your own space, is preferable.

The Arizal encouraged his students to continuously lift their heads up towards the Heavens, saying that through this they would attain greater measures of purity *(Ma'avar Yavak, 5; 17).* The mere act of looking upwards and contemplating the majesty, magnitude and mystery of the cosmos has a profound effect on a person's spiritual frequency.

One defining physical trait of the human being is that he stands erect. His head is positioned above his body and backside. As such, his head tilts easily upwards in order to observe what is above and beyond him. This is what makes him human, the ability to look upwards and perceive that which is above and beyond his immediate environment.

Along these same lines, we can detect a deeper reason why the human being has a natural inkling and desire to look upwards towards the stars, and why, by nature his head is positioned facing upwards in contrast to animals, whose heads are generally facing down towards the ground. According to many sages, this is because each creature faces their source, as it were *(Safer Hayashar, Shar 1. Rabbi Yoseph Yavatz Avos 3; 18. Rabbi Moshe Metrani (writing in the same time period and place as the Arizal, Tzfas in the mid-fifteen hundreds), Beis Elokim, Shar HaTefilah, 7)*.

The human being is comprised of both body and soul. The body comes from and returns to the earth, yet, the *Ruach/* Spirit of man is from the realms Above *(Even the* Nefesh, *the lowest part of the soul that is shared with all living beings, comes from the earth. Ramban, Bereishis, 1; 26)*. Everything gravitates towards its source. The body, naturally, is pulled by gravity towards the ground. Our soul, on the other hand, leaps upward. The tilting of our head upwards is a literal manifestation of the inner movement of our souls.

When we look upward we are awakening our higher/deeper levels of soul, the part of us that comes from beyond our immediate physical reality. There is a profound relationship between our bodies and our minds and psyche. The human is, in a sense, a biopsychic feedback loop, with the mind effecting the body and the body, in turn, effecting and influencing the mind, heart and psyche. The physical upward movement of the head stimulates an internal shift upward, a refocusing on matters of the spirit and beyond.

Here is a teaching from Rabbi Chaim Vital, the prime disciple of the Arizal.

To quote:

"My master, of blessed memory, used to tell me that it is good for man to live in a home that has windows opened to the Heavens so that he can lift his eyes upwards and peer out at all times. Looking upwards will inspire him to contemplate the wonders of creation and, by extension, its Creator, as it says, "When I look at the night sky and see the work of Your fingers — the moon and the stars you set in place" *(Tehilim, 8; 3)*. The act of looking out at the night sky inspires the psalmist to observe the Creator's hand.

The hidden Midrash *(Zohar 1, p, 113a)* speaks of the mighty ruler Nebuchadnezzar upon whom it says, "At the end of that time, I, Nebuchadnezzar, raised my eyes toward Heaven, and my sanity was restored" *(Daniel 4; 34)*. (In other words, it was by virtue of the fact that he looked upwards toward Heaven that his sanity and wisdom were restored).

It is therefore beneficial for man to continually look upwards toward the Heavens, for this act restores wisdom to a person and confirms within him a sense of awe and holiness."

(Shar Ruach HaKodesh, p. 35)

Rabbi Meir Papirosh *(1624-1662)*, one of the redactors

of the writings of the Arizal and a well-known Bohemian Kabbalist, writes that it is a good custom (in fact "a Mitz-vah") to look continually upward towards Heaven, for it fa-cilitates a deeper awareness and instills within man a sense of awe of the Creator" *(Hanhagas Tzadikim 1, p. 89).*

Many years before the Arizal, the moral and philosophical text *Chovos HaLevavos/*Duties of the Heart, written by the 10th century Spanish scholar Rabbi Bachya Ibn Pakudah *(1050 - 1120)*, states that wise men of the world have asked: "Where is G-d's presence to be found? The answer is *B'Tzipiah/*Through Looking or Gazing."

A genuine relationship with G-d demands that G-d is real to us. For G-d to be real to us, writes the *Chovos HaLevavos,* it is not sufficient to merely accept a certain belief system, whether based on formal education or something we have heard growing up in our homes. Rather, we need to actively contemplate and understand the Creator's existence. This, he suggests, comes through deeper observation of the won-drous marvels of creation. Whether we are contemplating the intricate details of our digestive system or the massive expanse of the cosmos, planets, or galaxies, the objective of such contemplation is to bring one to a deeper and a more intimate relationship with the Creator.

As mentioned, urban living may not allow for open roaming in the meadows or the most expansive stargazing. Perhaps it is not as easy for many people living in densely populated areas to look up to the skies. Perhaps one's private living quarters are not conducive for looking heavenward. And yet the sages state that the place where we collectively congregate to pray should be a space with windows and fresh air to clear and calm the mind, and so that we can look up to the heavens during prayer *(Berachos, 34b. So one can look upwards towards heaven. Rashi ad loc., Siddur R. Yaakov Emdin, Hakdamah, and experience a clear mind. Rabbienu Yona. Beis Yoseph, Orach Chayim 90. See also: Zohar 2, p. 251. Even a blind person should pray in a room with windows Kaf HaChayim, Orach Chayim, 90; 20).*

When we feel the need to muster some more intention and devotion in the midst of our prayers, all we need to do is look heavenwards to be inspired.

Prayer is not only reserved for set periods of time throughout the day. To be human is to pray. To be truly alive means to dream, to aspire, to long for something transcendent and beyond one's current situation or state. Some long for power, others for love, but in the depths of that which is most true, all yearning is ultimately for Unity — to connect with the Oneness of the Creator that interpenetrates all of life at every moment.

At various times throughout the day we may feel a need to pray, to reach out, to seek help from, make contact with, or acknowledge 'something' that is beyond and transcendent of us. In these very moments we aspire to sense that which is beneath or behind all of the mess, pain, confusion and apparent randomness of life.

Simply walking down the street and catching a glimpse of a star, the sun, the moon, or a beautiful ray of sun can stimulate and arouse an urge to feel a connection in our lives — a connection to our deeper selves, to our purpose, to our community, to the world around us, and ultimately to the Creator. It can be a catalyst for a real spiritual and inward reflective moment.

This is the tremendous virtue of looking upward and observing the continuous miracles of nature. Yet, as our sages teach: "One who walks along the way and interrupts his review of his Torah studies and exclaims, 'How beautiful is this tree!' Scripture accounts it to him as if he had forfeited his life" *(Avos 3:7)*. This statement seems contradictory to all the above teachings. To decode this apparent contradiction a more careful, subtle reading is in order.

For starters, this person has "forfeited his life" not because he was appreciating the wonders of the Creator's creation, but rather, because he was in the midst of reviewing his studies and interrupted his learning. The issue is one of neglect. He interrupted his Torah study. This reveals that he was ultimately in a scattered state of mind and not present with what he was doing. This reveals a certain lack of focus while in the midst of a meditative and contemplative practice.

On a deeper level, the language of this teaching is "one who walks…and *Mafsik*/Interrupts his studies to behold the beauty of nature." What he is doing is creating a false "separation" between Hashem's Torah that he is learning and Hashem's world that he is seeing. Because he is separating Torah from Nature and not seeing the unity and oneness of Creator and Creation, he too is "separated" from his Source, and he therefore forfeits his life.

A GLIMPSE BEYOND THE SUN:

In Hebrew, to catch a glimpse of something is called, *Tzipiah*, but to gaze at and deeply observe is called *Histaklus*. Histaklus occurs when a person is truly looking at the sunset, sunrise, a moving star, or just out into empty panoramic space and is then able to lose oneself and one's sense of time, ego, and body. One is then able to become completely absorbed in awe and wonder as they lose themselves within the visual landscape they are looking at — all without such admiration becoming idol worship.

It is perhaps even possible that while gazing at a sunrise, for example, one receives a mystical type of awareness where one experiences a sense that they are beholding the "reality" that is "behind" the sun. This type of awareness that transports a person to a realm beyond whatever object or image they are contemplating is essentially the goal of visually-based meditation.

THREE WAYS OF LOOKING:

To clarify and contextualize these ideas a little further we will now explore three different levels of Histaklus, or three ways of looking and observing. On the third tier of Histaklus the act itself becomes a medium for a deeper spiritual experience.

First, there is the act of looking, which is a purely biological function. You do so every waking moment, as millions of mostly subliminal images are being taken in. The second type of looking is when there is a conscious act of seeing, a proactive undertaking wherein you attempt to 'see' someone or something specific. In this second type of looking, whatever is looked at is interpreted through the prism of the viewer's cumulative prejudices and contextual thinking. Essentially, what is being seen is recreated by the mind in its own image. The third type of looking is gazing and this can only occur in a condition of complete nullification of any separate sense of "I". The gazer, through the mere act of losing him/herself in what is being observed, limits the internal static of the ego that normally prevents him from being unified with life and with the Creator of all life.

On this third level of Histaklus there is a unity that is achieved between the viewer and the object being viewed. There is a melding of the two into one wherein the viewer, the viewed, and the Creator of that which is viewed are experientially unified.

This is real 'awe,' when you lose yourself in something greater than yourself. Although, in this case it must be clarified that one is not aspiring to attain unity with the object per se, but rather, one uses the image to go beyond it to connect with the Infinite Imageless Creator of all life and of all form.

IMAGE FIVE: IDEA & PRACTICE

··

» LOOKING AT THE TEACHER, THE TZADIK

Earlier there was a discussion of the subtle negative effects that looking at a Rasha, a wicked or negative person, can have on the observer. Essentially, looking at a Rasha tunes you into their negative frequency. But, as mentioned, the reverse is also true, and in fact, even more so. Being in the presence and looking at the face of a Tzadik tunes one in to the spiritual frequency of the Tzadik.

In the words of the Baal Shem Tov:
> "Do not gaze upon the face of people whose thoughts are not continuously attached to the Creator even when speaking to them, for gazing at them will blemish your soul.
> As for fit people however, those whose thoughts are attached to the Creator, you ought to gaze at them and through this, enlarge the portion of holiness in your soul."
> *(Tzeva'as HaRivash, 50)*

Overall there is tremendous spiritual, mental and emotional value in looking upon the face of a true *Tzadik*/Righteous Person *(Reishis Chochmah, Shar Hakedusah. Chap 8)*. Beholding the face of a *Tzadik* arouses the observer to be more like that *Tzadik*. Great people inspire greatness in others. This is especially true when the *Tzadik* is teaching Torah.

Looking at your teacher while the teacher is transmitting Torah has a profoundly positive effect on the student. "Rebbe said *(Eiruvin, 13b)*, the reason I am sharper in Torah study than my friends is because I saw Rabbi Meir (when he was teaching Torah) from behind; and had I seen him from the front I would have been even sharper, as the verse states, "And your eyes shall see your teachers" *(Yeshayahu, 30; 20)*.

Rebbe is saying that since he sat in a row directly behind his teacher Rabbi Meir as he was teaching he gained more wisdom than his fellow students who were further away and unable to see R. Meir directly; but had he seen the face of his teacher as he was teaching he would have gained even greater insight and understanding from the subtle intricacies of his facial expressions *(D'rashos Ha'Ran, Derush 8. Maharsaha, Eiruvin, 13b)*. By seeing the face of the teacher the student becomes more attuned to the teacher's frequency and manner of thinking.

A teacher of Torah is not merely a scholar or someone who knows the material well. A good science teacher is someone that understands science well and has the ability to transmit scientific theory in an accessible manner. Not so with a teacher of Torah. To be an authentic teacher of Torah one needs to embody the qualities of the Torah. Our sages tell us that "if your teacher is like an angel of Hashem you should seek Torah from his mouth, and if not you should not seek Torah from his mouth" *(Chagigah, 15b. Mo'ed Katan, 17a).*

When a student of Torah looks at his teachers face when they are teaching Torah, besides just being able to pick up the subtleties of the facial expressions of his teacher and therefore understand the lesson better, the student is also able to receive some of the teacher's angelic light. In this way, the student receives much more than wisdom.

Rabbi Yonason Eybshitz, the famed Rabbi of Prague *(1690- 1764)*, writes that looking at a teacher while they are teaching Torah draws down goodness and blessings *(Ya'aros D'Vash 1, Derush 12)*. One receives goodness and blessings by merely looking at a person who embodies goodness and blessings.

Just as there is value to beholding the image of your teacher while studying Torah, there are also sources that speak of the value of looking at the face of a Tzadik during prayer *(Teshuvas Radbaz 3, Siman 472)*. When we surround ourselves with our teachers, or even loved ones, our hearts and minds are more open and we can be more sensitive and vulnerable during prayer. Not that we should actually look at another human being during our prayers, but rather, just before praying steal a quick glance at your Rebbe, teacher, or friend around you, and then, knowing that you are surrounded by people you love, admire and feel comfortable with, your prayers will be that much more focused and heartfelt.

Sometimes we can actually look at the face of the person teaching, but often we are repeating and reviewing what we learned to ourselves, or others while not in the presence of the teacher. Our sages tell us that when we are giving over a teaching from someone else we should conjure up the image of that person in our mind's eye *(Yerushalmi, Kedushin, 1; 7)*. When we are studying Gemarah (Talmud), for example, R. Elimelech of Lizhensk suggests *(Noam Elimelech, Igeres HaKodesh, 2)* that we should imagine the sage we are mentioning is alive and present, standing right in front of us. When we say, "Rabbi Akiva says," we should, according to this teaching, imagine Rabbi Akiva literally standing there in front of us saying these words.

The Jerusalem sage, Rabbi Chayim Yosef Dovid Azulai, known by his acronym the Chidah *(1724 –1806)*, speaks about forming a mental image of a Tzadik that you have seen in your mind *(Midbar Kadmos, Ma'areches Tzadik, Tziyur)*. He cites the writings of the Zohar, which speak of the sage Rav Aba who would conjure up the image of his illustrious master, Rabbi Shimon Bar Yochai. By doing so he would gain greater understanding of the studies he was pondering. Just thinking about his teacher and visualizing his image opened the student's mind to receive deeper levels of wisdom than he was able to access through expository thinking alone. This is an excellent example of how the subliminal imprint mechanism of the imagistic arts can supplement the more discursive cognitive methods in the process of achieving a more holistic integration of wisdom and experience.

Indeed, the Arizal teaches that when a person is having trouble understanding a passage in the Torah he should mentally visualize the image of his (primary) teacher and this will help him to unlock the concealed meaning of the text.

IMAGE SIX: IDEA & PRACTICE

» The Colors of Life

EVERY COLOR IS OUR TEACHER:

There are no coincidences. Everything that happens in our life, everything that we see, hear or experience is intended to be our teacher, telling us something about the world we live in and about ourselves.

There is a purpose to everything we hear or see in life. If we are simply walking down the street and chance upon a certain image we need to ask ourselves, why did we see it? What is it teaching me? What can I learn from what I have seen? And how can I grow from the experience?

That is not to say that every "message" is meant to be taken literally. We are not implying that everything contains some sort of coded directive for the way one should conduct their life at every moment. We are simply suggesting a more poetic or artful "read" of the reality one encounters. This approach to life would be more akin to a mystical reading of text, or to a deep engagement with a work of art. It is predicated on the idea that the relationship of the Creator to Creation is similar to a painter and his painting or a poet and his poem. There is craft, meaning, and purpose to the placement of details and digressions. The "messages" may be ambiguous and are often relative to one's inner experience in the moment. This type of awareness is therefore more about sensitizing oneself to these poetic 'traces' of the Creator within creation, as opposed to a more didactic or pedantic search for 'truths' within the imagery and aesthetics of the world.

"Every person needs a teacher," says Reb Bunim of Pshischah, "except for someone to whom everyone and everything is a teacher." According to this radical teaching, the role of a teacher is meant as a supplementary aid for someone who is not sensitive enough to perceive the hints and lessons being communicated to them through the world around them. The truth is that every person we encounter and every situation in life that we find ourselves in is our teacher, teaching us something about ourselves, about the world around us, and about our relationship with it.

The Baal Shem Tov taught that everything we see is for a purpose. If we see something 'negative' outside of ourselves, this indicates that there is something negative within us, otherwise we would not have seen or noticed any such external negativity. The reason we see and are shown the neg-ative image is so that we can become aware of what needs attention and alignment within our own souls.

Once the Baal Shem Tov saw a person desecrating the holy Shabbos. For a while he wondered why he had seen such an *Aveira*/Sin, until it became clear to him. A few days earlier he had asked a favor from one of his students, something that theoretically he could have done himself. Our sages say that a Torah scholar is analogous to the day of Shab-bos. "In a way," he thought, "I inconvenienced a student of mine who is also a Torah scholar. I myself thereby desecrat-ed "Shabbos" and that was the reason I saw Shabbos being desecrated. The external world is a mirror and it is thus showing and telling me to be more careful with my stu-dents. Do not place any extra burden upon them, otherwise, you too are desecrating the holy Shabbos."

Beyond learning from the images of the actual things we see, we can also learn from the colors in which these images appear. The shapes, colors, and textures of everything that we see have meaning and relevance.

Life is so full of sights, sounds, smells, images, colors and tunes. Someone that is truly alive and in touch with the vi-brations and creative forces of the Divine is able to perceive the animated fullness and presence within all of existence. For our purposes we will focus on the colors of life.

Once the Rebbe of Gur, the *Imrei Emes*, saw a groom walking to the *Chupah*/Marriage Canopy in the customary white *Kitel*/Robe; yet, as is the Chassidic custom, he was also wearing a black overcoat covering the *Kitel*. The white *Kitel* is worn to symbolize the atonement the groom is given for all his sins on the day of his wedding. White symbolizes purity and forgiveness *(Yeshayahu, 1; 18)*. The overcoat is worn so that the *Kitel* should be covered, so as not to stand out. This is an act of modesty on the part of the groom. The *Imrei Emes* said, "Look, here walks a living Torah. For as the Torah is 'Black fire on top of White Fire,' this groom too is black fire (the overcoat) on top of white fire (the *Kitel*)." This is such a rich observation. The Rebbe took an issue of modesty, as represented in someone's clothing and color coordination, and saw way beyond it. This is an example of how to see life as teaming with meaning and spiritual resonance, always inspiring and constantly provoking. It does not have to be a beautiful sunset or an awesome lightning storm that stimulates one's spiritual imagination. The mere color of the clothes another person is wearing can provide the same associative link to imaginal inspiration and deeper meaning.

In terms of seeing every color as our teacher the celebrated Chassidic Rebbe, Rabbi Tzvi Elimelech, the Rebbe of Dinov *(1783 – 1841)*, suggests *(Igra D'Pirka, 38)* that when we see a certain color we need to ask ourselves — why was this color shown to me? Why did I see this particular color? Besides the image itself, why did it appear to me in this color?

Every color says something. Every color resonates with a distinct energy arousing, awakening or even creating a psychophysical sensation within the observer. Some colors may arouse one's energy or passions, while others may have a calming effect. And of course we all have our own unique associations with different colors based on our own life experiences and personal narratives. In this way each color has a character of sorts or a particular quality that evokes certain emotional or associative responses within us. It is by paying attention to Hashem's colorful palette that we are able to appreciate the beauty of life, and then, even deeper, the symbolic meaning and poetic traces of the Creator within the canvas of Creation.

Here is an example that brings together the beauty of nature and the deeper meaning of Torah. There is an ancient art form called gemology, the theory of stones. The belief is that there are different stones with different colors, and each precious stone awakens a certain feeling or healing power within the person holding, looking at, or wearing the stone *(R. Gershon Ben Shlomo, Shar HaShamayim, Maamor 2; 3. R. Shem Tov Ibn Shem Tov, Sefer Ha'emunos, Shar 5; 1. See also: Sheivet HaMusar, 6; 10. Machir Yayin, p. 44).* In the Torah we find that the Breastplate that was worn by the High Priest contained four rows of precious stones, each row with three stones *(The Zohar correlates the particular colored stones with distinct Sefiros.*

Tikunei Zohar, Hakdamah 10). For example, one row contained "turquoise, lapis and emerald," while another contained "topaz, onyx and jasper" *(Shemos, 28; 15-20).* These twelve precious stones, with their unique energies and distinct colors, correspond to the twelve tribes of Israel. In this way we can see that the Torah itself suggests various symbolic associations between the colors as they manifest within the different gem stones and the qualities and concepts associated with the twelve tribes *(Rabbeinu Bachya, Shemos, 28; 15).*

In the realm of inquiry there is empirical evidence and experiential evidence. Experientially, there are particular sensations that are awakened when we see particular colors. Granted, this may be culturally conditioned, and perhaps fluctuates throughout the ages, yet, there does seem to be a kind of universal, almost innate response pattern regarding certain colors. Red, perhaps because it is the color of spilled blood, often arouses a sense of anger, wrath, and power. It seems to be universally acknowledged as a passionate and intense color, whereas blue feels quite different. Blue frequently induces a more watery or heavenly quality. Again, perhaps this is due to the fact that blue is the observable color of the sky and the sea. Based on both of these colors, blood-red and sky-blue, we can suggest that there are perhaps some basic universal associations with various fundamental colors that exist in nature and that are experienced by all humans in an ahistorical manner.

Additionally, there are colors that are more likely to be contextually determined and culturally loaded. To some, white feels harmonious and peaceful; whereas black seems dead and silent – like the color of something rotten. While for others, white feels empty and blinding, and black feels pregnant and mysterious. Yellow is often experienced as a gentle and compassionate color, such as the soft light of the sun, whereas silver seems transcendent and evokes clarity. But again, we must restate that our conceptions of each color are, in large part, conditioned by our cultural surroundings. There are in fact many culturally specific color codes that by no means adhere to ours. But we will for the most part in this text be focused on Kabbalistic conceptions of colors and their corresponding qualities.

For a more detailed discussion of the subtleties of color-coded meditations, see the "Advanced Visualizations" section of this book. For now we will present some of the very basics of this system. This should suffice for the reader to begin expanding his own perception of the colors of life that he encounters throughout his day.

There is a long tradition of Kabbalists attributing different colors to individual Sefiros. In fact, there are many such Kabbalistic color-coded correspondences developed throughout the ages, many of them differing quite significantly from previous and later systems. This must be noted at the outset, and just goes to show the contextual and experiential aspect of creative mystical theory and practice. There is no one 'right' color code of the Sefiros. It is up to each individual to find a system that speaks to them and to then apply it to their own experience as they seek out deeper meaning and connection to Hashem within their daily life.

The Kabbalistic paradigm and approach to the colors explores their experiential and meta-physical roots. In other words, in order to assign a specific color to a specific Sefira, Kabbalists posed questions such as, "why is blood red and the sky blue?" In such a way the Kabbalists are seeking meaning beyond scientific explanations, which are the external and empirical reasons for such phenomena. But the Kabbalists want to penetrate the deeper metaphysical reasons for such phenomena. For instance, in the world of the Kabbalists, blood is red because it is connected to a particular spiritual expression, a specific Sefira. Similarly, the sky is blue because it is connected to another spiritual expression and specific Sefira. In this way, the Kabbalists are positing that physical reality manifests in the way it does, in its particular garments and hues, as a reflection of its root within the meta-physical structure of supernal reality. Blood is therefore red because it is rooted within and expresses the energy of the Sefira of Gevurah, for instance, not the other way around.

It must also be stated that the Sefiros themselves do not

actually have any color or texture of their own. But rather, the colors appear to us as a reflection of the way in which we encounter and process the light of the Sefiros. This idea will be explored in much greater detail in the "Advanced Visualizations" section of this book. But in the meantime here is a general map of the Sefiros and their corresponding colors that we have compiled from various sources:

Keser – Desire and Will - Blinding White
(or, clear, colorless)
Chochmah – Wisdom and Intuition - Silver
(or, sapphire blue)
Binah – Reason and Cognition - Gold
Chesed – Kindness and Love - White
Gevurah – Strength and Restriction - Red
Tiferes – Beauty and Compassion -Yellow like a
ripening *Esrog*/Citron (or Green)
Netzach – Victory and Ambition - Light Pink
Hod – Devotion and Humility - Dark Pink
Yesod – Foundation and Relationship - Orange
Malchus – Royalty and Receptiveness – (dark) Blue

Being that every color we observe is associated with a particular Sefira, we need to ask ourselves when we observe a particular color: Why am I seeing this particular color at this very moment? What Sefira or spiritual quality am I being shown, and why? How does it relate to or inform my own process of spiritual development?

If it is white that is being shown to me this means I am being shown the Sefira of Chesed (loving kindness). This informs me that I may need to work more on my ability to express love towards myself, others, all of creation, and to the Creator of all life. If it is red that is being seen, then I am being shown the Sefira of Gevurah (strength and restriction). This may be revealing that I need more discipline or healthy boundaries in my life.

So, the question is not just, "why did I see this particular image," but also, "why did I see this particular image in this particular color?" "Why is Heaven showing me this color? Why am I seeing love and kindness," or "why am I seeing strength and restriction?" Every color resonates with a unique vibration, awakening and arousing a distinct emotion. "Why", we need to ask ourselves, "is this emotion or character trait being aroused at this time? Am I lacking this emotion? Is this emotion misdirected in my life? What can I do to access more of or balance this particular quality or character trait?"

IMAGE SEVEN: IDEA & PRACTICE

» A Spectrum of Visuals

There are many other possible visuals that one can use as a focus for meditation. Before we move into more aware-ness-oriented practices we will briefly mention a few more visuals that are discussed in traditional sources. These visuals range from helping to quiet the mind to actual healing.

REFLECTION OF LIGHT
ON METAL - HEALING:

The Zohar *(Terumah, 2, 172b)* teaches that there is a certain illness that causes a person's face to turn a greenish color. According to the Zohar the cure for this ailment is the making of a mirror-like object from sharp metal. Sparks of light then emanate from this object (when held in sun-light) and the healing occurs when a person looks at the metal as the metal is passed over his entire face. This may be understood magically, as it were, or perhaps this is de-scribing something like a case of jaundice in which a person benefits from exposure to sunlight in the course of healing. The point is that there was once a tradition to use this type of metal for healing. And in fact the healing came about through a person looking at the metal. It was therefore a visually induced healing.

MOVEMENT OF THE CLOCK – QUIETING THE MIND:

Another more practical use of a visual focus for meditation is the practice of watching the movement of the smaller second hand on a clock. Rabbi Klonimus Kalman of Peasetzna suggests that in order to quiet the mind and slow down the rush of one's mental activity, one should focus on the slow movement of the smaller hand of a clock. This will help one slow down the deluge of mental activity and inner narrative *(Derech Hamelech, p. 451).*

There is an assumption that most people make — that they actually control their thoughts. But if you think about it for a moment you will realize that more often than not your thoughts choose you.

If one were to just leave the mind alone to function on its own the mind would find what to think, reminisce, and daydream about ad infinitum. Even when a person consciously chooses a thought to think about, realistically how long can you hold that thought?

Imagine you decide to focus on a particular chosen thought on your walk from home to work. As you step out of your house you bring the thought to mind, but immediately the first thing you see, hear, smell or touch pops into your train of thought. Let's say you hear a siren going off in the distance and your mind instantly wonders about the siren. You notice the clouds, so you begin to wonder if it is going to rain. This sets off a whole chain of thoughts: Do I have an umbrella? Umbrellas are so expensive. I should really make more money. I don't like my boss — and so on and so forth. The thoughts slowly unravel and take over the driver's seat of your mind. In a short period of time, your mind has traveled on a wild goose chase comprised of loosely connected destinations. The unifying point for them all is that not one of them was chosen and not one of them was the original thought you decided to think about on your way to work.

Our thoughts are like "horse thoughts." To the best of our knowledge a horse (like all other animals) is always thinking about what is right in front of him at any given moment. Whether it is a basin of water or a pile of hay, the horse is thinking only of the basin of water or the pile of hay.

Whatever sensation is aroused, that is where the mind travels. You see something and you then think about what you are seeing; you see something else and you begin thinking about what you are seeing now; you hear something else, and now you think about that. Our mind seems to jump around like kernels of corn in a popcorn machine — a pop here, a pop there.

The mind seems utterly scattered and unfocused. And even when we try to focus on one thought, within ten or twenty seconds our mind is flooded with a deluge of unwanted and unrelated thoughts. How do we quiet down the mind and slow down this onrush of thoughts?

One visual suggestion, as mentioned, is to sit down in front of a clock and, before you are about to begin thinking over your chosen thought, give yourself a few moments to patiently observe the slow movements of the small second hand. For some people this can be unnerving and unsettling, but for many this works wonders. It slowly calms the mind down and thus allows you to introduce your chosen thought into a settled pool of water rather than a stormy sea, so to speak.

Another effective method is to sit opposite another person and look into each other's eyes for a set period of time, it could be ten minutes, a half hour, or even an hour. Each person should lock in their focus and gaze deeply into the other person's eyes.

The advantage of this technique over staring at an inanimate object is twofold: 1) there is palpable aliveness and clearly revealed depth in the other person's eyes so that it is more likely to hold your focus. Whereas, when staring at an inanimate object, although it too on a deeper level is "alive" and brimming with vitality and beauty, it is not as apparent. And parenthetically, the more you are actually able to gaze at the clock, for example, the more you will start to become sensitized to its aliveness and intrinsic beauty; and 2) since the other person is looking back at you there is a sense of accountability. In other words, if you are gazing at the movements of a clock and your eyes wander off it might take you a few seconds or more until you re-engage and focus your attention back on the clock, this is not so when another person is looking back at you. The moment your eyes begin to drift, the attention of the other person's eyes forces your focus back to them.

Try this and you will see how powerful of a method it is to help slow down the constant onrush of thoughts, to clear the mind, and ultimately to allow for, what the Peasetzna Rebbe call a Hashra'ah, a type of prophetic-like clarity and insight.

THE RISE OF SMOKE – CALMING ANGER:

There is another visual that is worth mentioning that can perhaps be helpful to many people — albeit in the modern era with our better understanding of the adverse effects of tobacco, maybe less so.

A disgruntled disciple once came to the famed Chassidic master, the *Choze*/Seer of Lublin, Rabbi Yaakov Yitzchak Horowitz *(1745-1825)*, and he asked the Choze for a remedy to conquer or squelch his anger. The Choze, who was known to take snuff during his prayers and smoked a pipe, suggested that he too take a smoke *(Erech Apayim, 10; 15, p. 289)*.

There are two elements at play here — the tobacco and the smoke that rises from the smoking itself.

One way to think about this suggestion is that the Choze was encouraging him to smoke tobacco. Studies today have shown that there may be a relationship between tobacco/ nicotine and managing one's negative emotions. There has been research that suggests that smokers with higher levels of hostility may use tobacco to deal with anger provoking situations, and that for some, total abstinence from smoking is associated with increased anger and irritability.

This may all be true for a person who is already a smoker. The trouble is that we also know today that smoking is damaging to your health and besides, if you have never smoked, there are studies that suggest that if you are more prone to anger or less naturally cheerful, you may also have a brain that is particularly susceptible to nicotine addiction. Which means that if you are a person susceptible to anger you may also be more likely to get hooked on nicotine and cigarettes.

In fact, despite the assumption that smoking can be calming, actually, it is often the reverse —nicotine makes many people even more aggressive.

So let us focus more on the smoke, not the tobacco, and its relationship to anger and its ability to help calm anger.

In the Torah smoke is associated with anger *(Devarim, 29; 20. Tehilim, 74; 1)*. In the experience of anger there is a kind of flaring up or billowing of flames of passion and furor.

And yet, paradoxically, a gentle rising of smoke can be used as a calming agent. Without cigarettes, tobacco or anything that is harmful to your body to inhale, the peaceful smoke that rises from a candle, for example, can be also used as a soothing device.

In the *Beis HaMikdash*/the Holy Temple, there was a special service dedicated to offering up the *Ketores*/Incense. The superficial "purpose" and reason for the Ketores was to eradicate the negative smells of the animal offerings *(Rambam, Morah Nevuchim, 3; 45)*. On a deeper level *(Likutei Sichos Vol. 14, p. 129. Emes VaEmunah, p. 125)*, the eradication of the negative smells represents and stimulates an eradication of all physical/emotional, mental and spiritual negativity *(Zohar Chadash, Shir HaShirim, 1; 4)*.

A fundamental aspect of the service of the incense was the

smoke that rose upward. This is especially true of the incense on Yom Kippur. On the holy day of Yom Kippur, the day of radical atonement, it was most essential that the smoke producing herb was included in the incense *(Rambam, Hilchos Avodas Yom Ha'Kipurim, 5; 25)*. The flowing upwards of the smoke as it rises and dissipates into thin air symbolizes and inwardly stimulates a letting go of negativity, as well as its elevation and complete nullification.

When a person feels like anger is flaring up, or that they are struggling with anger issues, they can use the advice of the Choze and use the gentle rising of smoke as a calming agent. If one is feeling angry, let the fire of your emotions dissolve in the smoke.

Not that you become one with the smoke, rather view the smoke as a vehicle to let out your steam and carry away your anger. As the intense red flame morphs into smoke, rises upwards, and then disappears, the same can be true for your anger. After a while of objectively observing the anger, you can see the anger rising up, dissipating, and dying out like the flame of a raging fire.

IMAGE EIGHT: IDEA & PRACTICE
....

» Yichudim – Acronyms & Scanning Sacred Letter Formations

There is another form of Kabbalistic meditation that will be explored in much greater detail in a further text that will focus on the teachings of the holy Arizal, Rabbi Yitzchak/ Isaac Luria. But here we will briefly touch upon this practice as it relates to visual-based meditation practices. We are referring to *Yichudim*, the practice of using a stream of Hebrew letters as a visual-focus device without actually pronouncing them audibly. This is based on the idea of creating a *Yichud*/Unification of various sacred names by combining them to create a larger compound name. This is similar to the idea of combining individual chemicals to create a reaction. The purpose of this practice is to allow the letters themselves to enter deeply into one's sub- and super-conscious in order to gain a more focused attention and advanced level of awareness by inducing a heightened state of trance-like sentience whereby one can even connect with righteous souls of the past.

The Arizal would on occasion give his students a particular Yichud to be practiced at the gravesite of past Tzadikim. When the students followed the Arizal's directions correctly they would merit mystical visions and spiritual unions with the souls of the *Tzadikim*/Righteous Ones that were buried in that location. On a deeper level, all the teachings of the Arizal are essentially forms of *Yichudim* (plural for *Yichud*) *(Leshem, Safer Ha'deah, Vol. 2. p. 137d)*.

YICHUDIM/UNIFICATION VISUALS:

The primary form of the *Yichud*/Unification practice is to combine a series of letters wherein various sacred names of G-d are joined as one. The different names and letters are written out on a page with the intention to be scanned (i.e., seen) but not pronounced (i.e., heard). For example, one Yichud would take the four letters in the name of Hashem, the *Yud-Hei-Vav-Hei*, and combine them with the four letters in the name, *Adon-ai, Aleph-Dalet-Nun-Yud*. The visual of this Yichud would be *Yud-Aleph-Hei-Dalet-Vav-Nun-Hei-Yud*.

Divine speech is the grand metaphor for the emergence of creation. Speech is differentiated sound revealed and encoded with meaning as letters and words. Essentially the letters are the primary conduits of energy. The letters of the *Aleph Beis*/Hebrew Alphabet are the building blocks of creation *(Sefer Yetzirah)*. The Torah describes creation as a process of Ten Divine Utterances *(Avos, 5; 1)*. It is through these primary utterances that creation emerges and is manifest. "G-d said, 'let there be light,' and there was light." The world of multiplicity begins with speech, when inner thought becomes externalized word.

Letters are the fundamental underlying vibrational patterns and energy structures of creation. There is a rhythm to creation. A Divine desire to create begins within the "thoughts" of the Creator. The thought then moves to become a Divine outbreath, which in turn flows as wind, becoming, ultimately, Divine speech, the "externalization" of the original thought.

This spiritual vibration evolves and gives rise to physical energy, which creates, sustains and enlivens creation.

Each distinct letter carries a particular resonance. When two, three or ten letters are streamed together in a particular sequence this is because on a meta-physical level the energy of the object or subject is related to those distinct vibrations and resonance patterns. This is similar to the function of sheet music. The manifest sound produced by the musician is contained within the code of the musical notation. The letters are essentially just that, a code that is utilized by the Ultimate Artist, the Creator, to conduct the Symphony of Creation.

Seen in this way, our sages saying that the Torah is the "blueprint of Creation" comes into more multi-dimensional focus. Especially when considered in conjunction with the Torah's statement that, "All of Torah is a song," *(Devarim 31; 19. Possibility, this reference to "song" refers to the entire Torah. Shu't Sha'agas Aryeh, Siman 34).* Meaning that the Torah is essentially the sheet music that Hashem used to sing/ speak the world into being.

Additionally, this takes on even more significance in the context of the practice of Yichudim when one adds a final layer to this gestalt, which is that, according to the Zohar, the Torah is also in fact considered one very long Name of Hashem. Poetically, one could then say that the world is Hashem's masterpiece and the Torah is Hashem's signature in the corner of the painting. Yichudim are thus our way of tapping back into that original creative impulse and energy contained within the letters themselves as we break down and recombine the raw elements and fundamental compounds of creation in order to more deeply understand and unlock the cosmic creative process of the Creator.

Seen from this perspective, the names of objects or subject are certainly not arbitrary. A father is called *Av* because the energy of a father is related to the letters *Aleph* and *Beis*, specifically in this order: first the Aleph and then the Beis, producing the word *Av*. There are specific combinations of letters, as it were, through which the Creator created the world *(Berachos, 55a).*

The sacred names of G-d are the "root" source vibrations, as it were, and the fundamental manifestations of the Divine into the world. One name reflects the revealing of an attribute we call 'kindness,' and another that we call 'strength.' When we combine the various names of Hashem we are creating new channels, as it were, to unlock new pathways and channels for blessings and Divine flows of abundance.

The letters that comprise the names of G-d and their particular sequences of letters carry immense power and sacred energy. The idea of the Yichud is to visually scan the newly formed unification of two or more names. It is a directed and structured visual exercise to scan these letter formations with one's eyes. The actual Yichud creates the 'connection' or 'unification,' so to speak. It is like a telephone number that one can use to call and connect with a particular aspect or attribute of the One, thereby tapping into and unlocking a deeper reality.

The objective of a Yichud is twofold. First there is making the actual connection, and then there is also the understanding of how such a connection works. To make the connection we do not need to understand the process of how it works. This is similar to dialing a telephone number or aligning a combination to unlock a safe. Whether or not one understands the mechanics of a telephone or not, the other person will still answer the call. In terms of the Yichudim, the Arizal revealed the combinations and all we need to do is use them. This is the path of the Sephardic, North African Kabbalists. According to them, the mere act of scanning the name is sufficient, even without understanding the meaning or mechanism of the Yichud.

Temunah/Picture is the name of this approach to the practice of Yichudim. The mere act of scanning the letters creates a picture of the Yichud within the mind of the meditator and thus awakens the level of *Malchus*/Doing within them. There is a positive effect on a person's soul and consciousness on the level of *Malchus*/Action. Simply (but not literally) translated, Malchus represents 'doing,' the world of action and physical manifestation. By 'dialing the number,' as it were, an alignment of energy is created which sparks and stimulates the person on this most manifest level of their being.

Yet, every letter and name represents a deeper spiritual quality, unlike a telephone number, which is merely a random strand of numbers. For this reason, the Ashkenazi/European Kabbalists stress the importance for a practitioner and meditator to understand what each name represents. While the scanning and picture-taking of the letters does have an effect on the level of "doing" (i.e., the outer/surface manifestations of the human being), through "thinking" about what the Yichud actually means and represents the mind itself is transformed. Encountered in this way there is a more subtle and internal transformation, which then also filters down and results in transformed actions.

This process is called *Tevunah*/Understanding, in contrast to *Temunah*/Picture. What differentiates the human from the animal is his capacity for abstract thought and his ability to transform his thoughts into words. Seeing and thinking about the Yichud initiates a deeper inward transformation than merely scanning it.

For example, the Yichud of two or three Divine Names is a synopsis and synthesis of multiple ideas or attributes in one long "word" comprised of a strung-together sequence of letters. The Yichud then encapsulates all the ideas of what these individual Names represent in one 'super-word.' Seeing the Yichud physically written out or seeing the Yichud as an internalized visual stimulates the mind to also think about the meaning of the Yichud. So there is the level of Temunah and the level of Tevunah. Action and Understanding are thus both transformed.

SEGULOS/OMENS AND KAMEIOS/AMULETS:

These types of scanning visuals, which are found in most Kabbalistic *Siddurim*/Prayer Books, are also connected to various *Segulos*, loosely translated as omens, and *Kameios*, also loosely translated as Amulets. It is beyond the scope of this text to get into all their various details, but suffice it to say that many Segulos or Kameios are related to particular verses in the Torah. They can either be orally recited or written down, and they are generally comprised of entire verses used for specific occasions, or acronyms formed of various verses combined and written out as a coded stream of letters.

One of the more cryptic texts written by Rabbi Chayim Vital, the primary student of the Arizal, is a text that has been called *Safer Ha'peulos*. It appears that Reb Chayim originally wrote the book as a personal diary of sorts, not intended for publication and mass consumption. Either way, there are many different Segulos that Reb Chayim records. Some of these still remain coded and clouded in mystery. Due to this, they may seem magical in nature, but a closer look at the text reveals certain patterns and illuminates a bit of the mechanics at work behind the spiritual technology of Segulos.

Take, for example, the Segula he proscribes as one of the first entries in the book for a person who is suffering from a headache. If a person is burdened with a bad headache he should take a cup of water (recite a blessing and drink a tiny sip), recite the verse from the Torah, "When you raise the head of the children of Israel..." *(Shemos, 30; 11)*, and then drink the entire cup of water.

Every letter, word, and verse of the Torah has spiritual

power. In fact, since the Creator looked into the Torah and only then created the world *(Medrash Rabbah, Bereishis, 1; 1)* and the Torah, as mentioned, is considered the blueprint of all of creation, all reality first exists in the Torah and only then in actuality. In this way, the Torah is actually the root of reality. The Torah is the Divine intelligence and working blue print through which reality is created. To simplify, imagine that you are an architect and you want to construct a building. Initially the idea of the building exists in your mind, then you create the plans as a blueprint, and only afterwards do you go ahead and build the structure. The Torah is the way the world/structure exists in the blueprint. The Torah is the interface between G-d and the world, between Creator and Creation.

The natural, physical reality is a derivative manifestation of spiritual reality. The Torah, as the *Shaloh HaKodesh* writes, is a *Roshem*/Imprint of Divinity and man (and by extension, creation) is an imprint of the Torah. All phenomena are rooted within the Torah. In the words of the Gaon of Vilna, "All that was, is, and will be, until the end of time is included within the Torah. Not only the general ideas, but all the details of every type of creation, and specifically every individual person, from the day of his birth to the moment of death, including all incarnations and all details of details…" *(Sifra De'tzniusa, Chap 5. See Ramban, Devarim, 32; 40).*

Therefore, when a person's head is weighed down and heavy

with pain, R. Chayim Vital suggests that one recite a verse in the Torah that speaks about the "raising of the head." Being that the Torah is the root of all "lifting(s) of the head," one should therefore recite Torah that is specifically related to a lifting of the head if and when the headache becomes unbearable *(Tosefos, Eiruvin, 54a)*. For this is the spiritual root of all types of "lifting the head," and in this meta-textual way one's headache will be lifted and alleviated *(Note; Eiruvin, 54a, Maharsha ad loc. Shavuos, 15b)*.

This is similar to the Segula for *Parnasah*/Livelihood and Material Wealth. For this blessing it is a common custom to read or recite the *Parsha*/Torah Portion that speaks of the Manna that sustained the nation of Israel in their journey through the desert. It is said that Reb Mendel of Rimanov *(1745-1815)* taught that a Segula for *Parnasah* is to read the verse in Hebrew twice, and then once more in the Aramaic translation of Unkelus, on the Tuesday preceding the Shabbos in which the portion is read. Being as it is that material sustenance is a perpetual concern there are even sources that speak of reading the portion of the Manna on a daily basis *(Shulchan Aruch, Orach Chayim, 1; 5)* as a Segula for *Parnasah (Yerushalmi, Berachos, Derisha on the Tur, ad loc., Mishna Berurah, 1; 1. In the name of the Tashbetz, 256. Although see Aruch Hashulchan, 1; 25)*. Of course, this needs to be done with *Tevunah*/Understanding, awareness and acknowledgment that our livelihood is ultimately in the hands of Heaven, and that even with all of our business acumen and strategizing, all blessings comes from Above and we, like our ancestors, are truly being fed from Hashem's abundance.

There is also another teaching from the *Choze*/Seer of Lublin who taught that when we read and recite the narrative of the Exodus from Egypt and the attendant miracles and wonders that occurred we too will experience a personal Exodus from all of our constrictions. In the words of the *Choze*: "Through the recitation of the letters in the Torah that speak about the miracle, we awaken the source of the miracle" *(Zos Zikaron, Beshalach)*.

When the Torah describes the splitting of the sea, the going out of Egypt, or the miraculous sustenance of the Manna, the Torah is not, as it were, merely describing the events that occurred on a physical/historical plane. Rather, the Torah is articulating and invoking the eternal spiritual Source of the event, and because there is a spiritual arousal of the event "above," there is also a correlating arousal below.

The idea of these Segulos is that the meta-source of all reality is encoded within the vibrational frequency of the Torah. The root of livelihood is the portion of the Manna. The root of miracles is the miracle of the Exodus from Egypt. Reading the Torah's description of the Israelite's going out from Egypt gives us the strength to go out of our own Egypt and draws down redemptive energy from all forms of oppression *(Chasam Sofer, Torah, Ekev, 7; 17)*. From this perspective every-thing and the whole of reality is all rooted within the Torah.

Parenthetically, this spiritual technology also works to eliminate negative energies or traits as well. For example, if a person lusts after or desires something that is not his to possess, ingest or experience, he should visualize the words of the Torah, "Do not covet," written out upon the inner screen of his vision and then repeat these words to himself *(Ohr Haganuz L'Tzadikim, Parshas Yisro. Darchei Tzedek, 1; 11)*. The visualization and audible repetition of this Torah phrase gives a person the power to overcome this self-centered and destructive desire.

As mentioned, many Segulos are related to recitations of specific verses in the Torah and indeed many Kameios are comprised of *Roshei Teivos*/Acronyms of Verses or words within a verse written out. For example, to arouse and inspire love a simple Kameia would be to take the verse *Va'ahavta L'reiacha KaMocha*/Love Your Fellow Neighbor As Yourself, and instead of writing out all these words, the first three Hebrew letters *(Vav, Lamed, and Kof)* would be written out as a kind of Kabalistic code and acronym used to represent the resident energies inherent within the phrase itself in its entirety. This is not to suggest that one should just go out and start writing random Kameios. But rather, this tiny teaching, which is just a tip of the iceberg, is merely meant for the reader to begin to get a sense of the nature and mechanics of a Kameia.

The acronym is a shorthand version of the verse or verses and all that they contain. The letters and words of the Torah resonate with powerful spiritual root vibrations, and the acronym encapsulates these forces. Its power does not lie in the 'rational' realm, but rather in the image itself, the *Temunah*. Although, as discussed, the Temunah is ultimately supposed to stimulate, according to the Ashkenazi Kabbalists, the process of *Tevunah*/Understanding wherein the mind achieves a heightened state of expanded awareness and simultaneously focused attention. Yet, overall the power of such a practice is also in the image itself.

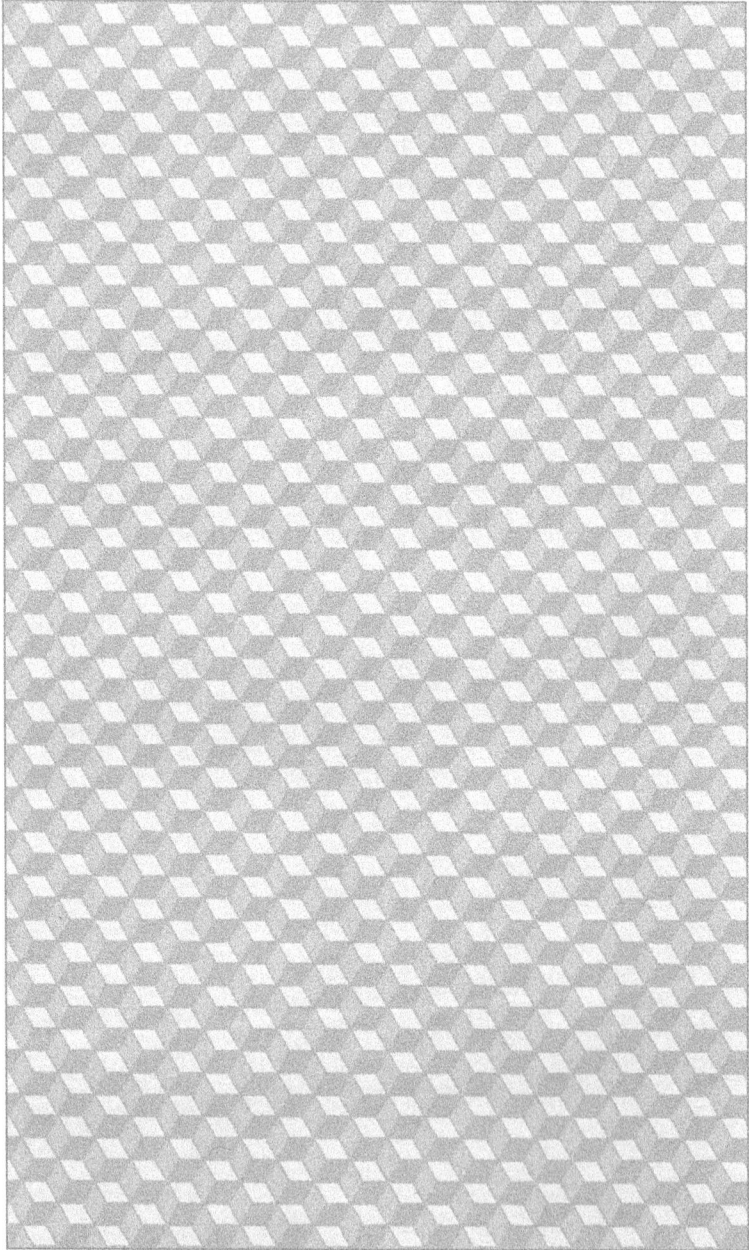

PART THREE

AWARENESS

VISUAL AWARENESS PRACTICES

....

OPENING

AS DETAILED IN THE PREVIOUS PAGES, THERE ARE MANY TYPES OF CREATIVE VISUALIZATIONS USED IN TORAH MEDITATION PRACTICES. There are those in which one uses his imagination and forms an image in his mind's eye. Then there are those in which one uses an actual external object as a visual focal point to observe and contemplate. And finally there is a third type of visual, which is focused more on developing a general sense of deeper awareness and presence through sensitizing oneself to various visual phenomena that are already present within one's field of consciousness.

In visual-based awareness meditation one trains oneself to become mindful of what already exists in the inner screen of the eye, whether it is colors, light patterns, or some sort of intrinsic inner reality.

This group of visualizations is more akin to realizations. These visuals are not generated by the imaginative mind, nor are they fixated on something external to the mind itself; rather, they are rooted in that which is always there. The techniques in the following chapters are merely meant to assist one in becoming aware of what is.

AWARENESS ONE: IDEA

» THE INNER LIGHTS

In the previously discussed methods of visualization one either actively generates an internal image within his mind's eye or focuses his gaze upon an external object. In the first form one creatively generates the imagery that one desires to visualize, this is a very active form of visualization. In the second form one focuses his sight on something that already exists outside of his mind. Although this kind of concentrated visualization takes energy and intention it is nevertheless a more passive form of imaginal exercise being that the object of one's visualization already exists as is. But there is a third form of visualization wherein one attempts to become aware of the colors, patterns and lights that arise within his inner field of vision when he closes his eyes.

This practice has two different levels. One in which a person first seeks to focus on these pre-existent patterns, and another in which one attempts to use the initial colors and lights to form other images to focus on. In this manner, this third form of visualization, which we will refer to as awareness visualizations, combines both of the previous forms of visualization. Similar to the object-based visualization practices it is based on becoming aware of an image that is pre-existent (i.e., not dependent upon one's active imagination). And similar to the creative visualization practices one then actively engages with the pre-existent raw material of the lights and colors that appear naturally behind his closed eyes and creatively forms them into self-selected imagery. In this way, these awareness visualizations are predicated upon seeing "what is," and then creatively engaging that reality with the intention of visualizing "what can be."

THE NATURAL COLORS:

First a few words about the natural inner lights and colors.

When you gently close your eyes you will notice that there is a screen that fills the space behind your eyelids and upon this screen there will often appear lights, shapes and colors.

This is the "inner screen" where various forms of light may appear in different shades and hues. These lights can appear as tiny particles or as elaborate patterns, as images or as waves of color.

Normally, as mentioned, colors appear. But sometimes no light or colors appear and the screen is intensely dark, tangibly black.

The Arizal teaches that these colors and their texture, transparency, or density reflect our state of consciousness at the present moment *(Shar Ruach Ha'kodesh, Derush 1)*. If a person sees lighter colors (assuming he or she is not facing a glaring light such as the sun) this means that they are experiencing a higher elevation of soul at that moment. And if, in the same or similar conditioning of light (not because they are sitting in pitch darkness) he or she sees a darker and denser spectrum of colors this is because, at this very moment, his state of consciousness is 'lower' and his spiritual energy is depleted.

These are very subtle states to be aware of. To truly know and get a good read of one's inner colors one needs to be exceptionally sensitive and self-aware, as well as being attuned to his surroundings so as to ensure that he is not just superimposing the state of the environment inward upon his state of mind. He needs to be aware of whether he was and/or is hungry or too full, tired or awake, for instance, because all of these conditions can contribute to the coloring of one's inner screen. Of course one must also take in to consideration the quality of the light of one's surroundings.

All of these factors are necessary to take into consideration because the hues that appear upon the inner screen can be affected by one's level of energy and external environment. One must sharpen his overall sensory and self-awareness before paying too much attention to the coloring of his inner screen. As a practice of quieting the mind, gently closing the eyes and just becoming aware of the swirling imagery, geometry and colors of the inner screen can work wonders for one's awareness and powers of perception. But interpreting the colors as a gauge to measure one's state of consciousness requires much training and discipline.

In either case, here is a general paradigm and color scheme that can be used to map the colors of one's inner screen to various states of consciousness.

THE FOUR COLORS: BLACK, RED, WHITE, BRILLIANT WHITE:

Overall there are four basic colors that can be seen upon one's inner screen: Black, red, white, and brilliant white. All the shades and variations of the colors of the spectrum are just variations of these. Denser colors are closer to black, while lighter colors are closer to white.

These four colors correspond to the "four inner worlds" of creation.

The process of creation, starting from the Infinite One and moving on into all (apparent) finite multiplicity, evolved in four stages: First there was a movement within the Mind of the Creator, a desire to create. This is the "world" of *Atzilus/*

Nearness, the world of the Spiritual. This is the most brilliant, almost transparent white.

Then there was the externalization of this desire in the form of an "idea." This is the "world" of *Beriah*/Creation, the "substance" of reality, the realm of the Mental. This is the color of white.

Then there was a process of the forming of the substance. This is the "world" of *Yetzirah*/Formation, the arena of the Emotions. This is the color of red.

And finally, there was the finished product, as it were. This is the "world" of *Asiyah*/Actualization, the world of the Physical. This is the color of black, where the screen seems blank of all colors.

> Brilliant White – *Atzilus* – Spiritual
> White – *Beriah* – Mental
> Red – *Yetzirah* – Emotional
> Black – *Asiyah* – Physical

If one closes his eyes one day and sees bright or even transparent colors and then on another day, in the same setting, during the same time of day, in relatively similar conditions as the previous time, he sees darker or denser colors, this suggests a depletion of energy and a lack of spiritual vitality. Clearly, the converse is also true. This wisdom can be used as a yardstick to measure one's spiritual temperature and perhaps even guide a person towards what they need to do or stop doing in order to achieve their maximal state of manifestation.

Here is a simple outline of a meditative practice in which one becomes more aware of the inner light that appears within the mind's eye when their eyes are closed.

AWARENESS ONE: PRACTICE

» BECOMING AWARE OF THE INNER LIGHT

Set a soft timer (or have someone else observe you) in order to fully enter this meditation without any worry of what needs to be done afterwards.

This is a time for being present. Allow yourself the gift of this experience.

For those new to meditation practice, it is recommended to start with anywhere from 10–20 minutes. This is not a competitive practice so if that amount of time feels overwhelming for you, best to start slowly and steadily build on a strong foundation.

Invite all of yourself into this space here and now. In a comfortable seat, preferably with your eyes closed, take a moment to let go of all the noise, chaos and movement in your life; simply be. Just as we need to minimize external stimuli via the sense of touch, the same is true with the other senses. To help with visualization, it is beneficial to gently close your eyes, shutting out the external world in order to move more inward to your inner field of vision.

You may notice various sounds, sensations, thoughts or feelings crossing your mind.

Sense everything without manipulating it; accept what is and relax from the urge to act.

Close your eyes. Focus your gaze upon the inner screen that comes in to view when your eyelids are drawn down.

As the screen fills with shades and patterns of light, focus your attention on the lights.

Take note of their colors, textures, and degree of transparency or density.

If your attention wanders, gently turn it back to the lights and colors as they dance behind your eyes.

Observe this for a few moments.

Gently open your eyes.

AWARENESS TWO: IDEA

» FORMING THE FOUR LETTERS WITH THE NATURAL INNER LIGHTS

Now that we have learned a bit about becoming aware of the lights, shapes and colors that appear within one's inner field of vision when one closes his eyes, let's move on to a more active and creative form of this practice — forming these lights and colors in to the four letters of Hashem's name.

As mentioned, there are colors that show up within one's inner screen of vision when the eyelids are closed as long as one is not sitting in utter darkness, and even then they can sometimes appear.

The first step to access or encounter these colors would be to close one's eyes and take notice of the lights, images, shapes and colors that appear behind one's eyelids. Taking notice of the colors, as explored earlier, is a method whereby one can begin to become aware of their level of soul at any moment. The lighter or more transparent colors are indicative of higher levels, and the darker or murkier colors represent lower levels of consciousness or energy.

The next step would be to gather the lights and colors in order to mold them and form the Four Letters of Hashem's Name.

As one's eyes are closed and one becomes aware of the lights/shapes/colors one should then compress all the lights/shapes/colors into a single small flame or ball of light. This is the letter *Yud* / ', the first letter in the four-letter name.

Once the image of the small *Yud* is secure, take that ball of fire, the *Yud*, and expand the image horizontally, forming a horizontal line. Then from the right corner of the horizontal line, move the light downwards forming a right leg, and from the left corner of the line suspend a left leg hanging in mid-air, together forming the letter *Hei* /ה.

Next take the expanded letter *Hei* and compress this image into one single line, one vertical beam of fire, this is the *Vav*/ ו. Or, one can also choose to allow the *Dalet*/ ד part of the *Hei* to merely fade away, leaving only the suspended left leg, which in essence is the *Vav*.

Take the vertical line of the *Vav*, the beam of fire, and rotate it into a horizontal position. Then from the right corner of the horizontal line, move the light downwards forming a right leg, and from the left corner of the line suspend a left leg, together forming the final *Hei* / ה.

Once one is able to form these letters in sequence (first the *Yud*, then the *Hei*, then the *Vav*, and then the final *Hei*), one can then attempt to form all four letters together and view them all in the mind's eye simultaneously from right to left.

As one is forming these letters one should take notice of how easy or difficult it was to form each one. Additionally, one should also be aware of how clear or smudged each letter appears. One should ask oneself: Were there any noticeable difficulties in creating any of the letters, and if so, which letters? And once the letters are formed, are they all clear or blotchy? Are some letters more transparent or opaque than others?

The difficulty or ease experienced while forming a letter – or letters, as well as the clarity or obscurity of the letters themselves once created, are both indicators of internal truths. Each letter embodies and represents another quality within (as will be explored shortly). When a letter is easily formed and appears clear and crisp, this suggests a balanced and well-adjusted quality on all levels — spiritually, mentally, emotionally, and physically. When there is difficulty in creating a particular letter, or when the letter is created but seems vague and inconsistent, this indicates that the corresponding quality of that letter is off balance, unhealthy and not functioning correctly.

It is important to keep in mind that this particular exercise of taking notice of the difficulty or easiness of forming each letter, and whether the letter is clear or opaque only works to reveal inner truths if this practice has been done in the past. One needs something to compare his present experience to, a baseline or previously established norm. For example, let's say that in the past this method was practiced and one was able to form the letter *Vav* with ease. Then one day he tries the practice again and he is now having trouble forming the letter *Vav*. This would suggest a defect, deficiency, or imbalance in the quality of the letter *Vav*. But if there is nothing in the past to compare it to, the fact that one is having trouble forming the *Vav* does not reveal anything significant except that one is having a hard time creating a vertical line in their inner field of vision.

By taking notice of the letters that were more easily formed as well as the ones that were more challenging one can understand, through comparison, what aspects or energies in one's life are "missing" and may need more attention and inner work.

THE FOUR (FIVE) LETTERS & THEIR CORRESPONDING QUALITIES:

In general there are four letters, each of which correspond to a unique inner quality. Looked at in more detail, the letter *Yud* has a small point, a crown as it were, above the letter. This point is known as the *Kotz Shel Yud*/Tip of the Yud.

This is the infinitesimal interface between all finite form and infinity. The *Yud, ʼ* , has a tiny point facing upward, so in actuality there are five "letters" with five corresponding qualities.

These four/five letters are analogous to the five stages of the unfolding creative process. Simply put, they mirror the cosmic process of creation and connect this process to our own consciousness.

Mirroring this cosmic process of creation, we too create in five stages. The first, almost imperceptible stage is represented by the "small point of the *Yud*." This is paradoxically both the crown and the foundation of the process, representing the will and desire to create. This is the intuitive impetus to move forward, to do something, to manifest.

This point of the *Yud* is also our basic belief system, our 'program' from which we operate. We all have a certain belief system. Sometimes these are positive, wholesome and life-affirming systems; and sometimes they are the opposite. In simple terms this means that we all operate from within a certain paradigm. For instance, one person's belief system, his point of the *Yud*, is based solely upon making money. All his thoughts and creative energies are therefore geared towards and focused on making money. Whereas another person's belief system might be to live a more spiritual life focused on coming ever closer to Hashem, and so this person's thoughts and primary creative activity are aimed at finding ways to self-refine and expand their own consciousness in relation to the Creator.

One person's "point of *Yud*" is optimistic and thus sees the world and him/herself in a positive light. This person might therefore live to draw more and more light into the world. Another person may be more pessimistic and therefore they see the world and him/herself in a correspondingly negative way. This person's modus operandi might then be to combat and fight the constantly encroaching negative energy that he/she perceive.

The point is that we all have a foundation from which we function based on a prism through which we perceive. This is our "small point of *Yud*," which is also represented as the crown of one's head.

From the paradigm and prism of our belief system stems and flows our intuition and creativity, our wisdom and the kernel of the thoughts we entertain. This seminal outburst of creativity is our inner *Yud*, not the point, but the actual body of the letter itself. This is reflected in the 'right' (creative) side of the brain.

Once we have an intuition or rudimentary idea of what we want to do, be, or create, we can then use our power to understand and thus organize and assimilate the idea. This stage allows us to take the creative outburst and make that information or idea useful. This is when we would draw up the actual plans of how we are going to implement the idea. This stage corresponds to the first and upper letter Hei. The 'left' side of the brain (connected to logic, language, and linear thought) is associated with the *Hei*, and so are the shoulders and arms.

The next stage is focused on actualizing the idea. First we organize the idea and formalize how exactly we are going to implement it. But then we need to move from theory to practice, making the leap from the world of ideas to the actual physical world. This process of actualization, which is the bridge between thought and manifestation, corresponds to the letter *Vav*. The torso/spine, which connects the upper and lower parts of the body, is associated with the letter *Vav*.

The process of actualization is a necessary step towards manifestation, but once we begin a project we need to complete it. The bringing to completion of an idea in actuality corresponds to the lower *Hei*. The lower part of the body, the hips and legs, represent the lower *Hei*.

IN SUMMARY:

LETTER	BODY	FUNCTION
POINT OF THE YUD	Crown of the head	Will/Desire/ Perspective
YUD	Right side of the brain	Intuition/ Wisdom/Passion
HEI	Left side of the brain (shoulders/ arms)	Organization/ Plan
VAV	Body/Torso	Actualization/ Doing/Process
HEI	Hips/legs	Completion/Be-ing/Product

These four/five stages encapsulate the way one moves an idea into reality. There are people who excel in generating ideas, but lack the power to systemize and put their ideas down on paper. Yet, there are also people who excel in the management and organization of ideas, but have little or no original ideas themselves. Then there are people who have good theories and are even able to organize these ideas, but have a hard time implementing them; they live in their heads. Then there are those who get excited about new projects, always beginning them with a lot of enthusiasm, but they tend to eventually run out of steam and have a hard time finishing things and completing projects. Some people simply do not have a strong belief system or base from which to start the whole process in general. But, in reality, to get anything accomplished, everyone needs to have a belief system, even if it is not such a good one, for it allows a person to move forward in life with conviction and clarity.

Within each individual person one of these five/four qualities are dominant. Some people are more creative and some are better with their hands, implementing abstract ideas. Some are good organizers and some know how to get things done and completed. A measure of all these is found in each and every one of us. We all have all these four/five qualities in varying proportions.

When we attempt to visualize the four letters of the Name of Hashem, the letters that we can form more easily and the ones that show up brightly tell us which area in our lives is functioning properly. Whereas, the letters we are having trouble forming, or the letters that appear blurry alert us to the areas that need work. This is in addition to taking notice of the colors of the letters, which was explored earlier.

For example, if one has difficulty forming the final *Hei* this suggests that one needs to work on the aspect of completing things. Perhaps you are very good at starting projects or entering relationships, but you struggle with completing things and taking ideas to their conclusion. Then this indeed is what you need to work on. Or if, for example, you can form the *Yud* and *Hei* but have trouble with the Vav, this indicates that you need to work on actualizing your ideas and putting them into motion outside your own head. Whenever a letter comes up with difficulty or is blurry or patchy, this suggests that this very area in your life needs work or *Tikkun*/Fixing.

The purpose of this meditative practice is therefore twofold: One is to become more G-d conscious, to literally place the name of Hashem in front of your mind's eye. Additionally, the ease or lack thereof with which one is able to visualize the letters, along with the clarity or blotchiness of the letters themselves, can inform and guide the meditator regarding what area of their life or soul needs to be worked on, fixed, or evolved. So, on one hand one is able to use this practice to become more G-d conscious, while at the same time one is able to use this practice to become more self-aware.

In terms of self-development, knowing the problem is half the solution. Defining one's issues clearly is the first and most important step in any process of evolution, refinement or growth. The blurry letters indicate one's deficiencies in a particular area in his life and thus one can begin to work on that area in an informed manner. One person needs to work on organizing their ideas or life, while another person needs to work on actualizing his ideas or dreams. One person needs to work on following his intuition, while another person needs to work on being better at following through and completing projects.

AWARENESS TWO: PRACTICE

» NOTICING THE SHAPE/COLOR AND CLARITY OF THE FOUR LETTERS

Set a soft timer (or have someone else observe you) in order to fully enter this meditation without any worry of what needs to be done afterwards.

This is a time for being present. Allow yourself the gift of this experience.

For those new to meditation practice, it is recommended to start with anywhere from 10-20 minutes. This is not a competitive practice, so if that amount of time feels overwhelming for you, best to start slowly, and steadily build on a strong foundation.

Invite all of yourself into this space here and now. In a comfortable seat, preferably with your eyes closed, take a moment to let go of all the noise, chaos and movement in your life; simply be. Just as we need to minimize external stimuli via the sense of touch, the same is true with the other senses. To help with visualization, it is beneficial to gently close your eyes, shutting out the external world in order to move more inward to your inner field of vision.

You may notice various sounds, sensations, thoughts or feelings crossing your mind.

Sense everything without manipulating it; accept what is and relax from the urge to act.

Begin by simply gazing at the inner screen that fills your vision when your eyelids are closed.

Notice the images or patterns of light and focus your attention on them.

Take note of the transparency or density of the colors.

If your mind drifts, softly bring your attention back to the lights and colors.

Gather all of the colors and lights in your scope of vision and compress them to form the letter Yud.

Notice whether it was easy or difficult to form the Yud.

Now that it is formed, does it appear clear or blotchy?

Sit with the Yud for a moment.

Then compress the Yud into one horizontal line, which from the two corners extend downward in the form of two legs, with the right side attached and the left suspended independently.

This is the letter Hei.

. . . .

Notice whether it was easy or difficult to form the Hei. Now that it is formed, does it appear clear or blotchy?

. . . .

Sit with the Hei for a moment.

. . . .

Next collapse the Hei into one line and then place the line vertically in your field of vision, like a beam of light.

. . . .

This is the letter Vav.

. . . .

Notice whether it was easy or difficult to form the Vav.

. . . .

Now that it is formed, does it appear clear or blotchy?

. . . .

Sit with the Vav for a moment.

. . . .

Take the vertical line of the letter Vav and rotate it into a horizontal line, which then extends downward from both corners in the form of two legs, with the right side attached and the left suspended independently.

. . . .

This is the letter Hei

. . . .

Notice whether it was easy or difficult to form the Hei. Now that it is formed, does it appear clear or blotchy?

. . . .

Sit with the Hei for a moment.

. . . .

Now arrange all four letters horizontally from right to left with the Yud on the right, then the Hei, then the Vav, and finally the second Hei.

....

Notice all the letters:

ה – ו – ה – י

....

Focus your attention on their details.
Which letters are clearest?

....

Which were most easily formed?
Which were most difficult?
Are the letters smooth and seamless or bumpy and broken-up?
Notice each letter's brilliance, texture, boldness and tone — note it all.

....

Sit for a few moments focused on the letters.

....

Gently open your eyes.

....

AWARENESS THREE: IDEA

» THE DIAGNOSTIC POWER OF THE DIVINE NAME

As previously explored, one way to become aware of whether there is a spiritual, mental, emotional, or even physical ailment that needs healing and correction is by first becoming aware of the colors and lights that appear within one's inner field of vision when the eyes are closed, and then in even more detail when one attempts to write or form the four letters of Hashem's name out of these lights and colors. One is able, through a self-reflective process of noticing the clarity or lack thereof of each letter, as well as how easy or difficult it was to create these letters, to become aware of his state of being and consciousness. In the actual formation of the letters one becomes more aware of themselves.

In addition, there is also another way of determining deficiencies using this visualization method and that is by taking the four letters that are formed and superimposing them over one's body in order to perform a body-scan through the prism of the letters, as taught by the Arizal *(Shar Ruach Ha'Kodesh, Derush 1)*.

To do this, one fastens an image of these four letters in their mind's eye, as formed out of the raw materials of color and light that exist behind one's eyelids and appear upon one's inner screen. The four letters should all be fused into one unit as one complete image. One then gently and meditatively begins to sweep this four-letter image across his body, starting from the top of the head and then moving over the eyes, nose, and mouth, eventually scanning the entire body.

The power of the four-letter name of Hashem is that it can detect and pick up any deformity, deficiency, or misalignment, although one does need an exceptionally refined self-awareness and heightened consciousness to truly diagnose these subtle inconsistencies. As you scan the letters over your body, try to notice if there is a difficulty in holding the image of the letters over a particular body part. This suggests that there is something spiritually (and perhaps even physically) amiss in this part of your system.

Let us take the liver as an example. If, when scanning the letters over the liver, the letters become vague and elusive, this indicates that there is a *Pegam*/Defect in either the liver, the blood, or in the spiritual capacity or quality that the liver represents. According to our sages the liver is the seat of anger *(Berachos, 61b)*. The liver is also physically and spiritually associated with blood and wrath *(Tikunei Zohar, Tikkun 21)*. If the four letters are not easily scanned over the liver this tells us that we need to work on and make a *Tikkun/* Fixing around our experience or expression of anger.

Again, as mentioned, this practice only works and reveals a *Pegam* if normally one can visualize the four letters and scan them over the body in a clear and strong way.

One who has trained himself in the art of meditation and focused awareness can also learn to scan the four letters over another person's body in order to diagnose what needs healing within the other person. This can be done with someone standing right next to or in front of you, or even a person who is not physically present. To do so demands extensive mental and spiritual training, but it is possible.

AWARENESS THREE: PRACTICE

» MENTALLY SCANNING THE FOUR LETTERS OVER THE BODY

Set a soft timer (or have someone else observe you) in order to fully enter this meditation without any worry of what needs to be done afterwards.

This is a time for being present. Allow yourself the gift of this experience.

For those new to meditation practice, it is recommended to start with anywhere from 10-20 minutes. This is not a competitive practice, so if that amount of time feels overwhelming for you, best to start slowly and steadily build on a strong foundation.

Invite all of yourself into this space here and now. In a comfortable seat, preferably with your eyes closed, take a moment to let go of all the noise, chaos and movement in your life; simply be. Just as we need to minimize external stimuli via the sense of touch, the same is true with the other senses. To help with visualization, it is beneficial to gently close your eyes, shutting out the external world in order to move more inward to your inner field of vision.

You may notice various sounds, sensations, thoughts or feelings crossing your mind.

Sense everything without manipulating it; accept what is and relax from the urge to act.

Close your eyes.

Notice the lights and colors that appear and dance behind your closed eyelids.

Begin by forming the four letters of Hashem's name in strong, sharp letters within the mind's eye. Arrange them horizontally, from right to left:

Yud to Hei to Vav to the final Hei.

ה – ו – ה – י

Now move the letters closer together as if you are squeezing out any empty space between them.

Take these four letters and begin to scan them over your body. Begin at the crown of your head; move down to your forehead, eyes, nose, and mouth, gradually scanning your entire body all the way down to your feet.

Take notice of where there is difficulty holding the letters steady and strong over any particular part of the body.

Over which part of the body are you having trouble scanning these letters?

One needs to do this slowly, with pauses to take note of the subtle sensations that may arise as you move the letters over various parts of your body.

Once the entire body has been scanned, sit for a few minutes and in the inner light of the Divine Name.

You may gently open your eyes.

THE ABOVE THREE PRACTICES AS ONE MEDITATION

Rabbi Chayim Vital maps out three separate practices: One is to notice the natural colors, lights and images that appear upon one's inner screen of vision when they close their eyes. Another is to form the four letters out of these natural colors, lights and images and notice which letters are clearer and more easily formed than the others. A third practice is to mentally take the four letters of Hashem's name and scan them over the entire body. This is done with the intention to detect any kind of psychophysical Pegam or spiritual defect in the body, which can also be manifest within one's overall system as an actual physical ailment. To simplify these three practices we will join them into one meditation.

Set a soft timer (or have someone else observe you) in order to fully enter this meditation without any worry of what needs to be done afterwards.

This is a time for being present. Allow yourself the gift of this experience.

For those new to meditation practice, it is recommended to start with anywhere from 10-20 minutes. This is not a competitive practice, so if that amount of time feels overwhelming for you, best to start slowly and steadily build on a strong foundation.

Invite all of yourself into this space here and now. In a comfortable seat, preferably with your eyes closed, take a moment to let go of all the noise, chaos and movement in your life; simply be. Just as we need to minimize external stimuli via the sense of touch, the same is true with the other senses. To help with visualization, it is beneficial to gently close your eyes, shutting out the external world in order to move more inward to your inner field of vision.

You may notice various sounds, sensations, thoughts or feelings crossing your mind.

Sense everything without manipulating it; accept what is and relax from the urge to act.

STEP 1:

As your eyes are closed, begin to take notice of the inner screen that fills your vision behind your eyelids.

Observe the images, colors or patterns of light that appear behind your closed eyes and focus your attention on these colors and lights.

Take note of the transparency or density of the colors.

If your mind drifts, gently bring your attention back to the lights and colors.

Sit and observe these lights and colors for a few moments.

STEP 2:

Gather all the images, colors or lights in your scope of vision and compress them together in order to form the small letter Yud.

Notice whether it was easy or difficult to form the Yud. Now that it is formed does it appear clear or blotchy?

Sit with the Yud for a moment.

Now expand the point of the Yud into one horizontal line, from which extend two legs from each end; the right leg remaining attached to the horizontal line and the left leg suspended independently just beneath it.

This is the letter Hei.

Notice whether it was easy or difficult to form the Hei. Now that it is formed does it appear clear or blotchy?

Sit with the Hei for a moment.

Next collapse the Hei into one vertical line and place it in front of you like a beam of light.

This is the letter Vav.

Notice whether it was easy or difficult to form the Vav. Now that it is formed does it appear clear or blotchy?

Sit with the Vav for a moment.

Now take the vertical line of the Vav and rotate it so it is horizontal. From the two ends of the line, extend two legs downward. The one on the right remains attached to the horizontal line, while the one on the left hangs suspended independently just beneath the horizontal line.

This is the letter Hei.

Notice whether it was easy or difficult to form the Hei. Now that it is formed does it appear clear or blotchy?

Sit with the Hei for a moment.

Now arrange all four letters from right to left, with the Yud on the far right, followed by the Hei to its left, then the Vav, and then the final Hei.

Notice the four letters together as one.
Focus your attention on their details.
Which letters are clearer than the others?

Which were more easily formed, which were more difficult? Which letters are patchy, if any, and which are seamless?

Sit for a few moments focusing on all four letters in sequence, from right to left: Yud-Hei-Vav-Hei

ה – ו – ה – י

STEP 3:

Take these four letters and secure them in your mind as one image.

Take the Divine Name and begin to scan it across your body.

Start with the crown of the head and move the image down over your forehead, eyes, nose, mouth, and gradually down your entire body piece by piece.

Ever so gently pass the image of the Divine Name over your entire body and attune yourself to subtly pick up any defects or inconsistencies.

Take notice of any part of the body where there is difficulty seeing or scanning the letters.

Pause at any part of the body in which there is difficulty holding the image.

Think about what is literally beneath the skin of that part

of the body. For example, if there is difficulty in maintaining the image of the letters over the chest, think about the physical functioning of the heart as well as the circulatory system of which it is the epicenter. Then also consider what that organ, body part or system represents spiritually and metaphorically in your life.

Resolve to investigate and work on any spiritual/mental/emotional/physical defect that you detect.

Sit with the image of the four letters for a moment.
Allow them to fill your inner field of vision.
Breather them in and blow them back out into the world.

Gently open your eyes.

AWARENESS FOUR: IDEA

» THE FOUR-LETTER NAME OF HASHEM (YUD-HEI-VAV-HEI) IN FRONT OF YOU AT ALL TIMES

We will now explore another awareness visualization practice based on the four letters of the Divine Name. But in this version one can either form the letters out of the lights and colors that are present within one's inner field of vision, or one can more creatively visualize the four letters in the mind's eye. In either case, the emphasis in this practice is not so much on becoming aware of what is present within one's inner field of vision, as much as on becoming aware of Hashem's presence within all creation, including both what is present within one's own mind's eye as well as what exists externally as well.

According to many great Kabbalists, because this name represents the eternal, transcendent, unceasing is-ness of the Infinite One it would be ideal if these four letters would be present within one's consciousness throughout the entire day. In this way, this name is not so much indicative of any one 'attribute or energy' of G-d as it is reflective of Pure

Perpetual Presence. For this reason it is particularly well suited for use in a visual-based awareness practice.

The letters *Yud-Hei-Vav-Hei* are not merely another name or aspect, as it were. Rather they are known as *Hashem*/The Name, and they are considered together as comprising the essence of all reality. This Name is present everywhere and is within everything, at all times and even beyond time.

This is therefore the highest and deepest name, the 'Be-er' of all being. In the image of the early Kabbalist, Rabbi Yoseph Gikatalia *(1248 – 1323)*, it is both the "seed and the actual tree in its totality." One way to refer to this name is *Ha'va'ya*, which is a permutation of the four letters that comprise this name. *Ha'va'ya* means literally *Haviya* or 'bringing being into being.' This refers to the Ultimate Being, which is the source and stuff of all being-ness; the Ultimate Being that does not depend on anything else to exist; Primordial being, which gives rise to all past, present and future manifestation, thereby bringing all "things" into existence ex nihilo — i.e. some-thing from no-thing.

The last three letters of this Name, *Hei-Vav-Hei*, create the word *Hoveh*. The root of this verb means, 'to bring into being.' The first letter, *Yud*, serves as a prefix to the word *Hoveh*, modifying the verb to imply that this is a perpetual action. The creation of all created being is constant and continuous.

The verse in Tehilim/Psalms says, "I have placed Hashem *(Yud-Hei-Vav-Hei)* before me at all times" *(16; 8)*. The simple meaning of these words is that one should envision that his or her life is being lived in the conscious presence of the Creator at all times.

This idea is reflected in the beginning of the *Shulchan Aruch*, the Code of Jewish Law, where it is written: "A fundamental principle of faith and the path of the righteous is to consciously and continuously walk as if they were in the presence of the Creator. For a person's manner of living, his demeanor and deeds, his speech and movements, when alone at home or in the intimate circle of his family and friends, are unlike those that he would exhibit were he to be in the presence of a great king. How much more so will his demeanor be considered upon reflecting on the ever-presence of Hashem, realizing that above him is the King of kings, the Holy One, blessed be He, watching his conduct and surveying his deeds" *(Ramah, ad loc.)*. *(This fundamental understanding of how we should live our lives, with a sensation of being in the presence of Hashem at all times, was first clearly delineated by the Rambam at the end of The Guide to the Perplexed, and the Shulchan Aruch quotes him.)*

As such, the directive, "I have placed Hashem before me at all times," is most often interpreted metaphorically, implying that one is to feel the gaze of Hashem at all times.

Yet this sentiment/suggestion could also be interpreted literally *(R. Yehudah Ashkenazi, Be'er Heitiv, ad loc.)*, meaning that a person should actually envision the four letters of the name of Hashem in front of the eyes at all times. In this way, not only is one aware of living within the constant gaze of Hashem, but he is also, in a way, actively returning the gaze as well.

Rabbi Yitzchak of Acco, a 13th century eclectic Kabbalist who was a student of the illustrious Ramban when the Ramban lived in Acco, Israel, writes that the placing of Hashem in front of one at all times means actually placing the four letters of the name of Hashem, the *Yud-Hei-Vav-Hei/* ה–ו–ה–י in front of one's vision constantly.

These four letters, he writes, should be visualized as written out in the script of the Torah. Each of these four letters should be infinitely large, filling one's entire inner screen of vision. While one's inner eye is gazing at these letters their mind/heart should be directed towards the Infinite One, the "Light" that is beyond all "Vessels," which, in this case, are the letters. Both the experience of *Habata/*Seeing (of the letters) and the *Machshava/*Thought and intention directed towards the Ultimate Reality beyond the letters should be simultaneous *(Meiras Einayim, Ekev, 11 – 22. R. Chayim Vital, Shaarei Kedusha, 4:5)*.

Sometime later, the renowned scholar and mystic Rabbi Yoseph Caro *(1488 – 1575)* heard the "voice" of the *Maggid*/Teller[1] of the Mishnah instructing him to place these four letters of the Name of Hashem in front of his eyes and visualize them as if they were written in black ink on white parchment *(Maggid Mesharim, Parshas Miketz and Parshas Vayikra. R. Chayim Vital, Shar Ruach Hakodesh, Derush 1. Shaarei Kedusha, Ch. 3, Shar 4)*. Similarly, the Torah is written with "black fire" (the ink) upon "white fire" (the parchment) *(Yerushalmi, Shekalim, 6; 1)*. And so when we visualize the Name of Hashem as written in a Torah scroll we see the letters as "black fire" imposed on "white fire," the backdrop and screen of our vision.

Some people may find it quite difficult to visualize four letters strung together as if written on a Torah scroll with black ink on white parchment. Often the harder you try to visualize something the more evasive and elusive the image becomes and one's frustration merely increases. Reb Klunimus Kalmish of Peasetzna addresses this problem and offers a solution. He suggests 'tricking' yourself by thinking

---

1 A Maggid is either an angelic teacher, as in a spirit guide, or the "spirit" of a sacred text that reveals deeper meaning and wisdom to the meditator. Every experience is an intermingling between the objective and the subjective. Accordingly, the "objective" Maggid manifests itself within the subjective person, triggering expressive acts of automatic writing or xenoglossia. In the case of R. Yoseph Caro the Maggid was also "audible" to all present, speaking through the lips of the Rabbi in a distinctive and loud voice heard by everyone present.

about a time that you were called up to the Torah. Remember being called up and reading the Torah and noticing the Name of Hashem in the scroll. So, instead of trying to create the image in your mind, think of a scenario when you observed the image and then focus on that which already exists within the mind *(Mova HaShearim - in Hachsharas Ha'Avreichim- Chap 10, p. 313- 315).*

INTERNAL IMAGE:

According to some sources there does appear to be the possibility of actually writing out the four letters of Hashem's name on a piece of paper and carrying it in your wallet or pocket in order to look at from time to time, much like how many synagogues have these four letters inscribed on top of the *Amud*/Stand where the *Chazan*/Prayer leader recites the prayers. One would then have an actual image of the letters to refer to before visualizing or recalling them within their mind's eye, similar to the practice noted above from the Peasetzna where on 'recalls' the image of The Name from seeing it written out in a Torah scroll. Yet, there are sources that warn of the spiritual risk of having Hashem's name written on a piece of paper meant to be carried around casually *(Sur M'rah, V'Asei Tov, p. 71).* Certainly, this is true regarding a simple-minded person who may think that they are looking at a divine image, or just as bad, forget that they are carrying it around at all and throw it out or treat it mindlessly in some way. As a result, many sources discourage the practice of inscribing the name of Hashem on the *Amud (Pnei Yehoshua, Gitin, 6b. Taz, Yorah De'ah, 283)*, and *Kal v'Chomer*/By Extension, they would also certainly discourage carrying around the Divine Name written out on a scrap of paper stuffed in one's wallet. For this reason the practice of constantly visualizing the Name of Hashem is presented here as a purely mental visual, to be 'carved' or 'sculpted' purely within the mind's eye.

THE PURPOSES OF THE VISUAL:

As mentioned, the objective of this continuous inner visualization is to ensure a perpetual state of G-d consciousness, generating an all-pervasive sense that our life is being lived within the presence of the Creator. This visual arouses us to live and experience all of life more fully — to eat, drink, and sleep with a heightened awareness and deeper consciousness filled with purpose and meaning.

Beyond this, placing the sacred Name of Hashem in front of our eyes transforms the way we look at every-thing including objects, subjects, life and people. We come to observe reality through "G-d colored glasses," so to speak, as the letters of the Creator's name are continuously super-imposed upon or uncovered within all creation.

If we look at things through the lens of the *Yud-Hei-Vav-Hei* we begin to see everything in a radically different light.

Via this visual we are able to see Hashem's presence within every-thing and everyone. Within everything we see, hear and experience we can begin to notice the subtle Divine message that is being imparted to us at any moment. Nothing seems random any longer. Although maybe not rationally understood we can start to get a spiritual sensation that it "all makes sense" and nothing is without its purpose.

The notion that one is to envision and place the letters of Hashem's name in front of the eyes at all times also has other benefits besides altering the prism of perception and making us more G-d conscious. There are sources that speak of how the visualization of the four-letter name can assist with memory *(Ohr Tzadikim, Chap. 22)*. In a certain sense all mental activity is beneficial to memory, therefore training the mind to hold an image (in this case the four-letter name) is a workout for the brain, and like all muscles of the body, the more the brain is worked the finer tuned it becomes. In addition to this general principle there is also a certain meta-physical power connected to this Divine Name. By using it as a visual focus in meditation, one is both exercising one's brain 'muscles' as well as receiving the influx of Divine energy attached to this particular and fundamental Name of Hashem.

This visual practice can also be used quite effectively as a device to block out all other extraneous thoughts. This could be exceptionally beneficial during times of increased mental focus such as prayer or study, for example. There is a distinct possibility that as one is about to pray, study, or meditate, the mind, as if on its own, may tend to wander and drift towards other areas of your conscious or even sub-conscious interest. Reb Elimelech of Lizhensk teaches that visualizing the four-letter name of Hashem is especially helpful in eradicating all non-consciously desired thoughts *(Tzetal Katan)*. Beyond the spiritual power of the Name to burn away and erase all negativity and extraneous thought, the mere act of filling the entire mind's eye with a visual image prevents other thoughts or images to enter in, thus clearing the mind from unwanted clutter and distraction.

Yet, the opposite is also true. In addition to helping one attain a state of intensified and hyper-focused attention, this visualization can also induce a relaxed and calm state of mind. There are sources that suggest that visualizing the Name of Hashem can help a person fall asleep *(Chidah, Avodas HaKodesh, Tziporan Shamir 8; 121)*. This may be due to the fact that the inability to fall asleep is often triggered by various anxieties related to a person's stability and security. Kabbalisitically speaking, this Name of Hashem is associat-ed with mercy and kindness, the qualities of nurturance and providing. By meditating on this name specifically, a person may come to relax in the awareness of Hashem's ultimate care and concern for his welfare, thus alleviating any excess anxiety.

Also, beyond the Name's inherent spiritual power, visualizing any mental image in one's mind to the exclusion of all other imagery blocks out extraneous thoughts and any external or internal stimuli. Thus, in essence, this visualization practice has the ability to gently quiet the mind and body thereby enabling and inducing a sleep state.

Anxiety, worry, doubt, and uncertainty are all the result of one's mind roaming endlessly into unpredictable and often alarming theoretical scenarios — the coulda, woulda, shouldas of one's past and future. This mental dereliction is what keeps people awake. The mental activity of visualizing these four sacred letters in the mind's eye relaxes a person and also enhances faith and trust in the Creator and orchestrator of all life. When we visualize these letters we ingrain the awareness that Hashem is truly with us at all times. A good sleeper, someone that sleeps peacefully and pleasantly, is someone that has a deep trust in life and in the Creator of life. In the wise words of the book of Proverbs: "If you rest, you will not worry; you will lie down and your sleep will be pleasant...for Hashem will be at your side" *(Mishlei 3; 24-26).*

Whether the act of the visualization flexes or relaxes the brain depends on how easily the image of the four letters forms or appears in one's imagination. If one has difficulty with this visual, or any other visual, carving the letters in the mind's eye and securing them will be an exertive exercise, one that keeps you more awake and sharpens the brain to be able to focus and memorize. But if you can visualize or sculpt the letters with ease it can have the opposite effect, relaxing the brain and emptying it of the onrush of random thoughts, thereby quieting and stilling the mind.

THE METHOD:

The simplest way to practice this visualization is to mentally write out these four letters in the mind's eye, moving horizontally from right to left. One begins by closing the eyes and perhaps visualizing his hand holding a flame in a white empty room, or, alternatively, holding a feather quill with ink in hand.

One walks into the empty room and begins by forming or writing the letter *Yud* - י. The letter is placed in the furthest right corner of the right eye. One then focuses all his attention on this *Yud*, expanding it and filling the entire screen of his inner vision with this single letter. Once the letter is secured and returned to its initial size and location in the right corner of one's inner field of vision, one then forms or writes the letter *Hei* - ה to the left of the letter *Yud*, placing it in the left corner of the right eye. One then expands this letter *Hei* and allows its form to fill his entire attention and awareness. Once the *Hei* is secured one returns it to its original size and place and then tries to visualize both of these letters together, the *Yud* on the far right and the *Hei* to its left.

At this point one forms or writes the letter *Vav* -ו, placing the letter in the right corner of their left eye. One allows the *Vav* to expand and fill his entire attention and focus. Once the *Vav* is fastened within his awareness and returned to its appropriate size and place, he proceeds to form or write the final *Hei* - ה, placing the letter on the left side of the left eye, and repeats the previous process.

Now in rapid succession begin to form or write all four letters from right to left, the Yud-י Hei-ה Vav-ו Hei-ה. *Yud–Hei* on the right, *Vav–Hei* on the left. Then as one seamless sequence bring the letters together as one to fill one's entire scope of vision with all four letters.

If it is difficult to visualize all four letters simultaneously, as just described, one can begin with one letter at a time, then two, and so on. First, carve the letter *Yud* in the mind's eye and allow this one letter to fill your entire screen of vision. Then let the *Yud* fade and allow the *Hei* to appear on its own. Next, let the *Hei* evaporate as well and let the *Vav* appear. Then the *Vav* dissolves and the final letter *Hei* is brought into view. Just try to visualize each letter, one at a time, without holding on to the previously visualized letters. Next, try two letters at a time. Visualize the *Yud* and the *Hei*. Let them fade and then visualize the *Vav* and *Hei*, two at a time, but not adding on to each other. Then try to visualize three letters, *Yud-Hei-Vav*. These letters also dissolve and the final *Hei* appears. Finally try to carve all four letters at once in one complete written out sequence.

Rabbi Chayim Vital elaborates on this technique as a formal meditative practice in greater detail in the fourth section of his work titled, *Shaarei Kedusha*/The Gates of Holiness. In that text he explains some general preparations required to effectively perform this meditation and how, as a prelude, one needs to purify himself physically. Furthermore, before even attempting the letter-based visualization, the meditator should begin by divesting himself of his attachment to his own materiality. (This practiced was explored earlier in the Creative Visualizations section, as Visual Two.)

Here is the relevant section from the Shaarei Kedusha, quoting an earlier Kabbalistic text:

> "One should purify his body and sanctify himself from all impurities, cleansing his hands from all forms of theft, cheating or bribery, as it says, "Who can ascend G-d's mountain? — One whose hands are clean" *(Tehilim, 24; 4)*. And then he must cleanse his inside as he cleansed his outside…
>
> In order to do this one should first ponder the meaning of the Mitzvos on a revealed level. Afterwards, a little delving into the inner mysteries of the Creator is in order. Other preparations for meditation include learn-

ing Torah, doing Mitzvos, refraining from idle speech throughout the entire day, and immersing oneself in a *Mikvah* on the day that one wants to perform the meditation. Furthermore, one should dress in white and place himself in a pure environment, distant from all impurities, away from any corpse or cemetery. Additionally, one should also distance himself from all worry, anxiety and depression, strengthening himself in joy.

One should divest from his materiality (his body) and, in one's mind, one should journey from one level of heaven (the sky) to the next, until one reaches the seventh Heaven...

At this point one should visualize that spread over the entire sky is a gigantic white tapestry and upon the tapestry there is the image of the four letters of the name of Hashem written in very big letters with the same script as in a Torah scroll, each letter like the size of a mountain – in the white color of snow.

And one should connect these four letters, first the *Yud* with the *Hei* and the *Hei* with the *Yud*.

Then the *Vav* with the *Hei* and the *Hei* with the *Vav*."

(Shaarei Kedusha, 4; 2 p. 6)

In addition to the purification process which R. Chayim speaks about and the divesting of oneself from the physical realm as one rises through the heavens upward, the visual that the meditator visualizes is the entire sky draped in a large white tapestry emblazoned with the four gigantic letters of the Name of Hashem. One visualizes the letters as large white mountains, or, as he later writes *(Shaarei Kedusha, 4; 3. p. 7)*, as deep valleys. One then completes this practice by connecting all four letters together.

Unlike the practice mentioned earlier, where one mentally writes the letters with a symbolic feather or candle, here one inwardly journeys upward and then beholds the four letters already carved into the sky as mountains or valleys.

This practice demands deep and disciplined inner work. One needs to divest themselves from the material world and inwardly journey all the way to the pure, infinite light of reality. The Kabbalist Rabbi Yehuda Albotini, writing in Israel in the 15th century, writes about various types of meditation that help a person 'leave' the 'domain of humanity' and enter into the 'domain of the Divine.' He writes that one should "Shut his eyes very tightly and clench his hands tightly with great fear and trembling, (with) sweat covering his body and his knees knocking against each other. He should take very long breaths, as long as possible… (and in due course) his entire body will be weakened, both the external and internal organs…without any sense of the material" *(Sulam Ha'aliyah, Chap 10, p. 102)*.

The resultant state of relaxation is paradoxically induced by heightened intensity. The intense closing of the eyes and clenching of the hands, while breathing very deeply, coupled with the inner visualization, releases a person from the sensations of the material.

Another way to practice this is by gently closing our eyes, releasing our attachment to our physical senses and gently relaxing the body allowing it to go limp, by, for example, having the arms dangling on our sides or loosely resting on a table. This is helpful in opening us to experiencing a release from the body, a type of *Hispashtus* or divestment from the physical.

In the meditation described by R. Albotini, which is connected with the 13th century R. Avraham Abulafia's method of combined head movement and chant, the end result is that the meditator literally "falls on the floor, almost like a dead corpse. He lies there and then wakes up" *(Ibid, p. 103)*. This is an extreme method of total divestment from the material, a death and resurrection practice, as it were. And yet, extreme as these practices may seem, if one truly desires to go deeper into these visuals one does need to experience some form of divestment.

Whichever method one chooses to use, it is extremely important to unify the letters, to create a *Yichud* and not, Heaven forbid, a *Pirud/*Separation or a dis-unity between the letters *(Rikanti, Ta'amei HaMitzvos, Lulav/Esrog. Rikanti, Torah, Parshas Emor. Beis Yoseph, Orach Chayim, 651)*. To do so, one first forms or perceives the letter *Yud* to the furthest right corner of his vision and then sees the *Hei* to its left. One then connects the *Yud* with the *Hei* and the *Hei* with the *Yud*. One then forms or perceives the letter *Vav* and, following that, the final *Hei*. One then connects the *Vav* with the *Hei* and the *Hei* with the *Vav*. And finally, one connects all four letters in one long sequence, as One Name.

Once one has done this practice — either by first divesting themselves from the physical world and journeying inwardly upwards and seeing the letters as mountains, or simply, by carving, forming and writing the letters in the screen of one's inner vision — when one opens his eyes he will perceive a radically altered world. By seeing the world "through" the lens of Hashem's name we begin to see the world aflame, alive, connected, unified, and filled with purpose and meaning. Nothing is random any longer. Within every-thing and everyone Hashem's presence is felt. This awareness awakens us to experience all of life more fully and with more intention. We are able to eat, drink, sleep, work, and perform all of our mundane activities with a heightened sense of spiritual purpose and direction.

SEEING & SENSING:

One final important point needs to be clarified before laying out the actual practice of visualizing the Name of Hashem and holding it in front of one's awareness at all times.

Overall there seem to be two levels of *Deveikus*/Cleaving to the Divine and closeness to the Creator. There is *Deveikus* "through the letters," and there is *Deveikus* "without the letters" *(Toldos Aaron, Vayechi)*. The first path is advocated by Kabbalists such as Rabbi Yitzchak of Acco and Rabbi Yoseph Caro, and the second path is advocated by philosophers such as the Rambam.

Essentially, it appears that there are those who need to see the Name of Hashem throughout all of creation in order to sense the immanence of the Divine presence, and there are those who are able to sense Hashem's presence within and through everything without the 'garb of the letters,' so to speak.

Seeing the world "through the letters" means that a person is inspired and G-d conscious and thus wherever they look they see the pattern and image of the Divine Name of Hashem. For example, a person looks at his body and sees the name of Hashem — his head is shaped like the letter *Yud*, his shoulders and arms are shaped like a *Hei* (*Hei* is numerically five, thus the five fingers on each hand), his torso is shaped like the letter *Vav*, and his hips and two legs make up the final *Hei*. Or, alternatively, when one performs an activity such as stitching a garment he sees the actual needle as the letter *Vav* (shaped like the letter *Vav*, which is a line), his two hands as the two *Hei's*, and the tiny hole where the needle penetrates is the small *Yud (Darchei Tzedek, 1; 79)*. Or, additionally, when one is writing a letter he sees the pen as a *Vav*, his hand holding the pen as one *Hei*, the other hand holding down the paper as the second *Hei*, and the *Yud* is the first dot on the paper that begins each letter *(Ohr Haganuz L'Tzadikim, Hazinu)*. In more modern terms: The keyboard is like the *Vav* (a line), the two hands typing are the *Heis*, and the *Yud* is each small letter on the computer screen.

This is one way of living. It is very visual, detail-oriented and focused on specifics. But, there is also another way, perhaps a broader and more general way, to sense the Divine Presence within all of creation without the need to see patterns and images of letters in all things. This is the approach of sensing or feeling the awesomeness of the Creator within all of creation at all times. The first approach is one of 'seeing,' and the second approach is one of 'sensing.'

From one perspective, these two paradigms seem to exist in a vertically oriented hierarchy, where one evolves from a fixation on the detailed specifics to a more general sensation. Yet, these two approaches can also be viewed as parallel paradigms that are horizontally aligned, rather than being developmentally understood. And, more accurately, they can even be thought of as different paradigms for different time periods in a person's life, or perhaps even for different times within one's day. We ought to use all tools at our disposal to ensure that we are living a truly inspired, awake, aware, intentional and mindful life.

We will now move on to the actual practice.

AWARENESS FOUR: PRACTICE

» CARVING THE FOUR LETTERS HORIZONTALLY

Set a soft timer (or have someone else observe you) in order to fully enter this meditation without any worry of what needs to be done afterwards.

This is a time for being present. Allow yourself the gift of this experience.

For those new to meditation practice, it is recommended to start with anywhere from 10-20 minutes. This is not a competitive practice, so if that amount of time feels overwhelming for you, best to start slowly, and steadily build on a strong foundation.

Invite all of yourself into this space here and now. In a comfortable seat, preferably with your eyes closed, take a moment to let go of all the noise, chaos and movement in your life; simply be. Just as we need to minimize external stimuli via the sense of touch, the same is true with the other senses. To help with visualizations, it is beneficial to gently close your eyes, shutting out the external world in order to move more inward to your inner field of vision.

You may notice various sounds, sensations, thoughts or feelings crossing your mind.

Sense everything without manipulating it; accept what is and relax from the urge to react.

Begin by closing your eyes and visualizing your hand holding a flame, or even a feather quill, in a white empty room. Then, in horizontal sequence, begin forming or writing out the Yud, then the Hei, then the Vav, then the final Hei.

Visualize a Yud in the right corner of the right eye – י

When focusing on the letter Yud think about the absolute Omnipresence of the Creator. There is no-place, no-thing, and no 'outside' that is not within the Oneness of the Creator, including you.

To the left of the Yud carve out the letter Hei – ה

When visualizing the letter Hei try to experience the creative power of the Creator. Think about how the entire cosmos, including you at this very moment, is being created anew, at this and every moment.

To the left of the Hei, write out a Vav- ו

When focusing on the Vav attempt to experience the entire cosmos as a whole, unified organism from above to below, you included.

To the left of the Vav, write out the final Hei – ה

When visualizing the second Hei try to experience the illusory independence of each aspect of creation, including your own independence, as yearning to reconnect with Primordial Unity and Transcendence.

Now bring the four letters together — this is very important. The letters need to be seen and understood as an inter-connected and interdependent whole system.

Observe the Yud in the furthest right corner and then see the Hei to its left, and then connect the Yud with the Hei and the Hei with the Yud.

Then perceive the letter Vav and the Hei to its left, connect the Vav with the Hei and the Hei with the Vav.

And finally connect all four letters in one long sequence, as One Name

ה – ו – ה – י

Sit with this awareness for a few moments.

Gently open your eyes and attempt to hold the image of the four letters in your mind's eye as you gaze out upon the world.

See all of creation through the prism of the Divine Name.

. . . .

Notice how the angles and contours of nature and the environment correspond to the archetypal geometries of the letters.

. . . .

Hold this perception for as long as you can.

. . . .

When it fades you can always close your eyes and recreate the letters again if you wish.

. . . .

The Divine Name of the Creator is always right there just waiting to be seen and acknowledged within all of creation.

. . . .

Aspire to live with this awareness.

. . . .

AWARENESS FIVE: IDEA

» The Four Letters & the Structure of the Human Body

THE FOUR LETTERS EMBODIED WITHIN THE HUMAN FORM:

In all the four-letter name visualizations mentioned until this point the visual is perceived as being outside of the body, so to speak. There is a "you" observing, carving or writing the Name and then looking at the Name. There is also another, more embodied practice where one becomes fully aligned and integrated with the four letters.

According to R. Eliezer Azikri, the human being standing upright is represented by the "line" of the letter *Vav*. The human being stands upon the vast expanse of the earth, which is the letter *Hei*, a letter that expands in both length and width.

An even closer examination of the human body reveals how the four letters are also congruent with and contained within the body itself. The shape and form of the human body parallels the four letters in the Name of Hashem. In this meditative practice one does not mentally or meditatively move his awareness upwards away from his body, but rather one experientially feels himself as being fully unified with the Name of Hashem. This is more of an embodied practice than an abstract or inward journey.

The structure of the human form replicates the four letters in the Name of Hashem *(Magid Mesharim, Parshas Chukas)*. The head embodies and resembles the small letter Yud - י. The straight shoulders and the two arms that extend downwards reflect and resemble the image of the letter Hei - ה. The aligned torso and spine is the letter Vav - ו. And the hips and two legs that extend downward are the lower Hei - ה. [1]

The human body is therefore an embodiment of the Divine Name of Hashem. This practice is geared towards empowering one to become more acutely aware of how the Name

---

1 This is but one image of how the name of Hashem is reflected within the human body. There are other ways the Arizal mentions how this same idea is revealed *(Mishnas Chassidim. See; Teshuas Chein, Lech Lecha)*. For example, the head is the Yud, the two hands are the two Hei's (Hei being the number five, represented by the five fingers of each hand), and the torso is the Vav. In the lower part of the body, the two legs/feet are the two Hei's (five toes each), the crown/corona above the male organ is (shaped as) the Yud, and the organ itself is (shaped like) the Vav.

of Hashem is within us at all times.

To begin, first one carves or writes the four letters of G-d's name in his mind's eye in a vertical formation, from top to bottom. Next, one focuses on the letter *Yud*. The entire internal screen becomes filled with the *Yud*. Then, one slowly draws the *Yud* towards his face and into his head. The energy and light of the *Yud* now fills his entire head.

Next, one does the same with the letter *Hei*. He fills the entire inner screen of his vision with the letter *Hei*. Then, he slowly begins to pull the *Hei* closer to his body all the way into his shoulders and arms in perfect alignment with the horizontal and vertical lines of the letter. Now that the *Hei* is filling one's shoulders and arms one begins to sense a subtle warmth and tingling as the upper body is embodied within the upper *Hei*.

After filling the upper body with the *Hei* one does the same with the letter *Vav*. First one forms or writes the letter *Vav* within his inner eye. Then one pulls the letter *Vav* towards himself as he lets it meld into his entire torso and spine, filling him with its inner alignment and energy.

Now, finally one can move his attention to the lower part of the body in order to carve or write the final *Hei* and allow it to fill the entire screen of his inner vision. At this point he can draw the letter *Hei* towards the lower part of his body, right in front of his hips and legs. Next he can merge the lower *Hei* into the lower half of his body and allow the *Hei's* light and energy to fill his hips and legs in perfect alignment with the horizontal and vertical lines of the Hei. As one is embodied within the Divine Name one experiences a sense of warmth and aliveness as he becomes the perfect vessel for Hashem's light to pour into and shine through.

At this point the entire body is resonating with the name of Hashem.

» THE TIKKUN HANEFESH/ SOUL ELEVATION PRACTICE:

This is a more advanced version of the above, skip ahead to the "practice" if the following is difficult to follow.

Instead of using one letter at a time, all four letters are used. In addition, the meditator meditates on a particular vowel and body part associated with that vowel.

First, visualize the four letter name of Hashem, the entire *Yud-Hei-Vav-Hei* with the vowel *Kamatz* underneath and place the image near the corresponding body part, the skull of the head, allowing the light to enter and fill the entire skull.

Next visualize the four letter name of Hashem with the

Patach vowel and place the image near the corresponding body part, the right hemisphere of the brain allowing the light of the name to infuse the entire right side of the brain. Following this, visualize the four letter name of Hashem with the *Tzeirei* vowel and place the image near the corresponding body part, the left hemisphere of the brain and allow the light to enter and permeate the entire left side of the brain.

For the eyes, nose, ears and mouth, the following methods are used:

For the eyes meditate on five sets of the name of Hashem. The name of Hashem is 26. 5 times 26=130 as the word *Ayin*/eye.

For the ears meditate on the name of Hashem spelled out, as in *Yud/Vav/Dalet*=20, *Hei/Yud*=15, *Vav/Aleph/Vav*=13, and *Hei/Hei*=10. 20+15+13+10=58. *Ozen*/Ear is numerically 58.

For the nose meditate on the name of Hashem spelled out, as in *Yud/Vav/Dalet*=20, *Hei/Yud*=15, *Vav/Aleph/Vav*=13, *Hei/Yud*=15. 20+15+13+15=63. *Chotem*/Nose is numerically 63.

For the mouth meditate on the name of Hashem spelled out, as in *Yud/Vav/Dalet*=20, *Hei/Yud*=15, *Vav/Aleph/*

Vav=13, *Hei/Yud*=15. 20+15+13+15=63. Since the mouth is the source of speech, also meditate on the 22 letters of the *Aleph-Beis*. 63+22=85. The word in *Hebrew* for mouth is *Peh* which numerically is 85.

Sit with this awareness for a few moments. Next visualize the four letter name of Hashem with the *Segol* vowel and place the image near the corresponding body part, the right arm and allow the light to enter and soak through the entire right arm.

Then visualize the four letter name of Hashem with the *Sh'va* vowel and place the image near the corresponding body part, the left arm and allow the light to enter and permeate the entire left arm.

Next visualizes the four letter name of Hashem with the *Cholam* vowel and place the image near the corresponding body part, the upper body and the torso and allow the light to infuse and saturate the entire upper body.

Sit with this awareness for a few moments and now move to the lower part of the body. First, visualizes the four letter name of Hashem with the *Chirik* vowel and place the image near the corresponding body part, the right leg allowing the light of the name to seep in and permeate the entire right leg.

Then visualizes the four letter name of Hashem with the *Kubutz* vowel and place the image near the corresponding body part, the left leg and allow the light to enter and infuse the entire left leg.

Next, visualize the four letter name of Hashem with the *Shuruk* vowel and place the image near the corresponding body part, the procreative organ and allow the light to fill-up and seep into the entire area. Conclude by visualizing the four letter name of Hashem with no-vowel and place the image near the corresponding body part, the feet, and allow the light to enter and saturate your entire being.

The following practice is a simpler version of the practice of embodying the name of Hashem, where one becomes a *Merkava*, a chariot for the Divine light, allowing one to feel and sense the light of the Creator permeating all his and the entire existence.

AWARENESS FIVE: PRACTICE

» Embodying the Four Letters within the Body

Set a soft timer (or have someone else observe you) in order to fully enter this meditation without any worry of what needs to be done afterwards.

This is a time for being present. Allow yourself the gift of the experience.

For those new to meditation practice, it is recommended to start with anywhere from 10-20 minutes. This is not a competitive practice, so if that amount of time feels overwhelming for you, best to start slowly, and steadily build on a strong foundation.

Invite all of yourself into this space here and now. In a comfortable seat, preferably with your eyes closed, take a moment to let go of all the noise, chaos and movement in your life; simply be. Just as we need to minimize external stimuli via the sense of touch, the same is true with the other senses. To help with visualization, it is beneficial to gently close your eyes, shutting out the external world in order to move more inward to your inner field of vision.

You may notice various sounds, sensations, thoughts or feelings crossing your mind.

Sense everything without manipulating it; accept what is and relax from the urge to act.

Begin by visualizing yourself standing in the place where you currently are.

Mentally write out these four letters in the mind's eye, from Yud to the final Hei, vertically aligned.

י

ה

ו

ה

First the Yud in front of you - י. Then underneath that, the Hei - ה. Below the Hei is the Vav - ו. And then at the base, the final Hei - ה

Set your concentration on the letters themselves, their meanings as well as their shapes.

Meditate on the image of these four letters and slowly bring each individual letter, one by one, right in front of you.

If these are letters of fire, feel the heat of the letters and sit in their warmth.

Focus on the Yud. Draw the Yud towards you until it enters and infuses your entire head.

. . . .

Next, focus on the Hei. Bring it towards your shoulders and arms, and then draw the Hei closer and allow it to literally fill your shoulders and arms.

. . . .

Now focus on the Vav. Place the Vav in front of your body and move it towards you until it fills your torso and the entire mid-section of your body.

. . . .

Then focus on the final Hei. Bring the Hei near the lower half of your body. Move it towards you and allow it to merge with your hips and legs, revealing how the shape of your lower body is analogous to the Hei.

. . . .

From head to toe you are the embodiment of the Name of Hashem: The Yud is your head, the Hei is your shoulders and arms, the Vav is your spine, and your hips and legs are the final Hei.

. . . .

Become aware of how your body is a reflection and embodiment of the Creative power of the universe, the Name of the Creator.

. . . .

Sit with this awareness for a few moments.

. . . .

Gently open your eyes and see your body for what it truly is — the 'seat' of your soul and a microcosm of the Infinite One.

. . . .

AWARENESS SIX: IDEA

» The Light of the Shechinah

Following the expulsion from Spain in the year 1492 many Spanish Jews migrated and were welcomed by the Ottoman Empire. Eventually many great poets, scholars, thinkers, kabbalists and Halachic deciders settled in Israel and many of them in northern Israel, in the town of Tzfas.

Rabbi Eliezer Azikri:

In the year 1533 Eliezer, the son of Moshe Azikri, was born to a Spanish family. It seems by all accounts that he was born in Tzfas. He grew up to become a noted Kabbalist, poet and writer. One of his most famous poems, *Yedid Nefesh*, is universally known and is recited by many worshippers on Friday evening right before Shabbos is welcomed in.

We know very little about his life. Although we do know that he was associated with the great mystics of that era such as Rabbis Shlomo Alkabatz, Yoseph Caro and the Arizal. He also seems to have studied under the Ramak, Rabbi Moshe Cordovero.

In 1588 Rabbi Eliezer either founded or at least was part of a group of Kabbalists who took it upon themselves to arouse their own and others' spiritual devotion. The group was called *Sukkas Shalom*, the Canopy of Peace.

Rabbi Eliezer passed from this world in 1600 and was buried in Tzfas in close proximity to the Arizal and the Ramak.

R. Eliezer penned a few books. His most well-known book is called *Sefer Chareidim*/The Book of the Scrupulous, which is a mystically inspired book of ethics revolving around the Mitzvos. In the introduction to this work he speaks about this group of friends that called themselves *Sukkas Shalom*. The primary ritual process and social structure of this group was predicated upon their gathering and admonishing of each other to do *Teshuvah*/Repentance or Return and to mend their ways. The experiences and expressions of this group were the inspiration and formed the basis for the book, *Safer Chareidim*.

The book itself is divided into three parts. The first part deals with the concept of knowing G-d and explores the inner workings of creation, including the interface between the Infinite Creator and finite creation. The second part of the book speaks about the *Mitzvos*/Commandments or Means of Connection. R. Eliezer focuses primarily on the Mitzvos that are still applicable today in exile. He divides the Mitzvos into eight categories, relating them to eight

different body parts. For instance, some Mitzvos are connected with the eyes; some Mitzvos are connected with the
ears, while other Mitzvos are connected with the hands,
and still others with the heart. The third part of the book
speaks almost entirely about *Teshuvah*, the notion of mend-
ing one's ways and pursuing the path of personal transformation and spiritual development.

This is the overall structure of the book. And yet there
seems to also be a sub-structure or hidden narrative that
develops a particular theme throughout the course of the
book, and that is the idea of the *Shechinah*, the Divine Presence that rests above one's head.

The Shechinah, in general, is understood as the indwelling presence of the Infinite Creator within creation. Yet,
as there are multiple realities, "worlds," perspectives and
states of consciousness, there are also many levels of the
Shechinah *(Ohr Hachayim, Bereishis, 46; 4)*. On a lower level
the Shechinah is not the Creator's Light per se, but rather
the "glory of creation," created solely for revelatory purposes. Specifically, this is a light that indicates to the observer
that the Creator is present and revealed *(Emunos V'Deios, 2;
10. Kuzari, 4; 3. Moreh Nevuchim, 1; 19, 1; 25)*. It is a medium
through which the message of Divine Immanence is made
known.

On a deeper level, however, the Shechinah is the "glory of

the Creator" *(Ramban Bereishis, 46; 1 Avodas HaKodesh, Ha'Ta-chlis, 30)*. On this level the Shechinah is actually understood as the indwelling presence of the Creator in whatever reality, world, perspective or state of consciousness one is in at that moment. In this way, the Shechinah is the message itself, made manifest through any number of mediums.

These two modes or methods of the Shechinah taken together create a two-tiered model through which we can encounter and engage the Divine Presence, as it were. On one level, there is the Shechinah's presence within tangible creation, the Malchus of our reality, in the present moment. And then there is also the aspect of the Shechinah that is "above" our heads, indicating the presence of a reality that is presently beyond us. The *Safer Chareidim* speaks particularly about cultivating an awareness of the aspect of the Shechinah that is above our heads.

Let us begin with a quote from the beginning of *Safer Chareidim*:

> "In general, all the nine Sefiros (from Keser to Yesod) are referred to as lighter lights, whereas Malchus (also called the Shechinah) is a darker (bluer) light which is the seat of the lighter lights. This is similar to the light of a candle where the higher parts of the flame are lighter, more transparent colors, and the lower parts of the flame are darker, bluer lights that serve as a seat for the lighter lights. And the nation that was chosen

was commanded to cleave their thoughts to this (dark) blue light. And they (their bodies) are like a wick upon which rests the blue light, and upon the blue light rests the white light."
(Safer Chareidim, Chap 2)

The higher/deeper Sefiros, the Sefiros closer to the original point of emanation from the *Ohr Ein Sof*/Infinite Light, appear (to the observer/meditator) as lighter and more transparent. The further removed one is from the Source, the more the "vessel" is pronounced as opposed to the light, and thus the darker and more opaque the colors appear.

The structure of the body parallels the ten Sefiros. The crown of the head is Keser, and Yesod and Malchus are the lower parts of the body, connected specifically to the procreative organs.

Here is a basic outline of the ten (eleven, counting Keser) Sefiros and their corresponding body parts.

KESER (desire, super-conscious) – the Crown of the Head*
CHOCHMAH (wisdom, intuition) – the Right Hemisphere of the Brain
BINAH (reason, cognition) –the Left Hemisphere of the Brain
DA'AS (knowledge, awareness) – the Frontal Lobes
CHESED (kindness, love) – Right Arm

GEVURAH (strength, restriction) – Left Arm
TIFERES (beauty, compassion) – Torso
NETZACH (victory, ambition) – Right Leg
HOD (devotion, humility) – Left Leg
YESOD (foundation, relationship) (masculine) – Procreative Organ
MALCHUS (royalty, receptivity) (feminine) – Procreative Organ*

Or the skull is Keser. The two ears are Chochmah and Binah. The forehead is Da'as. The two eyes are Chesed and Gevurah. The Nose is Tiferes. The two lips are Netzach and Hod. The tongue is Yesod. And the mouth is Malchus. Asara Ma'amaros, Maamar M'ein Ganim, 1.

The terms masculine and feminine procreative organs are used intentionally here as both males and females embody Yesod and Malchus within their bodies, in their own masculine and feminine areas. Yesod is the line, the masculine aspect, and Malchus is the circle, the feminine aspect.

The ten Sefiros are replicated throughout all of creation, from the highest point to the lowest. The ten Sefiros are the cosmic code of creation that is infinitely replicated within every dimension, including our own consciousness.

Each reality contains the entire structure of the ten Sefiros. When a person is standing upon the earth, for example, the earth is Malchus (the final *Hei*), and they are the nine Sefiros that connect earth (Malchus) to Heaven (*Keser*). Yet, within the body itself there is also Malchus (as outlined above). Furthermore, whereas the crown of the head is considered as Keser within the structure of one's body, right above the head, as it were, is the Malchus of a higher/deeper realm; and beyond that is an even higher/deeper reality, and so on, ad infinitum.

Malchus, the Shechinah, is perceived by the beholder/meditator as a dark blue light. For most people, unfortunately, the "light" of the Shechinah above their heads does not shine brightly or even at all. This is because 'they themselves do not shine,' as it were, and as a result, they are not consciously aware of or able to perceive the *Shechinah's* shining presence that is within them and above them at all times.

For a *Tzadik*/Holy and Righteous Individual, understood as one who "shines," this light is tangibly present, and thus their focused attention is directed towards this light.

To continue with the *Safer Chareidim*:
"For Righteous people this dark blue light shines above their heads…similar to the angels, as it says in the verse *(Bereishis, 19; 1)*, "And the two angels came (to Lot) and Lot saw…" The Zohar asks: What did Lot see? He saw the Shechinah…he saw a brilliant light that emanated above their heads…Even though this light is hidden to

most people...(a righteous person) should have complete faith that it is there, as if they are actually seeing it.
This is stated clearly in the Zohar's commentary on
the portion of Balak *(3, p. 187a)*, where it questions the
meaning of the scriptural verse, "The wise man's eyes are
in his head" *(Koheles, 2; 14)*. (The Zohar asks): If not in
the head, where else would a person's eyes be — on his
body or on his arms? So what does it mean that, "the
wise man's eyes are in his head?"
Why does the verse only speak of a wise man rather than
any other person? (Aren't all people's eyes in their head?)
The meaning of the verse is certainly this: It is as we have
learned — a person should not go about four paces with
his head uncovered. Why not? — Because the Shechinah dwells above his head. Every wise person's eyes and
his words are therefore "in his head." That is, they are
always occupied with that which dwells and exists within
and above his head."
(Safer Chareidim, Chap 3)

A little further on in the book R. Eliezer writes about a
person that focuses on the presence of the Shechinah above
his head and imagines that his body is a throne for the Creator's presence in this world.

To quote:
"A person is commanded to place the yoke of the Shechinah above him at all times...as the Shechinah is above

one's head. And he (or she) should imagine that he is a chariot and a throne for the Divine. The (Hebrew) word *Adam*/Humankind in small numerical value (i.e., only using single digits) is 9 (*Aleph*/1, *Dalet*/4, *Mem*/4 = 9), the same numerical value as the (Hebrew) word *Kisei*/Throne in small numerical value (*Kuf*/1, *Samach*/6, *Aleph*/1=9). His mind should therefore be constantly aware of this light that rests and hovers above him the entire day..."
(Sefer Chareidim, 35; 30)

Towards the end of the book R. Eliezer brings down a practice from the second Temple period in which the "pious ones" would begin their prayers by meditating on the light of the Shechinah that rests above a (righteous) person's head at all times. They would imagine themselves all seated and surrounded by the holy, warming, embracing and simultaneously overwhelming light of the Shechinah. This practice, suggested towards the end of his work, seems to be the culmination of all the previous references to the *Shechinah's* presence being above one's head, as here one actually performs a specific practice meant to animate and activate all the earlier teachings.

To quote:
"And this is what we learned *(Berachos, Chap 1; 5):* 'The early Chassidim would settle one hour and then pray in order to direct their hearts to the Creator.' The com-

mentators explain that this means that they would detach their thoughts from this world and attach them
to the Master of everything, may He be blessed, with
great awe and love. Meaning that for nine hours (each
day) they would discontinue their studies and dedicate
their time to the work of meditation (inner isolation)
and prayer (cleaving to their Creator). At this time they
would imagine the light of the Shechinah (reflected as
a dark-blue color) hovering above their heads. (And
then) as if it (the light) were flowing downward and
infusing the entire space around them, they would sit
and bask in the light…and they would naturally trem-
ble and rejoice in their trembling."
*(Safer Chareidim, Chap. 65. p. 227. See also: Maavar Yavak.
Shaloh, Meseches Yumah, Teshuvah 50. Ohr Haganuz L'Tzadikim, Vayeshev. Siddur Keser Nehurah, Hakdamah, Nesiv Mitz-
vosecha)*

Such is the understanding of this practice as found in the
oral tradition. Reb Yitzchak of Homel also writes that the
early pious ones would visualize the Shechinah surrounding
and enveloping them before, during and after their prayers
(Ma'amor Ha'Shiflus V'Ha'simcha, 8). The practice of imagining
oneself sitting in the presence of the Divine Light was also
strongly encouraged by the Baal Shem Tov and his students
*(Ohr Haganuz L'Tzadikim, Bereishis, Vayetze. Baal Shem Tov Torah,
Amud HaTefilah, 57).*

On one hand this is another type of awareness visualization where the refined practitioner becomes aware of the ever-presence of the Shechinah and, as a result, perceives the light shining within and surrounding his immediate space. And yet, beyond the visual, this is also a very visceral and embodied experience. There is an almost tangible sensation of being bathed, embraced and simultaneously overwhelmed in awe of the utter immanence of Divine reality. As a result of integrating the initial awareness of the hovering light of the Shechinah above one's head through the sensory embodiment of this light, the experience becomes much more 'real' to the practitioner than what is empirically observable or able to be expressed.

AWARENESS SIX: PRACTICE

» Sitting in the Light
of the Shechinah

Set a soft timer (or have someone else observe you) in order to fully enter this meditation without any worry of what needs to be done afterwards.

This is a time for being present. Allow yourself the gift of this experience.

For those new to meditation practice, it is recommended to start with anywhere from 10-20 minutes. This is not a competitive practice, so if that amount of time feels overwhelming for you, best to start slowly and steadily build on a strong foundation.

Invite all of yourself into this space here and now. In a comfortable seat, preferably with your eyes closed, take a moment to let go of all the noise, chaos and movement in your life; simply be. Just as we need to minimize external stimuli via the sense of touch, the same is true with the other senses. To help with visualization, it is beneficial to gently close your eyes, shutting out the external world in order to move more inward to your inner field of vision.

You may notice various sounds, sensations, thoughts or feelings crossing your mind.

Sense everything without manipulating it; accept what is and relax from the urge to act.

Now visualize yourself standing wherever you are currently.

Tilt your head upwards in an attempt to become aware of the Divine Presence of the Shechinah above your head. Ask humbly for this light and Divine Presence to be revealed to you. The Light of the Shechinah appears as a beneficent blue light, the deep color of the midnight sky.

Slowly and softly the light begins to descend upon you.

First the Shechinah's light encircles the top of your head. It then moves slowly downward encompassing your forehead.

Slowly the light encircles your entire head and you feel like you are being bathed in this holy light.

Then, the light gradually, but ever so gently, flows downwards encircling your arms, your shoulders, your torso and then the entire lower part of your body.

You are now completely surrounded by and embraced within the Shechinah's light from front to back, side-to-side, and top to bottom.

This dark blue light surrounds and embraces you. You are basking in its soft glow.

A sense of being protected and sheltered sets in as you feel yourself being bathed in this Divine Light.

This gives rise to immense waves of joy and contentment.

There seems to also be an overwhelming sensation of awe, fear and trepidation.

You are delighting in feeling this close to the Divine Presence, and yet you simultaneously feel overwhelmed and humbled.

A sense of rapture wells up within you as you get a taste of this radical awe and amazement.

There is a tangibly visceral sensation coursing through you. Your body is both excited and anxious.

At this point all your conflicting emotions morph into one single palpable sensation of being fully present, alive and deeply connected.

For a moment you stop feeling all together and you become one with the experience.

Sit for a few moments (or as long as the experience lasts) in this awareness of non-awareness.

Gently open your eyes.

PART FOUR

ADVANCED VISUALIZATIONS

ADVANCED ONE: IDEA

» The Four Letters Vertically: Journeying Upwards and Downwards

THE FOUR-LETTER NAME WRITTEN VERTICALLY:

Many of the previous visuals of the four letters were presented horizontally, placed in the mind's eye arranged from right to left (ה–ו–ה–י). But there is also the possibility of shifting the visual axis and ordering the letters in a vertical fashion with the *Yud* on top, followed by the *Hei* below it, the *Vav* below that, and finishing with the final *Hei* on the bottom, similar to the arrangement of the four letters when they are superimposed upon the human body:

י

ה

ו

ה

As mentioned, during the same time period as Rabbi Yoseph Caro the profound poet and ethicist Rabbi Eliezer Azikri also lived in Tzfas, Israel. In his classic work Safer Chareidim/The Book of the Scrupulous (Chap 66) he writes of how the lower Hei - ה represents the earthly realm of existence. The upright letter Vav- ו, situated above the Hei, represents the human being standing erect upon the surface of the earth. Above the human being's head is the upper Hei - ה, representing the Heavens, as it were, including the Throne of Glory. And above it all is the Yud - י, the revelation of the Creator that will only be fully manifest in the World to Come.

THE FOUR LETTERS & THE FOUR WORLDS:

This vertical arrangement of the four letters is very easily mapped onto the "Four Worlds." Without getting into all the details of what each of these four worlds/perspectives represent, here is a most basic synopsis: The lowest world represents Physical reality; above/within this reality/perspective is the Emotional world; even higher/deeper is the Mental world; and above/within that is the Spiritual world.

The process of creation, starting from the Infinite One and moving on into all (apparent) finite multiplicity, evolved in four stages: First there was a movement within the Mind of the Creator, a desire to create. This is the "world" of *Atzilus*/Nearness, the world of the Spiritual. Then there was the externalization of this desire in the form of an "idea." This is the "world" of *Beriah*/Creation, the "substance" of reality, the realm of the Mental. Then there was a process of working with the raw material of this substance. This is the "world" of *Yetzirah*/Formation, the arena of the Emotions. And finally, there was the finished product, as it were. This is the "world" of *Asiyah*/Actualization, the world of the Physical.

These Worlds are also states of consciousness or perspectival postures one can assume or inhabit as they encounter and engage reality. From an Atzilus paradigm, there is only One. The observer does not sense any separation from his Creator. Reality is beyond dissection and contextualization, it is simply the sensation of being at one with the One. From a Beriah paradigm, there is a subtle sense of separation. The observer feels himself to exist, and yet he also senses himself as being embedded deep within the Creator, like a fetus within the womb. From the Yetzirah paradigm, there is a more pronounced sense of separation. Yet, here too the observer feels himself being enveloped within and utterly embraced by the Creator, like a child suckling in the arms of its mother. From an Asiyah paradigm, there is a strong sensation of separation. There is a clear divide, and yet one still feels connected to his Creator and is able to sense how his existence is guided and influenced by his Creator, like a young adult after having left the house of his parents.

' - is connected to and revealed in the world of Atzilus.

ה - is connected to and revealed in the world of Beriah.
ו - is connected to and revealed in the world of Yetzirah.
ה - is connected to and revealed in the world of Asiyah.

The simplest way to practice this visualization is to mentally write out these four letters in the mind's eye, in large black letters, moving vertically from above to below, moving from the *Yud* to the final *Hei*. One begins by closing his eyes and visualizing himself holding a flame in a white empty room, or, alternatively, holding a feather with ink in hand ready to write the letters upon the inner screen of his vision. Then, in vertical sequence he begins forming or writing the *Yud* on top, then the *Hei* beneath it, followed by the *Vav*, and finishing with the final *Hei*.

י

ה

ו

ה

THE FOUR LETTERS & THE INWARD
JOURNEY UPWARDS AND DOWNWARDS:

The four letters of the Name of Hashem are also contained within the *Eitz Chayim*/Tree of Life, the meta-physical map of creation comprising the upper and inner worlds. One traditional meditation practice is to visualize these letters as superimposed upon the structure of this geometrical diagram, and then inwardly climb higher and deeper into the Tree.

In other words, the vertical formation of the four letters, when arranged in one's mental/visual field, can be used as a map for an upward/inward journey. One begins by entering into the root of the lower *Hei*, continuing to climb up the trunk of the *Vav*, on into the canopy of the upper *Hei*, and then perpetually higher, reaching the fruit of the *Yud*, and then even higher beyond all form, to the Infinite Light. The meditator continues to expand and elevate his finite self ever upwards and out into the Infinite Self of the One.

The Baal Shem Tov, of blessed memory *(1698-1760)*, taught that after visualizing these four letters one should meditatively "climb up" and ascend the letters, moving from the lower *Hei* all the way up until the *Yud*. And then, following the movement upward, one should then descend all the way back down into the consciousness of the body *(Siddur, Keser Nehurah, Hakdamah)*. (This is a prime example of the dynamic of *Ratzu v'Shuv*/Running and Returning that was explored earlier in this text).

When the letters are arranged vertically our consciousness is able to shift out of a flat-world reality as it were. In the horizontal perspective reality is conceived of as a series of linear movements gradually taking us from one place to another, from cause to effect, from past to future. But in the vertical paradigm our perception is altered to the point that we can perceive a different kind of movement that lifts us beyond the horizontal paradigm. This vertical image stimulates an inner movement beyond cause/effect, action/reaction, or past/future, to a place of limitless freedom. It lifts us up from the flat-world reality, and propels us into motion from below to above and then Beyond the Beyond. This is a kind of quantum leap of consciousness so to speak, wherein we can catapult ourselves to different states or levels of reality without moving at all. This kind of motion is not necessarily linear or gradual, but can happen in an instant and transport us far beyond our current state.

One begins this practice by becoming acutely aware of his body and its sensations. Gradually one begins to observe his consciousness slowly rising upward until he can view his own body from above. First he hovers above his body, then above the room, all the while observing his body in his seat or lying down. Then he continues moving out of the room, above the building, above the town and the city, into the clouds, above the clouds, and into the vast expanse of the cosmos. As his awareness is moving upward it is becoming lighter and lighter and floating higher and higher, leaving behind the pull of gravity and piercing through the atmosphere. At this stage one has elevated and propelled himself into the inner world of Asiyah, which reflects the most subtle realm of the final *Hei*.

At this point one has risen and traveled to the furthest ends of the observable cosmos and now one feels they have bumped up against a skycap, an ethereal wall of sorts. With the power of will and the determination of thought and imagination one then pierces through the skycap and elevates his awareness past this obstacle and into a vast expanse of brilliant lights and subtle, spiritual, emotional bliss. This is a world of angels and refined energetic consciousness. A reality where he feels completely embraced and enveloped within and by the Divine Presence. He has entered into the inner world of Yetzirah, the letter *Vav*.

Frolicking within the world of Yetzirah one rises to the furthest reaches of that world and senses that he has bumped up against another skycap, a ceiling of sorts. Yet, with tremendous effort, determination and perseverance, using his power of thought and imagination he pierces through this resistance and elevates his awareness beyond the boundary and is thrust into an even more brilliant, shining, sparkling reality of subtle mental and spiritual ecstasy. He enters into a world teeming with light and pure spirit, a world of souls and paradise. This is a reality where he feels himself swimming within the Divine womb, radically consumed within the Creator's embrace. He has entered into the inner world of Beriah, the upper letter *Hei*.

Floating within the world of Beriah one floats and rises upwards to the furthest reaches of that world and once again has the sensation that he has reached that world's end, its limit, a ceiling, an impenetrable surface. There is nowhere further to go and yet there is a burning desire to reach even higher, to pierce the limitation of the impermeable ceiling above him. Summoning the reservoirs of all of his strength, pent up energy, and unfulfilled spiritual hunger, he bursts through the upper limit and experiences a rush and flow of unimaginable, unfathomable, fantastical lights as they come streaming downward upon him. At the center of all the lights is one great infinite, blinding light. One begins to move towards that ever brilliant, warming and welcoming light. He has entered the world of Atzilus, the smallest "vessel", the letter *Yud*. The meditator's own vessel, his awareness of the experience, is nearly nullified and infinitesimal, like the *Yud*. He does not sense any independent existence or separation from the Creator's Light. The experience is beyond dissection and compartmentalization. It is simply the sensation of being at one with the One.

And yet, as one is drawn closer and closer to the Light there is an abrupt stop and his sense of materiality returns as he begins to feel that he is being pushed down through the inner worlds, back into his body. Just as one journeyed upward, one now begins the journey of return, taking all the enlightenment, illumination and awareness of such an elevated experience back with him into the world. One gradually descends from Atzilus (the *Yud*), into Beriah (the *Hei*), into Yetzirah (the *Vav*), and finally back into Asiyah (the final *Hei*), becoming enclothed again within his own skin and bodily awareness.

ADVANCED ONE: PRACTICE
....

» JOURNEYING ON THE FOUR LETTERS UPWARDS AND DOWNWARDS

Set a soft timer (or have someone else observe you) in order to fully enter this meditation without any worry of what needs to be done afterwards.

This is a time for being present. Allow yourself the gift of this experience.

For those new to this particular meditation practice, it is recommended to start with anywhere from 10-20 minutes. This is not a competitive practice, so if that amount of time feels overwhelming for you, best to start slowly, and steadily build on a strong foundation.

Invite all of yourself into this space here and now. In a comfortable seat, preferably with your eyes closed, take a moment to let go of all the noise, chaos and movement in your life; simply be. Just as we need to minimize external stimuli via the sense of touch, the same is true with the

other senses. To help with visualization, it is beneficial to gently close your eyes, shutting out the external world in order to move more inward to your inner field of vision.

You may notice various sounds, sensations, thoughts or feelings crossing your mind.

Sense everything without manipulating it; accept what is and relax from the urge to act.

Begin by visualizing yourself standing in the place where you currently are.

Mentally write out these four letters vertically arranged in the mind's eye in large black letters

י

ה

ו

ה

First the Yud in front of you - י. Then underneath that, the Hei - ה. Below the Hei is the Vav - ו. And then at the base, the final Hei - ה.

Meditate on the letters themselves and their individual meaning.

Focus your attention on their shape and structure. Now become aware of your body and its sensations, sensing your feet touching the ground.

Gradually begin to observe your consciousness slowly rising up your body until you can view your own body from above.

First you are hovering above your body, then above the room, above the building, the town, the city, and further up into the clouds, then above the clouds and off into the vast expanse of the cosmos.

As your awareness is moving progressively upwards it is becoming lighter and lighter and floating higher and higher into the inner world of Asiyah, the final Hei.

As you have risen to the furthest ends of the observable cosmos begin to sense that you have bumped up against a skycap, the roof of the letter Hei. Yet, with the power of your will and determination pierce through the upper horizontal line of the Hei and grab onto the Vav, thereby pulling yourself up into the vast expanse of brilliant lights and subtle, spiritual, emotional bliss. This is a world of angels and refined energetic consciousness. A reality where you feel completely embraced and enveloped within and by the Divine Presence. You have entered into the inner world of Yetzirah, the letter Vav.

You are rising higher and higher until you sense that you have hit the skycap, the 'top' of the Vav, and yet, with the power of your will and determination pierce through this limitation and grab onto the lower leg of the Hei and pull yourself up into a place of mental and spiritual ecstasy. This is a world teeming with light and pure spirit, a paradisal world of ancient and eternal souls. Sense yourself swimming within the Divine womb, completely contained within the Creator's embrace. This is the inner world of Beriah, the upper Hei.

Floating ever upwards through the world of the upper Hei begin to sense that you have reached the furthest ends of this world, the roof of the letter Hei. Yet, through deep yearning and determination you pierce through the upper horizontal line of the Hei and now take hold of the bottom tip of the small Yud and pull yourself up into the world of pure awareness and transcendence. Here you are in a world where you do not sense any independent self-existence or separation from the Creator's Light.

Slowly drift higher and higher into this world until you reach the upper edge of this world, the crown of the Yud, the space where Infinity touches finitude.

You are still holding on to the upper tip of the Yud as you slowly rise higher and higher. As you come to the very edge of the tip of the Yud you are emptied out into Infinity, beyond all expression, imagery or identity.

Suddenly there is an abrupt stop and a 360-degree change in trajectory. You are being pushed all the way back down through the inner worlds, from the Yud to the Hei to the Vav and then the final Hei, all the way down into your body and physical reality.

You feel invigorated and infused with illumination and expansive awareness. You now understand that the ultimate purpose of the soul is to be enclothed within the body.

. . . .

Sit for a moment with this realization and then gently open your eyes.

. . . .

ADVANCED TWO: IDEA

....

» The Sefiros & their Colors, Vowels, Directions, and Elements

We will now explore a multi-dimensional visualization practice that employs more technical Kabbalistic symbolism, particularly the structure of the Sefiros. We will build this practice layer by layer, adding texture and meaning to it as we go. It is important to note that the reader may at any time rest at any point along this process and engage a more simplified version of this practice. Due to its complex nature and multi-tiered structure this particular meditation demands a thorough discussion in order to fully understand it within its proper context.

Let us begin with a brief overview of what the Sefiros are. Then we can more confidently move forward to explore their multi-valent associations.

THE SEFIROS:

....

There is the *Ohr Ein Sof* — this is the Infinite, formless, undifferentiated Light and creative power of the Creator — and there is also the finite, time-space-consciousness reality of creation.

The ten Sefiros are the ten screens or filters, as it were, through which the Infinite Light pervades and permeates our finite reality.

The distinct forms, shapes, and colors of the Sefiros serve as filters through which the Infinite, colorless, formless, unified light is reflected and refracted into our world. Passing through the Sefiros causes the Light to appear differentiated and colored. But it is not. It is unified and infinite. It is absolutely necessary that one keep this in mind as we explore the qualities and properties of the Sefiros in the upcoming pages.

The word *Sefira* is from the grammatical root, *Safar*, which means 'counting' *(Pardes Rimonim, 1; 1. Gra, Yahel Ohr, 6d)* or 'telling' *(Sefer Yetzirah)*. It is also related to the word meaning, 'edge', as in the edge of a city or encampment. As each Sefira is defined by and possesses a measured, counted, finite edge, so to speak. The Sefiros are the screens that allow the Infinite Light to be 'measured' and moderated as it passes into the finite realm of creation. Thus, they tell the *Sipur/* Story of the transformation of the Infinite Light as it journeys towards finite manifestation in order to illuminate our world. Fittingly, the word Sefira is also related to the word

Sappir, meaning to illuminate *(Zohar Chadash, Yisro, 41b)*.

The *Seder*/Structure of the Sefiros is as follows:

Keser – crown; desire, super-conscious

*

Chochmah – wisdom, intuition
Binah – understanding, cognition
Da'as – knowledge, awareness

Chesed – kindness, love
Gevurah – strength, restriction
Tiferes – beauty, compassion

Netzach – victory, ambition
Hod – devotion, humility
Yesod – foundation, relationship

Malchus – royalty, receptiveness

There are only ten Sefiros, and yet in the list above the reader may have noticed that eleven were listed; that is because Keser and Da'as are interchangeable. They are understood as higher and lower expressions of a unifying agent. Keser is the meta-level that allows for and houses the fundamental paradoxes of life. It is the liminal interface between the Infinite and finite reality. Keser encompasses and connects the various dimensions of all reality. Da'as, on the other hand, bridges and connects the various dimensions of human consciousness. It is the liminal interface between intellect and emotion. When Keser is counted among the Ten, then Da'as is not counted; and when Da'as is counted, then Keser is not.

The system of the Sefiros is organized along a right, left, and middle column structure.

The 'right column' is the giving, expanding, reaching out reality (extroversion). The 'left column' is the restrictive, boundary defining, inward-oriented reality (introversion). The 'middle column' is the balance between these two polar processes and proclivities - balance between opposites.

Chochmah (wisdom, intuition, flash of inspiration) is a right column reality. Binah (reason, logic, cognition, breaking down ideas into details) is a left column reality. Da'as is the middle column that unites the two and connects them to the rest of the human psycho-emotional spectrum.

Chochmah is associated with the nonverbal, right hemisphere of the brain. It is in a sense above and beyond verbalization. It is the kernel of the creative thought in the manner it existed prior to its descent into verbalization. This is the initial burst of inspiration right before expression. This is the right column.

The power of Binah is associated with the verbal capacity of the left hemisphere. This is characterized cognitively as the ability to break down ideas into defined categories and language. This is a left-column ability.

Da'as is the middle column, which connects intuition and creativity with understanding. Da'as is, in a sense, an act of identification. Da'as is the attachment of the mind to the idea it is contemplating. The Torah uses the term Da'as to connote the idea of attachment, connection, and union. The word Da'as essentially means to internalize a thought or concept in an attempt to make an associative identification with the idea. In the level of Da'as consciousness the boundary that usually separates the knower from the known is eliminated.

Personal reality resides in Da'as. Until opinions, notions, ideas and concepts reach that level they remain abstract, theoretical and inconsequential. The concretization of thought occurs in the realm of Da'as. It is the creation of conviction, making thoughts real. It is the realm of making choices and decisions as to how to bring ideas down into reality.

After the three mental Sefiros, there arise the three primary emotional Sefiros — Chesed, Gevurah, and Tiferes — also known by the acronym, *Cha'gas*.

On the right expansive column is *Chesed*, kindness and love. Chesed is not about the 'other'. Rather it is related to the internal desire to express and give irrespective of the capacity of the other to receive.

On the left restrictive column is Gevurah, strength and restriction. Gevurah is also referred to as *Din*, judgment or justice, because when you use your strength to restrict or resist something you are making a judgment. This Sefira is restrictive, and yet in Gevurah there is a stronger awareness of the 'other' than in Chesed, which is pure unidirectional giving. This is based on the simple fact that the very act of creating of boundaries defines the borders of self in relation to 'other.'

Between Chesed and Gevurah is their synthesis Tiferes, beauty and compassion, the middle column. Tiferes is characterized by a sense of giving coupled with an enhanced sensitivity to the needs of the recipient. This is manifest in the consideration of how much the 'receiver' could receive, as well as how much they need to receive. This is true compassion. It is not only about how much you want to give, but also about how much the other person needs. This balance creates harmony and beauty and is the synthesis between giving all you have and withholding completely.

This is the difference between compassion and kindness, Tiferes and Chesed. At its root, kindness is ultimately selfish. I give to you because I want to give, or it feels good to give, therefore I want to give you. Although positive, this impetus is actually somewhat selfish. In the modality of Gevurah I may be aware that you should not get what I may have to give because you will further abuse yourself with what I give you, therefore I withhold what I have to give out of consideration for your capacity to receive and your wellbeing. Tiferes is thus a balance of the two in which I will give to you, but I will give to you in the manner and amount that you need or that is beneficial for you. This is why Tiferes is called beauty — it harmonizes and brings the two parties together as one, the giver with the receiver. When there is harmony achieved between two opposites it is considered something beautiful. It is like art, wherein at least two contrasting lines or colors harmonize into a third, creating a beautiful tapestry or image.

The 'outer' implementing emotions, the *Na'hi*, are also divided into three. On the right expansive column is Netzach, victory and ambition. Netzach is outwardly directed movement. On the left constrictive column is Hod, devotion and humility. Hod is inwardly oriented. In the middle column is the unifying agent connecting the outward and the inward. This is the Sefira of *Yesod*, foundation and relationship.

If I am in a Chesed mode and I want to give, the question is: in what way should I give, how should this internal emotion manifest outwardly? The internal desire can behaviorally manifest in either a right column Netzach manner, or in a left column Hod manner. Netzach is empowerment and confidence. Hod is submission and humility. These Sefiros are therefore not the emotions themselves, but rather the expression of the emotions. The emotion is Chesed or Gevurah. The expression of that emotion is manifest through Netzach, empowerment, or Hod, humility.

Yesod is the middle column. The idea of the middle column is that it unifies. The Sefira of Yesod is where something is actually being expressed or given over to the receiver. This is the point in the process that makes the connection between the internal desire to connect or communicate and the actualization of that desire. In summary, Netzach and Hod are the ways in which something is given or expressed, and Yesod is the actual giving or expression.

Malchus, or kingship, is receptiveness. It represents the vessel that receives from the preceding nine Sefiros. Malchus re-channels all these energies downward into itself, thus becoming the 'crown' (*Keser*) for the subsequent structure of Sefiros, as the image of ten just keeps on replicating itself throughout all possible realities.

THE OHR EIN SOF & THE SEFIROS:

As mentioned, the root of the structure of the Sefiros, which is comprised of differentiated 'finite' vessels, exists within the deepest depths of Hashem's Ultimate Unity. And yet, as the Sefiros are revealed the Infinite Light and finite vessel appear as distinct and separate from each other with the Light giving and the vessel receiving. But in truth the Light is One and it is only the vessels that create any sense of apparent distinction. This is an ontological paradox that defies logic, but as we are reminded by R. Azriel of Gerona, "Just as Hashem has the potential of Infinity, Hashem also has the potential of finitude, otherwise Hashem would be limited in being" *(R. Azriel of Gerona, Biur Eser Sefiros)*.

The Infinite Light of Hashem is always the same *(Rikanti, Safer HaMitzvos. Chayit, Chap 3 on the Ma'areches Elokus. Distinctions are only in the Sefiros; yet, others argue. Ma'areches Elokus, Chap 3. Radbaz, Magen David, Hakdamah. R. Meir Ben Gabbai, Avodas Hakodesh, 1:2. Once the Infinite Light is expressed in the vessels of the Sefiros it too assumes 'form' Pardes Rimonim, Shar 4, Chap 4. Or paradoxically, Hashem is expressed in both form and formlessness, and is beyond them both).* But sometimes this light appears to be hidden or restricted (Gevurah), and sometimes this light seems expansive and benevolent (Chesed), while at other times this light appears powerful (Netzach), and sometimes compassionate (Tiferes).

The particular distinctions of the ONE Light are only perceived through the prism of the Sefiros, the vessels. But from the perspective of the Light there is always only One. There is thus 'our perspective' and the 'Creator's perspective,' as it were. From our perspective there is a world of separation and Hashem's Light is revealed to us through the prism of multiplicity and individuation.

One way to conceptualize this idea is to think about a colorless, undifferentiated ray of sunlight that is filtered through various colored glasses, or as colorless water that is placed in colored glasses *(The Ramak, Pardes Rimonim, Shar 4; 4. The Arizal, Shar Hakdamos, Hakdamah 4).* When one looks at the colorless water through the prism of the glass it will appear as if it is actually colored. If it is placed in a red glass, the water looks red, and if the clear water is placed in a blue glass, it appears blue. This is only from the perspective of the vessels. However, from the perspective of the Light, the 'water' is always the same colorless water. Nothing has changed. It is the same colorless water within each colorful vessel. But due to the fact that from our perspective we do indeed perceive the unique qualities of each individual Sefira, working with their corresponding colors is an effective way to remember and relate to their various properties and relationships within the unified structure of the Infinite One.

THE CORRELATION BETWEEN COLORS & THE SEFIROS:

Here is a basic map of the Sefiros and some corresponding colors culled from various Kabbalistic sources - particularly the Sefer Yetzirah along with its commentaries, and the Ramak's Pardes Rimonim:

Keser – transparent, blinding white, or colorless
Chochmah – transparent sapphire, blue or silver (also either black or white, colors that include or exclude all other colors)
Binah – yellow, gold, or green like grass
Da'as – transparent
Chesed – white or silver with a bluish tinge
Gevurah – red or gold
Tiferes – yellow like a ripening *Esrog* (citron), purple, or green (or pinkish)
Netzach – light pink
Hod – dark pink
Yesod – orange, or a rainbow of hues including blue, red, yellow
Malchus – dark blue with purple tinge, almost black.

ABOUT THE COLORS & THE SEFIROS:

Before moving forward, there is one initial point that must be addressed: As evidenced by the above table of *Sefiros* and their colors, there is no one-size-fits-all system of Sefira-Color correspondence. There are multiple systems promulgated by various Kabbalists in numerous texts. For example, Tiferes is considered yellow, or pinkish; and yet in the Zohar, Tiferes is green *(Zohar, Acharei Mos. Alternatively, the Shushan Sodos (a student of Ramban, p. 94) writes that Binah is green and Tiferes is pinkish).* This is an important point that has relevance beyond our immediate discussion of the Sefiros and their colors. Namely, that there is no one 'right' system, as it were, and that each one is 'right' in their own way. There are various systems and structures created by various teachers at various times for various purposes. Students of Kabbalah are always in danger of becoming even more rigid and unyielding in their thinking and understanding rather than more flexible and sensitive, which is one of the goals of Kabbalistic study. The ability to hold multiple definitions or valences for any particular Sefira depending upon context is the mark of a mature and agile mind, which is exactly what is needed in the quest to 'know' Hashem, as if that were even possible.

Now, although there are various systems of Sefiros and their colors there is a general consensus among all Kabbalists that the lighter more transparent colors are higher on the Tree of Life, whereas the denser and darker colors are lower. In addition the harsher or stronger colors are attributed to left-column Sefiros, and the softer, more diffuse colors are attributed to right-column Sefiros. Either Chesed is white or silver; Gevurah is either red or gold. Chesed, on the Tree of Life diagram, is 'higher' than Gevurah, and thus is attributed a lighter color. In addition, Chesed is a right-column Sefira and Gevurah is on the left, accounting for the difference in color tone between soft silver and bright gold.

The same dynamic holds true with the positioning of the Sefiros themselves. The right-column Sefiros are the more open, giving, expansive Sefiros, whereas the left-column Sefiros are the more restrictive, inward-directed Sefiros. For example, Chesed is a right-column Sefira and is generally white, while Gevurah is a left-column Sefira and is generally red. The mix of red and white produces pink. So Netzach, which is a (lower) right-column Sefira, is light pink, a color that contains more white (Chesed) than red (Gevurah). And Hod, which is a (lower) left-column Sefira and thus has more Gevurah (red) than Chesed (white), is represented in dark pink.

The reason the denser colors are lower and the lighter colors are higher is because, as explored earlier, the Light is transparent, Infinite, boundless, and unified. The vessels are the screens through which the Light of the *Ein Sof* reaches and influences the worlds. The denser the vessel, the less the light is revealed. Until, ultimately, the light (i.e., the Divine animating force and purpose of life) is almost completely concealed. That is when the vessels are densest and darkest towards the bottom of the Tree.

This is the inner reason why the higher Sefiros are more transparent and the lower Sefiros are more opaque, until Malchus is very dark blue.

The *Ohr Ein Sof*, the Infinite Light, is beyond all vessels. So the most appropriate way to speak of it would be as 'clear' water or clear light.

The vessels (i.e., the Sefiros) make the One Light appear to us as various expressions — at one time as Chesed, at another time as Gevurah. But it is ultimately the same Light. The vessel is what creates the apparent differentiation.

The more the Light is revealed, the less the vessel is perceived. And the more strongly the vessel is perceived, the less the Light is revealed.

This is the reason why there is more Light within the higher Sefiros. The Light is more revealed because there is less vessel. Therefore, the color is more brilliant. One can see through the vessel more clearly.

This is true in life as well. The more Light (connection, unity, oneness), the less vessel. For example, if your child is leaning on you and her weight is 50 pounds, it will feel relatively light. Contrast that to a stranger falling asleep on your shoulder on the plane. His head, which only weighs 15 pounds, will feel relatively heavy. This is because in relation to your child, you are perceiving more light, love, connection, unity, and less vessel. Whereas, in relation to a complete stranger on the plane you are connecting more to his vessel, and less to his light.

The more we experience Light, the less we experience vessel.

DIFFERENT COLORS
TO THE SEFIROS:

Now that we have covered the reason for the higher–lower, clear and cloudy color schemes of the Sefiros, we can attempt to address the discrepancies between color correspondences in different Kabbalistic systems. Why, according to certain paradigms is Chesed white, and according to another it is silver? Why is Gevurah red or gold depending on the system? Which color is it?

The most important idea to understand is that the Sefiros really do not have any color whatsoever. Attributing colors to the Sefiros is merely a metaphor, an image, or a manner of speaking intended to render the ethereal Sefiros more accessible and tangible.

And since there is no inherent color to any Sefira it is more easily understood why different teachers have attributed different colors to the Sefiros. Colors themselves and what they represent and embody are not indigenous to the Sefiros. Particular colors mean different things in different periods of times. Take the color pink, for example. Pink is a color related to both Netzach and Hod. Many years ago in America pink was considered a more masculine color. People would dress their little boys in pink. Today pink is most commonly considered a feminine color, and one dresses their little girls in pink. A baby boy dressed in pink these days is often mistaken for a girl.

This is the reason why certain Kabbalists, speaking from within their own historical, geographical, and cultural experience speak about a certain Sefira in one color; whereas other Kabbalists, speaking from within their own experience, speak of that same Sefira in another color.

It is of the utmost importance to remember that the colors and their relationships to the Sefiros are not literal. The colors are not inherent to the Sefiros. Their properties and the ways in which they are understood and arranged in correspondence is simply an expression of experience. What the color red meant to those earlier teachers, and what it means to you in the present, may or may not be analogous.

SIMPLE COLOR COORDINATION BETWEEN THE SEFIROS & COLORS:

For our purposes, we will present the reader with a simplified color correspondence table for the Sefiros, counting Keser instead of Da'as. This is so that we will have a common structure from which to work with, as well as to acclimate the reader with utilizing a color-coded correspondence system with the Sefiros. In time, once the reader has become more familiar with the Sefiros, and has done his own inner work to identify his own symbolic relationships to different colors, he may even tweak the system of correspondences to work with.

Beginning above Keser there is a pure Infinite Light, colorless as it were.

The Light becomes more colored as it descends.

Keser – Blinding White
Chochmah – Silver
Binah – Gold
Chesed – White
Gevurah – Red
Tiferes – Yellow
Netzach – Light Pink
Hod – Dark Pink
Yesod – Orange
Malchus – Dark Blue

EMBODYING THE SEFIROS THROUGH THEIR COLORS:

Clearly, as mentioned, the Sefiros have no intrinsic color. The correspondence is a mere symbolic association. That is why different colors are attributed to different Sefiros. And yet, to our mind, when we think about a Sefira, a particular color comes up; a color that we naturally or culturally associate with a certain feeling tone, or a color that resonates with a particular energy according to our current paradigm.

Throughout the years many Kabbalists have used the Sefiros and their corresponding colors as a tool for visualization and meditation practice. The intention of such a practice is, essentially, to become embodied within, or embody, a particular Sefira, or series of Sefiros, during one's prayers. So, for example, if one was praying for Chesed to be more revealed or expressed in his life he would visualize and 'enter' into the 'white' space of Chesed. Similarly if he desires to access more Gevurah he would visualize and 'enter' into the 'red' space of Gevurah. We will explore this practice in more detail shortly.

TO HASHEM ALONE
OUR PRAYERS ARE DIRECTED:

But before we continue we must address one more important issue and that is the fact that our prayers need to always be directed to the Creator alone, and never to the actual Sefiros as independent entities.

"We pray to Hashem alone, and not to Hashem's attributes" *(Sifri, see; Pardes Rimonim, Shar 32; 2. See also: Rambam, Pirush HaMishnayos, Sanhedrin Chap. 10. In the words of the Jerusalem Talmud: "to G-d alone you cry out but you do not cry out to the angel*

Michael nor Gavriel." *Berachos Chap 9).* And yet, on the other hand, the Medrash asks, "Why are the prayers of the people of Israel not answered? — Because they do not know the Name" *(Midrash Tehilim 91; 8).* This cryptic statement suggests that we need to know 'the name' of the specific Sefira (attribute) we wish to draw down into our lives. We need to articulate that which we want to draw down into our lives, we need to 'name' it, but we also need to 'source' it, so to speak.

These ideas do not contradict each other. An example is provided in the case of a subject requesting something of his master, the king *(Teshuvahs Rivash, Teshuvah, 157).* Just as if one were to request justice from the king, he would petition the king to order his magistrate to dispense judgment; he would not seek help from the treasurer. And similarly if he wanted a gift he would ask the king to order his treasurer, not the magistrate. If he desired bread he would ask the king to command his baker, and wine he would seek from the wine-maker. As the below mirrors the above, when we ask for mercy from Hashem we keep in mind the Emanation/*Sefira* of mercy, and for justice the Emanation/*Sefira* of strength. And yet all the while our focus and request is directed to Hashem alone.

Although an analogy has been drawn, a clear distinction must be made, as the Tzemach Tzedek explains *(Shoresh Mitzvas Ha'Tefilah Chap 8).* In the case of the earthly king and his ministers they are in fact two separate beings and it is the minister who carries out the decrees of the king. With regards to Hashem, however, there is no separation, only unity. Hashem, the Infinite One alone is the King and the treasurer and the magistrate. The relationship between the formless Infinite One and the finite Sefiros is simply that the Infinite, as it were, uses the Sefiros as tools to reveal the Divine Will. The "vessel" of Chesed is used to manifest Hashem's quality of kindness, just as Gevurah is used to channel stringency. But there are no independent existences. And, in fact, on a deeper level there is only Hashem, period.

EMBODYING THE SEFIRA:

But for our purposes, while keeping in mind the absolute unity of Hashem, we will now explore some Kabbalistic practices of color-coded meditations and visualizations. Essentially the goal of the practice is to visualize and become embodied within the color of the Sefira one wishes to draw down into one's life.

To quote from the Pardes Rimonim of the Ramak:
"There are many times that a person who ponders the texts of Kabbalah and the Zohar (notices) that there is a correlation between certain colors and the Sefiros and that every Sefira has a particular color.

It is important for the person who ponders such ideas to be careful. He should not think in his heart that this (color scheme) is literal, Heaven forbid. For color is a physical thing and therefore labors under the laws of physicality. But regarding something that is not physical (i.e., the Sefiros), it is impossible to describe it in terms of physical properties, Heaven forbid. Therefore, a person who thinks that a Sefira actually has color is destroying the world and its boundaries that were put in place by the early ones, and he is [guilty of] materializing [the immaterial], Heaven forbid.

One who ponders this should therefore be careful. The intention of the colors is a metaphor for actions that are drawn down from higher sources. For example, regarding the powerful who are victorious in battle, it is appropriate to speak of them as 'red' as they draw red blood in battle. Also, red represents the qualities of cruelty, anger, and fury. Red is the color of angry men, as a person turns red in anger; this is (self) explanatory. Therefore, the quality of harsh Din (judgment) is associated with redness. Also, there is no doubt that the things that are red are connected to this quality and originate in this source as explained later on.

The same dynamic is present in relation to the color white. Things that are white represent peace and harmony. This includes the nature of people that are white-haired (i.e., elderly). As older people with white hair are generally more compassionate and open than fiery youngsters. It is not the nature of an older person to go out to battle.

Therefore when you want to make a color-correspondence to represent peace, kindness, and compassion, you say that this is the color of white. There is no doubt that things that are white come from this quality and source as explained later on…

For this reason, when a person is trying to draw down Chesed from the place of kindness he should visualize the name of the appropriate Sefira in the garb of the appropriate color. If you want pure kindness then meditate and imagine pure white, if you want kindness with strength and power then think of white that is a little off white.

And if a person needs to perform an act or behave in a manner that requires an influx of the attribute of Din (judgment, power) then he should dress in red garments and meditate on the Name of Hashem (the four letter Name) in the color of red.

The same is true for all required actions and desired attributes.

When one needs Chesed and compassion one should garb himself in white.

Proof of this comes from the Cohanim/Priests who are rooted in Chesed. Their garments are correspondingly white, to represent peace.

This is the same reason why the High Priest wore white on Yom Kippur. On Yom Kippur he would take off his gold clothes and put on white garments because the service of the day would primarily be concerned with seeking Hashem's kindness and mercy....

...do not dismiss this concept, for even the 'masters of nature' speak of this and say, that looking at running water awakens 'white bile'...This is part of the reason the Early pious ones, in the time of drought, would spill water in front of them while praying. This was done so that their hearts (minds) would focus on this (Chesed) and their souls would be aroused (to pray for Chesed) thus drawing down Divine Chesed.

There is no doubt that this is the reason why people in mourning dress in black, so that they should be moved by the lack of light and darkness which is dominant during a time of loss..."
(Pardes Rimonim, Shar Gevanim –Shar 10; 1.
Siddur Shaloh, Minhagei Leil Rosh Hashanah)

Essentially the practice is twofold. The first step is for one to literally dress oneself in the color of the Sefira one wants to draw down (for Chesed dress in white, for Gevurah dress in red, and so forth). In this way one physically embodies the color of the Sefira one wishes to access and amplify *(Note, Imrei Pinchas, Likutim 89).*

The second step is to visualize and meditate on the name

of the Sefira in its corresponding color. For Chesed visualize the name of the Sefira: *Ches – Samach – Dalet* written out in white letters. This can also be accomplished by visualizing the four-letter Name of Hashem (instead of the name of the particular Sefira) in the color corresponding to the Sefira you want to access or awaken; visualizing the Tetragrammaton in white for Chesed, or red for Gevurah, for example.

It is thus both a physical and a visual practice. The idea is for the entire body and mind to resonate with the *Sefirotic* energy one wishes to call forth and draw down.

Colors are evocative. They speak to us and create something within us. And so if it is Chesed that we desire to draw down, one should dress in and meditate upon its corresponding color. In many Kabbalistic systems this is the color white, but as mentioned before, it can be whatever lighter color works for you and your particular paradigm. By both thinking about and dressing in the color that we associate with a particular Sefira, we will be opened up and inspired to create a psycho-magnetic field that draws down Divine Chesed into our lives.

Through color-coded physical action and visualization we create the vessel of Chesed in order to draw down that particular quality. The 'external' act of 'looking' like Chesed, coupled with the internal practice of visualizing Chesed, inspires us, even if only unconsciously, to access and activate more Chesed in our lives.

Elsewhere, the Ramak *(in Tomer Devorah)* also speaks strongly about how, in addition to these two practices mentioned above, we also need to 'be' and 'do' actual deeds of Chesed in order to truly draw down Chesed into our lives. He explains that it is not enough to recite the "thirteen Divine attributes of mercy" to draw down Divine mercy, but that we need to actually embody the qualities of the "thirteen attributes" in order to fully draw them down.

Yet often it is the external that inspires the internal. What moves us to 'do' more Chesed may in fact be to dress like and meditate on Chesed. If we 'look' like Chesed and 'visualize' Chesed by using the *Sefirotic* color-code that will very likely stimulate us to act more in the spirit of Chesed. And when we look, think, feel, and act like Chesed we create a fitting vessel to receive an abundance of the Divine flow of Chesed into our lives.

We need to first embody and visualize the quality and attribute we seek to draw down into our lives. In this way we become the vessel to receive the light of that attribute.

We are using Chesed as an example but this is true for any of the Sefiros. You think it, visualize it, wear it, do it, be it, and you will then draw down even more of it into your life.

Everything of the macrocosm is reflected in the microcosm. "*Olam Katan Zeh Ha'adam*/The human being is a tiny world". The entire structure of the Divine creative process, as represented by the Sefiros for example, is embodied within the human being. And so by us visualizing and wearing the 'finite' expressions of Chesed we evoke and help draw down the Divine, Infinite expression of Chesed into our lives.

VOWELS/SOUNDS AND THE SEFIROS:

In addition to the ten Sefiros and their corresponding colors, which provide a visual way to embody each Sefira, the Ramak also talks about how each Sefira is connected to a *Nekudah*/Vowel Sound. In Hebrew, a Semitic language whose alphabet is comprised solely of consonants, a vowel is what moves a letter into a particular sound *(Pardes Rimonim, Shar 19 and Shar 28, Shar Kavanos)*. For example, take the word *Aleph*, the name of the first letter of the Hebrew alphabet. It is spelled with 3 letters — an *Aleph*, a *Lamed*, and a *Peh*. On their own the letters have no sound. Those 3 letters can therefore be pronounced in numerous ways. When pronouncing the name of the letter *Aleph* we pronounce the *Aleph* (first letter) with an 'Ah' sound, and the *Lamed* (second letter) with an 'Eh' sound, so we get the word '*Aleph*.' But, as mentioned, this is only one way to pronounce these 3 letters together. If one places an 'Ee' vowel underneath the *Aleph* (first letter), and an 'Uh' under the *Lamed* (second letter), the word '*Aleph*' would then be pronounced as EeLuph.

R. Avraham Abulafia and the Tikunei Zohar both speak of five primary or king vowels *(Hakdamah, Tikunei Zohar, 4b).* These are considered the main vowel sounds, although, in fact there are nine vowels (ten including silence).

Let us now explore how the system of vowel sounds and their corresponding semiotic signifiers can be integrated into the color-coded visualization practice that we have been exploring.

Note: Despite the fact that language in general and vowels in particular are designed to function audibly, in the context of this practice we will primarily be using the visual symbols that represent the vowel sounds as an aid in strengthening the visualization. This is because most of the meditations we will be exploring use the Tetragrammaton, which is 'unpronounceable.' On the other hand, if one were to use the names of the Sefiros themselves, rather than the Divine Name, one could then both visualize the vowel signs under the letter and sound out the word. Either way, for our purposes in visualization practice, it is important to visualize the vowel signs. The method is primarily based on pairing the various vowel signifiers with their corresponding Sefiros and their colors, as explored.

Let us begin with the most iconic letter-based visual icon, the unpronounceable four-letter name of Hashem (Note: This is why we are avoiding using the actual sounds of the vowels in the context of our meditation. We do not want to 'voice' the un-voicable Name. We will therefore confine our use of the vowels to their visual cues, rather than their audio signatures.).

To begin, pair the four-letter Name with one of the 9 (10) vowels signs, which, as mentioned, each correspond to a particular Sefira and color (*Sefirotic*/Vowel table included below). As one visualizes the Name of Hashem, the *Yud-Hei-Vav-Hei* ה–ו–ה–י, then one will also visualize it with the desired vowel symbol beneath the letters in the color with which it is associated.

For example, white is the color of Chesed and Chesed is associated with the Segol vowel, which produces the 'Eh' sound. The Segol is comprised of three dots in the shape of a triangle. In this practice one visualizes the four-letter Name of Hashem with the Segol vowel underneath each letter. Furthermore, one visualizes the vowels in the color white, which we have designated as the corresponding color of Chesed.

As one is dressed in white, one begins by visualizing and entering into a general surrounding ambiance of white. One then visualizes the Tetragrammaton written in white with the Segol vowel placed underneath each letter of the Divine name. The letter Yud has a Segol vowel and corresponding Eh sound, so Yud is Yeh (without pronouncing the actual letter). The letter Hei has a Segol vowel, so Hei is Heh. The same is true for the letter Vav; Vav is Veh, and the final Hei, which becomes Heh. All the while there is an undertone ambient 'Ehhhhhhh' sound.

Although this is a purely visual meditation, primarily utilizing the symbols of the vowels, which are intrinsically connected to sound, there is still the vibrational residue of the sound associated with the particular vowel. Therefore, one can still 'hear' or sense a feeling tone or sympathetic resonance of the particular sound represented by the chosen vowel. There is still the trace of the silent sound that is able to be 'heard' within the inner ear, even though it is not actually sounded out loud.

The same steps would be followed (with a different color and vowel combination of course) for the Sefira of Gevurah, or any other Sefira.

THE SEFIROS AND THEIR CORRESPONDING VOWELS:

Here is a list of the Sefiros with their corresponding vowels:

1. Kametz (aw) **ָ** **KESER:** *deep desire & primordial will*

2. Patach (ah) **ַ** **CHOCHMAH:** *wisdom and intuition*

3. Tzeirei (ei) **ֵ** **BINAH:** *reason and cognition*

4. Segol (eh) **ֶ** **CHESED:** *kindness and love*

5. Sh'va (uh) **ְ** **GEVURAH:** *strength and boundaries*

6. Cholam (oy) **וֹ** **TIFERES:** *beauty and compassion*

7. Chirik (ee) **ִ** **NETZACH:** *victory and perseverance*

8. Kubutz **ֻ** **HOD:** *splendor and humility*

9. Shuruk **וּ** **YESOD:** *foundation and relationship*

10. No vowels (silence)

   MALCHUS: *kingship and receptiveness*

KESER: *Kamatz* is the *Aw* sound, the vowel sign formed by the meeting of two perpendicular lines under a letter.

CHOCHMAH: *Patach* is the *Ah* sound. Essentially, the Patach is a flat horizontal line under a letter.

BINAH: *Tzeirei* is the *Ei* sound. It is in the shape of two horizontal dots placed underneath a letter.

CHESED: *Segol* is the *Eh* sound. It is comprised of three dots in the shape of a downward facing triangle, which is placed underneath a letter.

GEVURAH: *Sh'va* is the guttural stop sound. It is in the shape of two vertical dots and placed underneath a letter.

TIFERES: *Cholam* is the *Oh* sound. It is in the shape of a dot placed on the top of a letter.

NETZACH: *Chirik* is the *Ee* sound. It is in the shape of a single dot at the bottom of a letter.

HOD: *Kubutz* is the *Uu* sound. It is formed by three dots arranged along a diagonal plane and placed underneath a letter.

YESOD: *Shuruk* is also an *Uu* sound. It is in the shape of a Vav with a dot to the left of it placed to the left of the letter that carries its sound.

MALCHUS: No vowel, silent.

To make this a little more comprehensible let us delve a bit deeper into the actual sounds and symbolism of the vowels in order to uncover their connection to the corresponding Sefiros.

Although it is also important to note that sounds, like colors, mean different things to different people in different places at different times. For example, as explained earlier, pink can be seen as both a masculine and a feminine color depending on the culture and time period. The same is true with sounds. Certain sounds can mean one thing to one people during one era in history, and mean something quite different in another era to another people.

KAMATZ:

The highest Sefira is Keser, which corresponds to the *Kamatz* vowel sound/symbol *("Kamatz is 'above and high,' higher than Patach." R. Bachya, Vayeira, 18; 3)*. Kamatz is the sound of 'Awe.' It is considered a 'closed sound,' the sound of 'not releasing.' Kamatz actually means, "closed" *(Vayikra, 5; 12. Tikunei Zohar, 5. Ohr Torah, 433)*.

The reason it is considered a 'tight-fisted' sound, as it were, is because sound is a product of movement, and movement suggests a separation from Unity. The *Ein Sof* is One, Unified whole. There is no interior and exterior, no higher or lower, there is only One. The Sefiros are the 'finite' screens through which the One is projected into and perceived by the many. This implies a gradual process of separation. Keser is the bridge between the *Ein Sof* and all the lower Sefiros. Therefore, it exists at the dynamic intersection between Unity and multiplicity, or stillness and movement. Being as it is in this intermediary position it contains both the initial stirrings of sound as well as the anxiety of expressing sound, like a seed about to burst forth from its enclosed shell into the process of blossoming and individuation.

The Maggid of Mezritch teaches that the Kamatz comes from the saying *"K'motz Picha/* Close your mouth (from speaking)" *(Rashi, Devarim 32; 50)*. There is a *Peh*/Mouth, whose normative function is to speak and generate sound, and yet, the passage orders one to 'close your mouth.' The Kamatz is thus is the space between sound and silence, between movement and stillness, on the cusp of finite fullness and infinite emptiness.

Patach:

Patach is Chochmah, wisdom and intuition. In Chochmah there is the beginning of a true opening. The word Patach actually means "opening." Patach is an "Ah" sound, as in something opening up and revealing itself, "ahhh..." It is the continuation of the opening that began with the Kamatz, although with the Kamatz there was a certain tension, apprehension, and strain in the release of the sound *(*According to certain sources there is a possibility that Patach is actually a Kamatz sound. Haskamas R. Yehudah Leib Me'yanavitch Siddur Torah Ohr. See also: Rashi, Berachos. 47a. Ha'gaas Yaavatz).*

Tzeirei:

Tzeirei is Binah. Binah is understanding. Tzeirei is an "Ei" sound, which is associated with the point in the cognitive process when something begins to make sense. After the initial "Ahhh" sound, there is a corresponding "Ei" sound. This shift in vibrational frequency represents the movement from an initial intuitive grasp of an idea on the big picture level, to a more thorough understanding of its constituent parts. This takes patience and a certain degree of the critical faculty represented by the "Ei" sound.

In addition, Tzeirei is comprised of two dots. The two dots suggest a process of understanding through the drawing of parallels, analogy, association and analysis.

Segol:

Segol is Chesed. Chesed is loving-kindness. Segol is the "Eh" sound. The "Eh" sound is an expressive sound, a sound of release. In addition to its sound, the shape of the vowel is also significant. The Segol is in the shape of a triangle made up of three dots, with two on top and one on the bottom. This formation is a depiction of the process of synthesis. It illustrates the coming together of two distinct points through the founding of a harmonic 'third way.' It shows that something higher wants to lower and offer itself to the other.

Sh'va:

Sh'va is Gevurah. Gevurah is strength and boundary. Sh'va is a guttural stop that produces its own very short sound. It is an inward moving sound. The Sh'va indicates that you are taking a pause in order to reflect. It is the pause before further letting go. The root of the word Sh'va means to sit or to settle (i.e. to stop).

CHOLAM:

Cholam is Tiferes. Tiferes is beauty. Cholam is the "Oh" or "Oy" sound. This is the sound of feeling compassionate, empathetic and merciful.

CHIRIK:

Chirik is Netzach. Netzach is Victory. Chirik is the "Ee" sound. It is an enduring and penetrating sound. It is a sound of perseverance.

KUBUTZ:

Kubutz is Hod. Hod is thankfulness and humility. Kubutz is the "Uu" sound. It is a sound of wonderment and splendor. This is the essence of Hod — a person being overawed, experiencing a 'wow' moment. Being in awe is to be humbled by the majesty of both creation and Creator.

SHURUK:

Shuruk is *Yesod*, foundation and relationship. This too is an 'Uu' sound. But this vowel is placed to the left of the letter, unlike the Kubutz, which is under the letter. This suggests a movement outward. This is the idea of Yesod, connecting to others and forming relationships.

No Vowel:

No vowel — Malchus. Malchus is kingdom, the world, tangible reality. It is not about "you," but about the other. Malchus is the ultimate "other," the receiver. It has no sound of its own. It only receives sound as it is acted upon.

DIRECTIONS & THE SEFIROS:

As one can begin to appreciate, there are many dimensions to this visualization and embodiment practice. For example, so far we have covered three ways of interacting with the color of a particular *Sefira*/quality/attribute that one desires to draw down into his life in more abundance or balance. To recap, those are: dressing in the color associated with the particular Sefira, visualizing a kind of colored aura of light that one can enter into during prayer or meditation, and visualizing the Tetragrammaton coupled with the correspondingly colored vowel symbols of the particular Sefira that one wants to activate and embody. All this is done to expand the vessel of the Sefira in one's own life in order to receive more of Hashem's light filtered through that particular channel.

There are two more layers to this meditation that we can add to aid one in more fully entering into the energy of the Sefira, they are the directions and the elements.

Wherever we are, there is the center of the cosmic cube of consciousness comprised of six directions or faces — up-down, right-left, front-back — which surrounds us at all times.

These seven aspects of physical space (including the center) are a physical reflection of the seven 'emotional/expressive' Sefiros.

It is through the seven lower Sefiros that the physical world is manifest, hence the seven days of creation and the seven-day cycle of the week (i.e., space and time). Each day another Sefira predominates.

East is considered the "front" of the "face" *(Shemos, 38; 13. Rashi ad loc.).* West is thus the backside. In other words, the proper orientation of one in prayer or meditation is facing east. This indeed is the original orientation of the human being in general. The primordial man, Adam, was created, our sages tell us, with his head to the east, feet to the west, right hand to the south, and left hand to the north *(Chagigah, 12a, Rashi (M'sof) ad loc. Shar HaMitzvos, Bereishis 4a).*

In general, and specifically on the fall and spring equinoxes, the sun rises in the east and sets in the west. Therefore, east represents the newness of creation as it manifests every new day *(Maharal, Gevurahs Hashem, Hakdamah 3).*

East is where the "light" comes from. West is where "darkness" resides *(Pirkei D'Rabbi Eliezer, 3).*

To the right of the east is the south, Chesed, the source of blessings.

To its left is the north, Gevurah, the place of thunder, hail, and negative influences (Ibid).

When one is facing east, the directional orientation of the seven Sefiros are as follows:

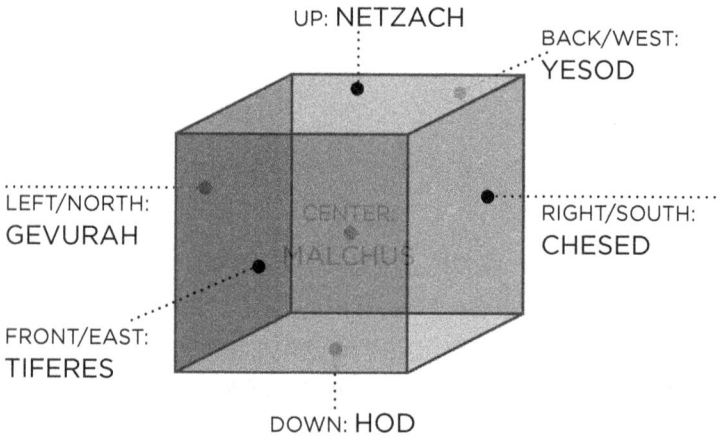

UP: NETZACH
BACK/WEST: YESOD
LEFT/NORTH: GEVURAH
CENTER: MALCHUS
RIGHT/SOUTH: CHESED
FRONT/EAST: TIFERES
DOWN: HOD

Now, in the context of our visualization and embodiment practice, as one is engaged in being, doing, thinking, dressing, dreaming, and visualizing Chesed, for example, along with its corresponding color (white) one can, while facing east, gently tilt or turn his head to the right, in the direction of the south. This is a physical gesture and movement to assist one as they seek to enter into the inner essence and 'space' of Chesed. One would do the same in relation to any of the Sefiros he desires to connect with or access.

FOUR DIRECTIONS & THE FOUR ELEMENTS:

In addition, the four horizontal directions are also associated with the four elements and basic 'ingredients' of creation. They are: fire, wind, water and earth; or, alternatively: hot, cold, moist and dry. Everything within this universe is said to contain some component and proportion of these four elements/states.

Note that the terms earth, water, air and fire are not meant to be taken literally, as in clods of earth or buckets of water, but rather as primordial elements or ingredients of creation.

The four elements and their corresponding four directions are:

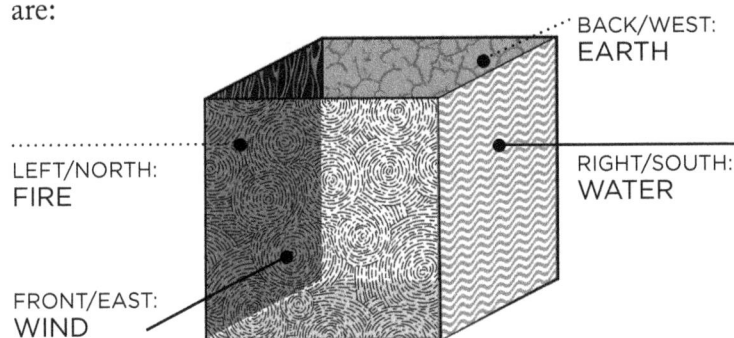

BACK/WEST:
EARTH

LEFT/NORTH:
FIRE

RIGHT/SOUTH:
WATER

FRONT/EAST:
WIND

In addition to tilting or turning one's head in the direction of a particular Sefira, one can also imagine a sensation of the corresponding element, such as the sensation of moistness for Chesed (water), or of heat for Gevurah (fire), for example.

Furthermore, to take it a step further, one could also visualize the Four-Letter Name with the particular Sefirotic vowels in their corresponding color, 'written' in the medium of the particular element. For instance, while one is facing east and wearing all white (the color of Chesed), he can turn his head to the right/south (the direction of Chesed) and visualize Hashem's Name with the corresponding vowel symbols written in pure water or crystalline ice, while attempting to 'feel' the sensation of moistness.

The same practice could be used to access Gevurah. One would then stand facing east, dressed all in red, turn his head to the left/north, and visualize the Four-Letter Name along with the appropriate vowel signs written in pillars of fire, while attempting to 'feel' the sensation of heat.

For Tiferes, one would face forward/east, dress in yellow, and visualize the Four–Letter Name along with the appropriate vowel symbols 'written' with the wind, while conjuring up the sensation of a cool breeze caressing his skin.

And for Yesod, one would face forward/east, dress in orange, tilt or turn his head back, and visualize the Four-Letter Name along with the corresponding vowels signs written in earth or sand, while conjuring up the feeling of one's feet planted firmly in the dirt, enabling him to sense the dryness of the earth.

ADVANCED TWO: PRACTICE

» Being Embodied within a Sefira

NOTE: This particular practice is performed using the Sefira of Chesed/Divine kindness and Love, but it is a blueprint that can be used to work with any of the ten Sefiros. For example, instead of being dressed in white, in a white room, with the element of water, and sensing Divine kindness and love, one could dress in red, in a red room, with a blazing fire, sensing Gevurah/Divine Power and Strength.

Set a soft timer (or have someone else observe you) in order to fully enter this meditation without any worry of what needs to be done afterwards. This time is for being present. Allow yourself the gift of this experience.

For those new to this particular meditation practice, it is recommended to start with anywhere from 10-20 minutes. This is not a competitive practice, so if that amount of time feels overwhelming for you, best to start slowly, and steadily build on a strong foundation.

Invite all of yourself into this space here and now. In a comfortable seat, preferably with your eyes closed, take a moment to let go of all the noise, chaos and movement in your life; simply be.

Just as we need to minimize external stimuli via the sense of touch, the same is true with the other senses. To help with visualization, it is beneficial to gently close your eyes, shutting out the external world in order to access and activate your inner field of vision.

You may notice various sounds, sensations, thoughts or feelings crossing your mind.

Sense everything without manipulating it; accept what is and relax from the urge to act.

With a deep exhalation, focus on the breath leaving your body naturally and effortlessly. Inhalation is the body's instinctive response to exhalation, effortlessly being drawn into the lungs from the power of the pressure created by exhaling.

Visualize yourself dressed in white from head to toe. All the items of clothing you are wearing are white. (You can also do this in actuality, i.e., dress all in white). Meditatively turn to the right and step into a room. (You may also move your head instead of turning your whole body).

Everything in the room is white — the walls, the floor, the ceiling. Navigate your way through the room and try to sense its water-like quality.

. . . .

This room is curved, damp and soft; there are no sharp angles to be found. Feel the sensation of wetness on your skin, the soothing sound of running water reminding you of where you are.

. . . .

Nearby, you see the letters Ches, Samach, and Dalet, the three letters that spell the word Chesed, written in white and shaped within snow or carved in ice. (Alternatively, you may visualize the four letters of the Name of Hashem, the Yud, Hei, Vav, and Hei, written in white snow or ice).

. . . .

The letters have the vowel of Segol underneath them and from a distance you hear a soft "eh" sound. This is the sound of loving kindness (Chesed). This sound expresses release, moving beyond limitation, the letting go that comes with moving forward.

. . . .

You are calling forth and evoking the Divine quality of kindness and love.

. . . .

You feel the Divine Chesed flowing towards you, enveloping you, and surrounding you from all sides, in a total embrace.

. . . .

You feel infused with Divine love.

. . . .

The love of Hashem vibrates throughout your entire being.

......

You are the embodiment of Chesed. If flows through you
and guides your movement in life gracefully. Everywhere
you go, offer yourself fully.

....

Sit with this awareness for a few moments and then gently open your eyes.

....

ADVANCED THREE: IDEA

» IN THE LIGHTS OF THE SEFIROS & ANGELS

Earlier there was conversation about different colors and their relationship with the Sefiros (although it is important to remind the reader that the Sefiros do not have actual colors themselves, the colors are only in the mind of the perceiver), the spatial dimensions and four directions, the primordial four elements, and the four letters of Hashem's name. We will now add another element to this associative symbolic matrix, the angelic reality.

SIX/SEVEN SEFIROS-SIX/SEVEN DAYS OF THE WEEK:

Broadly speaking, our physically manifest world, brought into being through the seven days of creation, embodies the seven lower "emotional" Sefiros, which are — Chesed (kindness, love); Gevurah (strength, restriction); Tiferes (beauty, compassion); Netzach (victory, ambition); Hod (devotion, humility); Yesod (foundation, relationship); and Malchus (royalty, receptiveness). Every day of the six days of the week expresses another one of the "masculine" Sefiros: Sunday/Chesed, Monday/Gevurah, and so forth.

Shabbos, the seventh day, the day from which all weekdays both flow into and out from, embodies the feminine quality of Malchus.

THE SEFIROS & THEIR SPATIAL DIMENSIONS:

Just as these six/seven Sefiros are expressed in the dimension of time, the days of the week, they can also be expressed in terms of space. Malchus, as mentioned earlier, is the presence of the Divine in reality as it is. It is the center point, the place where you are at this very moment. The other six Sefiros are expressed and embodied within the six directions: up-down, right-left, front-back.

The psycho-spiritual orientation of the human being is facing East. In the world of the Sefiros, East (forward) is Tiferes/Beauty and Compassion. To the right (South) is Chesed/Kindness and Love. To the left (North) is Gevurah/Strength and Restriction. To the back (West) is Yesod/Foundation and Relationship. The above and below, which are normally Netzach and Hod respectively will be left out of our current conversation, as here we will focus on the aspect of Malchus/Shechinah as being above the head, rather than the aspect of Malchus within the center of one's reality.

Chesed –Right/South
Gevurah – Left/North

Tiferes – Front /East
Yesod – Back/West
Malchus – (of the higher realm) Above

THE SEFIROS & THEIR CORRESPONDING COLORS:

The basic color scheme of the Sefiros that we will use for this practice is as follows:

Chesed – (Right) White
Gevurah – (Left) Red
Tiferes – (Front) Yellow
Yesod – (Back) Orange
Malchus (the Shechinah) – (Above) Dark Blue

A more in depth understanding of the relationship between the Sefiros and the colors was explored in the previous chapter. The template listed above is simply a basic outline that can be used for this specific exercise.

THE SEFIROS & THE ELEMENTS:

Beyond the directions and colors there is also the aspect of the elements. There are a number of elemental ingredients that compose the universe. If one looks at any modern scientific textbook that deals with the building blocks of matter, one finds a catalogue including a considerable number of elements. Today, in the periodic table for instance, there are over one hundred chemical components listed — an element being a substance that is chemically irreducible.

But fundamentally and philosophically understood, there are four basic elements. They are fire, wind, water and earth; or alternatively, hot, cold, moist and dry. In modern scientific language these may be analogized as hydrogen, nitrogen, oxygen and carbon — the predominant components of the four elements respectively.

Everything within the universe contains some component of these four elements*. Some things are predominantly fire-oriented, while others contain more wind, some more water, while others more earth. Of course, what we are talking about are the generic "elements," the primordial stuff of life if you will, which in turn can be broken down into greater detail. But for our purposes, this will suffice.

*Note: The terms earth, water, air and fire are not meant to be taken literally, as in clods of earth, buckets of water, air in the atmosphere, or the flame of a candle. Rather, these are to be regarded as constituent units of primary, primordial matter.

All things contain each of these four basic elements in varying proportions, yet some contain one that is more dominant. Mountains are predominantly earth, while rivers are obviously more water. For this reason, the physical fire we observe, for example, is not the element of fire itself, but rather the kinetic expression of its energy and essence. Some stones, which are primarily earth-oriented, contain more of the element of fire than other stones, and therefore when rubbed together they release fire. Similarly, some kinds of wood show the same tendencies, being more easily ignited and releasing their own resident fire. This is also true with certain kinds of wood and stones that release water when struck, compressed or rubbed together.

These four primordial elements are primary potentials, as they exist in their root. From primordial fire comes literal fire, and from primordial water evolves (or devolves) actual water; the same is true for wind and earth as well.

As with the other symbol sets previously explored, there are also correspondences between the elements and the Sefiros. There are models that arrange them hierarchically and vertically, with earth being the 'lowest' element, with the others 'above' it. And there is also the model that situates them horizontally and spatially, related to the four directions.

East / Front - Wind
West / Back - Earth
South/ Right - Water
North / Left - Fire
(Pardes Rimonim, Shar 21; 16. Midrash Talpiyos, Anaf Yesodos. Zohar 3, 24a)

As outlined above, to one's right is Chesed, understood as the giving and extending column. In terms of the elements, the right, when one is facing east (as proscribed), is represented by the south corresponding to the element of water, which nurtures and flows downwards. The left side (as established) is Gevurah (strength and restriction), which corresponds to the north and the element of fire. Yet, in this arrangement, there is a seeming contradiction. The "south" is typically considered the hot side of the planet, and the "north" is thought of as the colder half of the planet. According to this physically based analysis it appears that the correspondences should be the opposite or inverse of what they are (with fire in the south and water in the north). This requires explanation.

From a simple vantage point, water and fire seem to be total opposites of each other. Water is cold and wet, while fire is hot and dry. So the question is what unifies them? How do they relate to each other and ultimately come together? There are two ideas that explain such a seeming paradox: 1) They are either intrinsically connected because they both share a common root or denominator or, 2) they are connected because opposites attract; this is the principle of magnetism.

In this case (regarding the relationship of fire and water), according to the common denominator paradigm, the unifying element is Wind/*Avir*. Wind is considered to be both hot (as is the element of fire) and wet (as is the element of water), and so it contains traces of both fire and water and can thus draw them both together. Wind/Air is therefore the elemental bridge between fire and water.

On the other hand, the idea behind magnetism, as mentioned, is that opposites attract. Water, by virtue of its position of polarity, pulls fire towards it; and, in an equal and opposite manner, fire pulls water towards itself. It is for this reason that the South, which is hot and dry, is represented by the element of water. Due to the balancing mechanism of creation, the element of water, which is considered cold and wet, is paired with the direction of the south, which is physically hot and dry; and similarly the element of fire, which is considered hot and dry, is paired with the direction of the north, which is naturally cold and wet. This is a classic spiritual technique, wherein a counter-intuitive pairing of symbols or concepts is enacted in order to achieve a kind of meta-physical balance, equilibrium, or unification of polarities within the context of a greater systemic whole. From this perspective there is an 'elemental' balancing act going on throughout creation. One extreme is constantly seeking its opposite counter-weight through which to achieve its equilibrium.

THE SEFIROS & THE ARCHANGELS:

In addition to the relationship between the Sefiros and the

colors, directions, and elements there is also the aspect of angels. Our sages speak of each person's surrounding angels *(Shabbos, 119a. Pesikta Rabasi 44; 8)*. The Zohar teaches that wherever we are, we are always surrounded by the angelic hosts *(Hakdamah p. 12b–13a. Zohar 11 p. 199a. See also: Pardes Rimonim 31; 3. Zohar 3, p. 118b)*. Angels are spiritual, subtle energetic forces that surround us at all times. They are channels and transmitters of energy. These angelic forces that surround us do not determine our life or force choices upon us. Rather, they channel energy to and from us, and help us continue along the path that we have freely chosen.

Broadly speaking, there are four archangels and conduits of Divine flow into this world. There is Michae-l (Michael) to the right, Gavrie-l (Gabriel) to the left, Urie-l (or Nurie-l) in the front, and Refae-l (Rafael) in the back *(Zohar 3, p. 125a. p. 127b. See also: Pirkei D'Rabbi Eliezer, 4. .R. Menachem Rikanti, Bamidbar. Note the image of Michae-l in the middle, Gavrie-l to the right and Refae-l on the left. Yumah, 37a)*. Interestingly, the acronym of these four archangels is GeMaR'Ah, the Talmud.

The suffix of all the angel's names is E-l. The Divine name E-l is expressive, outgoing, creative, and giving. This is the essence of the angelic dimension as each angelic entity goes out of its way to express Hashem's desire for us, as well as assisting us in co-creating our own reality by transmitting the charge and quality of our intentions back out into the world. Thus, the Hebrew word for angel is Malach, which also means Messenger. The angels are essentially messengers that traffic between the human and Divine realms, carrying messages, prayers, intentions and blessings back and forth between the worlds.

There is the angel Michae-l, which corresponds to the attribute and is the conduit of Chesed. The name Michae-l is *Mi'Cha'e-l*/Who is Like E-l? Michae-l acts as the interface between pure, spiritual and unrestricted Divine Chesed, and Chesed as it is revealed and expressed in the physical realm, well defined and appropriately proportioned.

Gavrie-l is *Gevurah E-l*, the Gevurah (strength and restricting element) of the Divine. Gavrie-l serves as an interface between the pure, spiritual and unrestrained Divine Gevurah, and the way that Gevurah is revealed in the physical world, as G-d's strength and power never exceed what we can withstand.

Urie-l is *Ohr E-l*/The Light of the Divine. Urie-l acts as a conduit and interface between the pure, spiritual, infinite Light of Divine Compassion (the attribute of Tiferes), and the way that this Light is manifest within our physical reality.

Refae-l is *Rofe-E-l*/The Healing Power of the Divine. Refae-l serves as the interface between the pure, abstract, spiritual power of the Divine to heal, and the way that this healing flows into our physical reality and literally heals the sick on all levels — physically, mentally, emotionally, and spiritually.

There is a passage that is often quoted, and many have the custom to recite it before retiring to bed: "To my right is Michae-l, to my left is Gavrie-l, in front of me is Urie-l, behind me is Refae-l, and above me is Shechinah E-l" *(Siddur R. Yaakov Emdin)*.

As we are sitting in the center of the world as it were (and wherever we are in the present moment is in fact the center of our world), to our right is Michae-l and to our left is Gavrie-l, in front of us is Urie-l and behind us is Refae-l, and always right above us is the presence of the holy Shechinah.

East / Front – Urie-l
West / Back – Refae-l
South/ Right – Michae-l
North / Left – Gavrie-l
Above –Shechinah

THE DIRECTIONS & THE LETTERS IN THE NAME OF HASHEM:

As explored earlier, the Arizal teaches that the four letters of the Name of Hashem, the Yud-Hei-Vav-Hei, are also expressed in the four directions. Yud is to the right, the South. The upper Hei is to the left, the North. In front, to the East, is the letter Vav. And the final Hei is to the back, West.

Wherever we are present, we are within the orb of the Divine name and Hashem's presence.

Parenthetically, based upon another model, wherein we are the center, representing Malchus, and the six Sefiros are represented by the six spatial dimensions (4 directions and up/down) we can meditate on the shape of a cube as being our spiritual container or vehicle. The total structure of a cube has 8 vertices (points), 12 lines connecting them, and 6 sides or faces (the 4 directions and up/down). In total this equals 26, the numerical value of Hashem's name (8+12+6=26) (Gra, Sefer Yetzirah). Wherever we are our consciousness is heightened by the awareness that the total dimensions of the cube, our surrounding space, equals 26, the name of Hashem.

Here is a table of all the spatially related dimensions and their correspondences:

Right/South: Chesed –Yud - White – Water – Michae-l
Left/North: Gevurah – Hei - Red – Fire – Gavrie-l
Front/East: Tiferes – Vav - Yellow – Wind – Urie-l
Back/West: Yesod – Hei – Orange – Earth – Refae-l

Above: Malchus – Dark Blue – Yuli (aether or pure potential) – The Shechinah

In the practice explored earlier, the pious of old would meditate on the blue light above their head, i.e., the presence of the Shechinah. For our purposes, with the intention of entering fully and experientially into a self-defined sacred space so as to feel embraced within the Divine cocoon, we can employ all the imagery explored above including the textures and sensations of the elements and the imagery of the colors.

The truth is that in order to fully enter into a deep inward space that is dedicated to being vulnerable and open to ourselves, our desires, our aspirations, our inclinations and our shortcomings so that we can authentically feel the presence of the Creator in a very real way, we need to first ascertain that our immediate surrounding space is safe and secure. This means that we feel protected on a literal and physical level, providing us the safe space within which we can let down our guards and defenses.

We need to create a protective Makif/Surrounding Space so that we can enter this inner space feeling protected and open to being honest and vulnerable. The greatest, widest, deepest and most expansive possible Makif is the awareness that we are standing in the presence of the Master of the Universe and that Hashem surrounds, protects and is with us at all times. The Maggid of Mezritch teaches *(Likutei Yekarim, p. 2)* that we are able to experience being within the midst of the Divine presence so intensely that it is literally a visceral sensation of being embraced and enveloped from all sides.

This heightened awareness can serve us well at all times, not only when we want to open up, pray or practice some form of meditation. This awareness allows us to feel close and intimate with our Creator, and yet simultaneously to feel humbled and in awe. Try to feel that Hashem's presence is closer to you than your own body and yet, paradoxically, sense that Hashem's presence is utterly removed and Transcendent, always observing and protecting you.

How do we do this? How do we induce and inculcate a sensation that we are being both observed from a distance and embraced within the Divine reality? How do we create this sacred cocoon? We can achieve this by utilizing the symbolic associations, intentions and visualizations outlined above. By culling from and employing all the structures and patterns illustrated earlier, including the colors, the letters, the directions, the elements and the angels, we can create a tangible, sensational reality wherein our relationship with the Creator is real, relevant and alive.

ADVANCED THREE: PRACTICE

··

» SITTING IN SACRED SPACE

Set a soft timer (or have someone else observe you) in order to fully enter this meditation without any worry of what needs to be done afterwards.

This is a time for being present. Allow yourself the gift of this experience.

For those new to this particular meditation practice, it is recommended to start with anywhere from 10-20 minutes. This is not a competitive practice, so if that amount of time feels overwhelming for you, best to start slowly and steadily build on a strong foundation.

Invite all of yourself into this space here and now. In a comfortable seat, preferably with your eyes closed, take a moment to let go of all the noise, chaos and movement in your life; simply be. Just as we need to minimize external stimuli via the sense of touch, the same is true with the other senses. To help with visualization, it is beneficial to gently close your eyes, shutting out the external world in order to move more inward to your inner field of vision.

··

You may notice various sounds, sensations, thoughts or feelings crossing your mind.

····························

Sense everything without manipulating it; accept what is and relax from the urge to act.

Begin by facing East. Bring your awareness to the right side of your being. If it helps you to literally turn your head gently to the right you may do so, but for the primary purpose of bringing your inner awareness to that space. Become aware of the angelic reality of Michae-l, the aspect of Chesed, kindness and openness on your right.

Imagine yourself dressed in white and feel the texture of this color on your skin.

Allow the sensations of being near the primordial element of water to arise.

In the presence of Divine kindness meditate on the white watery letter Yud. Now gently turn your awareness (or your head) to your left in order to become aware of the angelic reality of Gavrie-l, the aspect of Gevurah, strength and power.

Imagine yourself dressed in red and feel the texture of this color. Feel the heat of the primordial element of fire to arise.

In the presence of Divine strength meditate on the fiery

red letter Hei. Now turn your awareness to face forward and become aware of Urie-l, the attribute of Tiferes — beauty, light and compassion.

. . . .

Imagine yourself dressed in a subtle yellow garment and feel its texture on your skin. Sense the element of wind swirling around you.

. . . .

In the presence of Divine light meditate on the yellow letter Vav carved out of wind. Now gently tilt your head back and become aware of Refae-l, the attribute of Yesod — connection, healing and alignment.

. . . .

Imagine yourself dressed in orange and feel the texture of this color on your skin.

. . . .

Visualize yourself sitting or standing upon the element of earth, in a vast expanse of sand.

. . . .

In the presence of Divine healing meditate on the orange/ brown letter Hei carved out of the earth. You are now and always surrounded by Hashem's loving-kindness to your right, Gentle Strength to your left, Beautiful Light in front of you, and Holistic Healing behind you. Now that your awareness is focused on the Divine expressions of kindness, strength, compassion and connectedness sur- rounding you, recognize that you are the foundation of this sacred space.

. . . .

Your body is the throne of the Shechinah. Your body is

the wick for her flame. Tilt your head gently upward and acknowledge the Shechinah's Blue Light.

Visualize a gentle blue light slowly descending from above all around you, suffusing the sacred space, including your entire body, with its brilliant, protective, all-encompassing light and love.

You feel love and awe simultaneously.

Bask in this light, holding this blessed space for a few moments.

Absorb the experience.

And when you are ready, slowly open your eyes.

ADVANCED FOUR: IDEA

....

» MOVING FROM DARK BLUE TO PURE BLINDING LIGHT AND BEYOND:

In a previous meditation the (lower seven) Sefiros were arranged horizontally and three-dimensionally, with each Sefira representing another direction — right-left, front-back, up-down, and center.

In this practice we will arrange the Sefiros in a more two-dimensional vertical alignment, moving from the lower more opaque color of Malchus up to the more transparent color of Keser. This is similar to climbing a ladder with each rung's colors becoming ever brighter and more transparent until one dissolves into the Infinite, formless, colorless Light above Keser and then beyond even that.

Here again is the order of the Sefiros and their corresponding colors as explored above:

Keser – Blinding White
Chochmah –Silver
Binah –Gold
Chesed – White
Gevurah – Red

Tiferes –Yellow
Netzach – Light Pink
Hod – Dark Pink
Yesod – Orange
Malchus – Dark Blue

SHADES OF LIGHTS:

In addition to the colors of the Sefiros there are medieval sources that also correlate various shades or qualities of light with the different Sefiros. One such tradition is from the school of R. Azriel of Gerona. R. Azriel was one of the teachers of the Ramban and the author of Biur Eser Sefiros, a fundamental text that elucidates why there are in fact ten — not nine or eleven — Sefiros.

R. Azriel, or someone connected with his school of thought, composed a slim booklet called *Sha'ar Ha'Kavahna*/Gate of Kavanah. This text was incorporated by R. Chayim Vital as the fourth section in his *Sha'arei Kedusha*/Gates of Holiness, which is a tremendous resource of older Kabbalistic practices.

The text speaks about a meditation where one first imagines oneself as a body of light, and then uses the various shades of light to enter into and be empowered by each of the Sefiros.

R. Chayim Vital also suggests a relationship between these subtle shades of light and the Sefiros and then quotes another version of this practice that details their relationship with the vowels. Here is the basic relationship between the Sefiros and the shades of light:

Keser - Infinite Light
Chochmah and Binah (or Yesod) is called Chayim –Living Light
Chesed is called Tov – Good Light
Gevurah is called Nogah – Glowing Light
Tiferes is called Kavod – Glorious Light
Netzach is called Bahir – Brilliant Light
Hod is called Zohar – Radiant Light
Yesod (or, Chochmah and Binah) is called Chayim – Living Light
Malchus is the Kisei – Throne of Light

While it is not perfectly clear what the relationship is between these shades of light and the Sefiros, what is clear is that they were used for a meditation practice with the intention of drawing down blessings into one's life.

To quote from the original text:

"Whoever sets his mind on something with a firm resolution to understand or achieve it will merit that the essence (of that idea) will return to him. Therefore, if one prays or desires to understand something deeply, [this will enhance the possibility that they will in fact achieve such a breakthrough]. [In order to do this] imagine that you are light and that all of your surroundings on every side and in every direction are light.

In the middle of this light is a throne of light (Malchus).

Above (the throne) is the light of Nogah/Glowing Light.

Facing this is (another throne) and above this throne is the light of Tov/Good Light.

(Visualize yourself) standing between them.

(Now, if you wish) to take revenge, turn to the light of Nogah (as Nogah is Gevurah).

And if (you wish) to offer compassion, turn to the light of Tov (as Tov is Chesed).

And the words you speak shall be directed towards the face (of the lights).

Turn yourself to the right and you will find (the attribute of) Netzach, which is the light of Bahir/Brilliance.

Turn to the left and you will find (the attribute of) Hod, which is the light that is Zohar/Radiant.

Above and in between them is the light of Ka-vod/Glory (Tiferes).

Around (this light of Kavod) is the light of Chay-im/Life (Chochmah and Binah).

And above (this light) is Keser.

(The) light (of Keser) crowns the desires of the mind and sheds light on the path of imagination, enhancing the clarity of one's vision.

And from the glory of its perfection (comes forth) desire, blessing, life, peace, and all good things to those who keep the way of its unification.

And from those who turn from the path of light, it (i.e., the light of Keser) disappears and is trans-formed into its opposite, (becoming the cause of) harsh rebuke.

(Sha'ar Ha'Kavahna. R. Chayim Vital, Sha'arei Kedu-sha, 4, Shaar 2; 12)

The practice detailed above is similar to the technique of the Ramak, wherein one turns towards and enters into the Lights of Chesed or Gevurah, depending upon what one's desired outcome is. If it is to arouse within oneself the at-tribute of compassion, then one turns and enters into the direction/light of Chesed; and if for purposes of Gevurah, then one turns and enters into the direction/light of Gevu-rah.

Our text then continues to speak about the movement of the lights in a vertical fashion, moving from lower to higher until one reaches (not literally) the *Ohr Ein Sof*/Infinite Light, the place of the Supernal Will.

In this process, as described, one is completely comprised of light and is also surrounded by light. It is within this surrounding light that one then encounters and engages the various shades of light in order to perpetually elevate his consciousness from one level of light to the next. One continues to ascend until he reaches the pure transparent Infinite light, as it were, and becomes a vessel to draw down all blessings.

To continue the quote:

"Indeed, it is a straight path corresponding to the *Kavanah*/Intention of the person who knows how to concentrate with truth and the utter cleaving of his thoughts and desires with all the strength of his being…

Therefore, an individual who ascends with the power of his intention from one thing to the next until he reaches the *Ohr Ein Sof* must focus his intention in a manner appropriate to reaching its perfection.

So that the Supernal Will should be vested within his Will, and not merely that his Will is vested within the Supernal Will.

The higher Will and lower Will are then joined...

And when one approaches in this manner, the Supernal Will draws closer to him and gives him more strength and desire to achieve and complete anything (he so chooses)...

This is the straight path.

One who desires to do anything — to pray or bless, or even the opposite — needs to imagine with his mind that he is pure light [and that he is surrounded by light].

And around this light is a throne of light.

And above (the throne of light) is the image of the order of the lights (Sefiros), as is known.

He must have intention to rise from one level to the next, from lower to higher, in the order of their emanation until the *Ohr Ein Sof*/Infinite Light.

(Sha'ar Ha'Kavahna. R. Chayim Vital, Sha'arei Kedu- sha 4: Shaar 2; 12)

Essentially, a person must direct his intention, first focusing on the throne (Malchus), and then slowly moving from the lower, denser shades of light (i.e., "life" to "radiance" to "brilliance" to "glory" to "glow" to "good") to the higher shades of light, to Keser and beyond.

For this, one needs to concentrate with deep Kavanah upon each set of lights, staying focused on them and nothing else. In this way one may move upwards from light to light until reaching the pure transcendent Light, and then even beyond all forms of light.

*Note: Included at the end of this chapter is a more accessible variation of this practice without the advanced objective of elevating to Keser and Beyond in order to draw down blessing and abundance from the Supernal Highest Will, but instead with the simple Kavanah/Intention of attaining some small measure or sense of connection to the Transcendent Realm. But first let's explore one more variation of this practice as brought down in the name of the Baal Shem Tov.

FROM MANY LIGHTS TO ONE LIGHT AND BEYOND:

There is another practice that is similar to the one explored above expressed in the teachings of the Baal Shem Tov. In this practice the objective is also to move from one level or Sefira to the next in a vertical fashion. But in this exercise the primary imagery is not based on the movement from dense/dark/opaque light to subtle/bright/transparent light, but from many lights to one light, and beyond. And in this version of the meditation, the vehicle or vessel for

the lights is not the Sefiros but rather the letters of the Hebrew Aleph-Bet.

The Baal Shem Tov teaches that the first letter in the Hebrew Alphabet is the letter Aleph, which equals one and is
therefore intrinsically connected to The One. In this manner the second letter, Beis, which equals two, is essentially
a devolved state of Aleph (i.e., primordial Unity). Beis is,
therefore, really two Alephs (representing the first stage of
the emergence of multiplicity, which is duality). The third
letter, Gimel, which equals three, is then three Alephs. The
last letter of the Aleph-Beis is the letter Tav, which numerically equals four hundred; it is thus four hundred Alephs
(Baal Shem Tov Torah, Amud HaTefila, 110).

The first nine letters in the Aleph-Beis parallel the single
digits, from one till nine. The second nine letters parallel
the double digits, from ten till ninety. The next four letters
are the triple digits, from one hundred till four hundred,
with Tav, the final letter, being four hundred. In addition
to the twenty-two letters there are also the five "final letters." These five letters move, in numerical value, from five
hundred to nine hundred. The highest number/letter is the
final Tzadi (known as Tzadik), which is nine hundred. Taking the highest number for each set of letters — the nine
from the single digits, the ninety from the double digits,
and the nine hundred from the triple digits — the largest
number in the Aleph-Beis is 999.

One thousand is called *Eleph*, which is the same spelling as the letter Aleph, but with different vowels. One thousand is thus considered "beyond" the set of cardinal or ordinal numbers, representing eternity and infinity. In essence, the *Eleph* is linked back to the Aleph, the One.

Parenthetically, the name "Yisrael Baal Shem Tov" has the numerical value of 1,000. The Baal Shem Tov's life mission was to reveal how the "One," the Aleph, permeates all of the multiplicity of creation, all the way up/down to the Eleph/1,000.

Letters are conduits of creative energy and light. They are the vessels and containers of the light of creation. Each letter has its own unique quantity and quality. The letters of the Aleph-Beis are thus the transmitters or vehicles that move the limitless Divine light into finite creation, as each letter resonates with a particular frequency and vibration. The closer the letter is to its Source in Unity the more unified and singular it is. Aleph (one) is thus considered the highest letter, as it is the closest numeric approximation to unity. Tav and the five final letters are the furthest removed, as they are all the more distant from this original state of unity.

The Zohar *(2, p. 214a)* teaches that, "in matters of holiness, the less letters the more holiness." This is another way of saying that the less vessel, the more light. The less letters there are, or the less numeric value a word has based on what letters it is comprised of, the closer the word is to its Source, which is the Infinite Light of One.

Alphabetically speaking this construct outlines a process of moving one's awareness from Tav back to Aleph, or from the many to the One. Additionally, the trajectory of this process simultaneously moves in the opposite direction as well, from Aleph to Eleph (from 1 to 1,000), revealing the Infinite One within the world's finite multiplicity.

Now let us see how this process works in a visual sense as a form of meditation. Take prayer as an example. In prayer, one is aspiring to experience a living and vibrant dialogue and relationship with the Infinite One. In the realm of the emotions (Yetzirah) this may make sense on an intuitive relational level. But in the realm of the intellect (Beriah) this is a paradoxical and totally abstract concept. How can One be Infinite? And how can we (who are just a part of the One) form a relationship with the One, of which we are an integral part?

In order to address these subtle existential questions the Kabbalists relied more on actual experience than ideas alone. This is a defining aspect of the mystical path, as opposed to the strictly philosophical approach to ascertaining the Truth. For these essential questions, which ride the fine line between epistemology and cosmology, are the very questions that take one to the apex of ideas and language itself, so to speak. At this crossroads of paradox and logical contradiction the normative rational mind breaks down. Therefore the Kabbalists employed experiential practices such as creative visualizations and meditation to equip the aspirant with keys to unlock the higher realms beyond the mind enabling one to enter into the more subtle world of Atzilus.

With this transcendent process in mind the Kabbalists were actually very practical in their diagnosis of human consciousness as it strives to expand and evolve beyond its own self-imposed limitations. For even though a soul may start its journey from within the Heavenly realm of the Aleph (Infinite Oneness with no separation between subject and object), as the mind develops it inevitably defines itself against the 'otherness' of the world, including its myriads of seemingly independent subjects and objects, represented by the multitudinous world of the Tav (and including all letters that follow the Aleph). So, theoretically by the time one begins a path of meditation and spiritual practice they are fully immersed in the world of multiplicity, and they are, at this point, seeking to return to the state of primordial unity from which they emerged. Therefore, the Kabbalists employed experiential practices such as creative visualization techniques that are designed to take the meditator on a journey from the many back to the One, so to speak. This is understood as moving from the subjective world of imagery to the highest level of imageless abstraction and existential identification with the Immanent Divine Presence.

This process-oriented approach is based on the Kabbalists' understanding that it would be more effective to gradually move the aspirant's awareness from a set of images through a process of refinement until they finally arrive at the ultimate experience of the Imageless Infinite One. This is due to the fact that human consciousness is, by nature, built upon a foundation of imagery. The human mind recognizes, generates and attaches itself to various images in order to identify ideas and entities within its world, and as a result one's emotions are then activated and triggered by this imagery and it's often unconscious narrative associations. Because the Kabbalists sought to include all of one's being within the awareness and experience of G-d's Infinite Oneness, it was not enough to merely contemplate the abstract idea of an imageless G-d. This idea, crystallized as it is within the mind of the adept, would not suffice to stimulate one to reach out and pray with all his heart and soul to the One Who Hears All Prayer. Prayer requires all of oneself, including one's emotions and senses, which must be refined and transformed in order to align themselves with the abstract and imageless essence of G-d's Ultimate Unity. When one is able to bring all of themselves into harmonious alignment with the One this is what is referred to as the spiritual experience of Atzilus.

In order to initiate this process of moving the meditator's awareness from the many to the One, one may in fact need to start with a certain conception or image of sorts with which to identify with and relate to. Simply put, let's say that you are praying to Hashem and you want the experience to be real and visceral, what visual would you entertain while you are conversing with and pouring your heart out to Hashem? Granted, on the deepest level there is no image that contains or defines the imageless reality of the Divine, but you are human and you think in a visually oriented, four-dimensional paradigm — so what is the "image" that you intuitively gravitate towards, what moves you? This is akin to asking, "What metaphor do you use to relate to Hashem?" Is it a King, a Queen, an aspect of Nature, a Friend, a Lover, a Father or Mother Figure? The Torah, both Oral and Written, is replete with these kinds of metaphors and images used to 'describe' the indescribable essence of Hashem. So, rest assured you are not alone in your attempt to imagine the imageless.

Rabbi Klunimus Kalmish, the Peasetzna Rebbe, taught that although the Rambam (Maimonides) calls someone that imagines the Creator in any kind of anthropomorphic form a heretic, the Ravad (R. Avraham ben Dovid, 12th century) counter-argues that, "There are many people greater than he who did in fact engage in such a practice and adhere to such a belief" *(Rambam Hilchos Teshuvah 3; 7. Ravad ad loc.).* Therefore, for the mentally immature and less abstract

thinkers, one may in fact begin his process of spiritual refinement with an "image" in mind, so to speak. In this way,
one may begin with a very literal or classical image, such
as a powerful and benevolent king sitting on a throne. But
slowly, and with meditation and mental maturity, this image will begin to fade and one will be left with increasingly
more abstract imagery until one transcends the need for
imagery altogether *(Bnei Machshava Tova, 7)*.

This requires explanation. In essence, the image that one
employs at the initial stage of his prayer is meant to help
the mind and heart grasp onto something during prayer
so that one can slowly expand and deepen his awareness,
allowing his thoughts and emotions to grow stronger and
ever more subtle as he strives to reach the level of Ein Sof
or Divine nothingness. Developmentally speaking one is
using the image as a stepping-stone towards the imageless,
and thus he is slowly training the mind to apprehend in-
creasing levels of abstraction. One is, in effect, harnessing
the mind to transcend itself. Otherwise, the rational, concrete mind will continually place imaginal and ideological
obstacles before the aspirant, constantly drawing them back
to the limited and limiting realm of Asiyah.

After a period of utilizing this initial imagery to connect
and relate to Hashem (such as a royal or parental figure),
one may find that his awareness and understanding of the
Divine has become ever more refined and subtle. At this

stage, they may not need to see an actual anthropomorphic image — but they still see "something." Often, once one has reached this intermediate stage of spiritual development, in between anthropomorphism and pure imageless abstraction, he will enter into the world of light(s), such as we explored earlier in this chapter. This may manifest as a visual or visceral sensation of light, or perhaps of a plethora of lights showering down upon them and filling the entire field of vision.

Starting from an anthropomorphic image and going through a process of ideational and imaginal refinement, one's visual conception becomes ever more subtle until it morphs into an image and experience of infinite light and love. To quote the Maggid of Mezritch: "One places his entire focus of thought and energy into the words he utters until he "sees" the *Oros*/Lights that emanate out from the words and notices how they sparkle and illuminate one another, and from these sparks more and more Oros/Lights are born" *(Maggid Devarav L'Yaakov, 47)*. And as one continues along the spiritual path towards imageless abstraction, gradually, from the many lights there arises one great light; this is the Aleph emerging from the many lights of the Tav and all the other letters.

In other words, as one goes deeper and deeper into this path of visual meditation or prayer, the various lights/letters will eventually all merge into one great, awesome, indescribable light/letter — a light of infinite proportions. This is a light like one has never seen before, billions of times brighter than looking straight at the sun. Within such a light there is so much power, and yet it is also so gentle and welcoming. At this stage, the one massive, brilliant light eclipses the entire screen of one's vision. All one senses at this point is light, love, awe, and a deep yearning to connect and unify with the Source of all Light and Life.

Eventually, even the Aleph — that one great indescribable light — fades as well and all one is left with, is that which lies beyond the image of light.

From anthropomorphic imagery, to a very strong vision of multiple lights, to an encounter and identification with one giant indescribable light, one gradually refines the mind to 'grasp' pure imageless abstraction. This is the process, described by the Maggid of Mezritch, of reversing creation and turning something back into nothing.

To summarize: First, the crude anthropomorphic imagery falls away and the 'king' morphs into lights. Then those are also refined and condensed into one great ball of light. Then, slowly, that light also dissipates and one is left with a pure, almost prophetic like awareness. At this point there is a sensation that one has 'arrived,' a visceral sense of *Deveikus*/Cleaving and a collapsing of the small individual 'i' of the self within the Infinite I/*Anochi* of Hashem.

The point is ultimately to move from the image to the imageless, from the many lights to the one great light, and then beyond all light and imagery into Pure Presence and Infinite Unity.

ADVANCED FOUR: PRACTICE

....

» Moving Through the Lights — Climbing the Divine Ladder

Set a soft timer (or have someone else observe you) in order to fully enter this meditation without any worry of what needs to be done afterwards. This time is for being present. Allow yourself the gift of this experience.

For those new to this particular meditation practice, it is recommended to start with anywhere from 10-20 minutes. This is not a competitive practice, so if that amount of time feels overwhelming for you, best to start slowly, and steadily build on a strong foundation.

Invite all of yourself into this space here and now. In a comfortable seat, preferably with your eyes closed, take a moment to let go of all the noise, chaos and movement in your life; simply be. Just as we need to minimize external stimuli via the sense of touch, the same is true with the other senses. To help with visualization, it is beneficial to gently close your eyes, shutting out the external world in order to activate your inner field of vision.

....

You may notice various sounds, sensations, thoughts or feelings crossing your mind.

....

Sense everything without manipulating it; accept what is and relax from the urge to act.

. . . .

With a deep exhalation, focus on the breath leaving your body naturally and effortlessly. Inhalation is the body's instinctive response to exhalation, effortlessly being drawn into the lungs from the power of the pressure created by exhaling.

. . . .

Begin with a deep out breath. Focus on the breath leaving your body, pushing itself out of your body.

. . . .

Visualize your body as a body of light.

. . . .

Allow your light to be penetrated by a series of even more brilliant lights arranged in the geometric pattern of the Tree of Life, shining from the center point outwards. Each light represents a Sefira, as they ascend ever higher into the spiritual realms.

. . . .

You open yourself up to receive the light of each Sefira. You are filled with each individual light to the point of overflowing, one after the next as you rise up the Tree of Life.

. . . .

With each rung that you ascend, the quality of the light becomes more transparent and luminous, as does your body, which is comprised entirely of light. The higher you climb up the ladder of light, the more brilliant you become.

. . . .

Above you, the brightest light that you have ever seen shines brilliantly. Move towards and into this light, becoming one with it.

....

And now above that, you sense an even more brilliant light. You move towards and into that light, becoming one with it as well.

....

This goes on and on until the light above you is so subtle that it is totally colorless and utterly transparent.

....

You become one with this transparent light. But you then sense that there is something even higher and more transcendent — beyond all form, light, color, or conception.

....

This is the space of pure Divine Reality where your own light merges completely with the unified field of surrounding Light. Here, there is only Oneness. It is neither Light nor Dark. It just Is.

....

Settle into this sacred space for a few moments before returning all the way back down the ladder of lights. Then begin your descent, moving from pure light and energy all the way down into your physical body. Gently open your eyes.

....

OTHER BOOKS
BY RAV DOVBER PINSON

REINCARNATION AND JUDAISM
The Journey of the Soul

A fascinating analysis of the concept of reincarnation as it appears in the works of the Kabbalistic masters, as well as how it is discussed by the great thinkers throughout history. Dipping into the fountain of ancient wisdom and modern understanding, the book addresses and answers such basic questions as: What is reincarnation? Why does it occur? And how does it affect us personally?

INNER RHYTHMS
The Kabbalah of Music

Exploring the inner dimension of sound and music, and particularly, how music permeates all aspects of life. The topics range from Deveikus/ Unity, Yichudim/ Unifications, to the more personal issues, such as Simcha/Happiness, and Marirus/ sadness.

MEDITATION AND JUDAISM
Exploring the Jewish Meditative Paths

A comprehensive work on Jewish meditation, encompassing the entire spectrum of Jewish thought--from the early Kabbalists to the modern Chassidic and Mussar masters, the sages of the Talmud to the modern philosophers. The book is both a scholarly, in-depth study of meditative practices, and a practical, easy to follow guide for any person interested in meditating the Jewish way. In addition, the book broadens our view of meditation, demonstrating that in addition to the traditional methods of meditation, meditation is prevalent within so many of the common Jewish practices.

TOWARD THE INFINITE
The Way of Kabbalistic Meditation

A book focusing exclusively on the Kabbalistic – Chassidic, Hisbonenus approach to meditation. Encompassing the entire meditative experience, it takes the reader on a comprehensive and engaging journey through meditation. The book explores the various states of consciousness that a person encounters in the course of the meditation, beginning at a level of extreme self-awareness and concluding with a total state of non-awareness.

JEWISH WISDOM OF THE AFTERLIFE
The Myths, the Mysteries & Meanings

What happens to us after we physically die? What is consciousness? And can it survive without a physical brain? What is a soul? Can we remember our past lives? Do near-death-experiences prove the immortality of the soul? Drawing from the fountain of ancient Jewish wisdom and modern understanding of what consciousness is, this book explores the possibilities of surviving death, the near-death-experience, and a possible glimpse of the peace and unconditional love that awaits, empowering the reader to live their day-to-day life with these great spiritual truths.

UPSHERIN
Exploring the Laws, Customs & Meanings
of a Boy's First Haircut

What is the meaning of Upsherin, the traditional celebration of a boy's first haircut at the age of three? This in-depth answer to that question explores as well the questions: Why is a boy's hair allowed to grow freely for his first three years? What is the kabbalistic import of hair in all its lengths and varieties? What is the mystical meaning of hair coverings? Rav Pinson answers these questions with his trademark deep learning and spiritual sensitivity. Includes a guide to conducting an Upsherin ceremony.

THIRTY-TWO GATES OF WISDOM
Awakening through Kabbalah

Kabbalah holds the secrets to a path of conscious awareness. In this compact book, Rav Pinson presents 32 key
concepts of Kabbalah and shows their value in opening the
gates of perception.

THE PURIM READER
The Holiday of Purim Explored

With a Persian name, a costuming dress code and a wom-
an as the heroine, Purim is certainly unusual amongst the
Jewish holidays. Most people are very familiar with the
costumes, Megilah and revelry, but are mystified by their
significance. Rav Pinson offers a glimpse into the unknown
world of Purim, uncovering the mysteries and offering a
deeper understanding of this unique holiday.

EIGHT LIGHTS
8 Meditations for Chanukah

What is the meaning and message of Chanukah? What
is the spiritual significance of the Lights of the Menorah?
What are the Lights telling us? What is the deeper dimen-

sion of the Dreidel? Rav Pinson, with his trademark deep learning and spiritual sensitivity guides us through eight meditations relating to the Lights of the Menorah and the eight days of Chanukah, and a deeper exploration of the Dreidel.

Includes a detailed how-to guide for lighting the Chanukah Menorah

....

THE IYYUN HAGADAH
An Introduction to the Haggadah

In this beautifully written introduction to Passover and the Haggadah, Rav DovBer Pinson, guides us through the major themes of Passover and the Seder night. Rav Pinson addresses the important questions, such as: What is the big deal of Chametz? What are we trying to achieve through conducting a Seder? What's with all that stuff on the Seder Plate? And most importantly, how is this all related to freedom? His answers will surprise even those who think they already know the answers to these questions.

....

THE MYSTERY OF KADDISH
Understanding the Mourner's Kaddish

The Mystery of Kaddish is an in-depth and Kabbalistic exploration into the Mourner's Kaddish Prayer. Throughout

Jewish history, there have been many rites and rituals associated with loss and mourning, yet none have prevailed quite like the Mourner's Kaddish Prayer - which has become the definitive ritual of mourning. The book explores the source of this prayer and deconstructs the meaning to better understand the grieving process and how the Kaddish prayer supports and uplifts the bereaved through their own personal journey to healing.

RECLAIMING THE SELF
The Way of Teshuvah

Teshuvah is one of the great gifts of life. It speaks of a hope for a better today and empowers us to choose a brighter tomorrow. But what exactly is Teshuvah? And how does it work? How can we undo our past and how do we deal with guilt? And what is healthy regret without eroding our self-esteem? In this fascinating and empowering book, world-renowned teacher and thinker, Rav DovBer Pinson lays out a path for genuine transformation and a way to include all of our past in the powerful moment of the now.

PASSPORT TO KABBALAH
A Journey of Inner Transformation

Life is a journey full of ups and downs, inside-outs, and unexpected detours. There are times when we think we know exactly where we want to be headed, and other times when we are so lost we don't even know where we are. Rooted in the teachings of Kabbalah, this book provides readers with a passport of sorts to help them through any obstacles along their path of self-refinement, reflection, and self-transformation.

....

THE FOUR SPECIES
The Symbolism of the Lulav & Esrog

The Four Species have inspired countless commentaries and traditions and intrigued scholars and mystics alike. In this little masterpiece of wisdom both profound and practical - Rav DovBer Pinson explores the deep symbolic roots and nature of the Four Species. The Na'anuim, or ritual of the Lulav movement, is meticulously detailed and Kavanos, or meditations, are offered for use with the practice. Includes an illustrated guide to the Lulav Movements.

....

A BOND FOR ETERNITY
Understanding the Bris Milah

What is the Bris Milah – the covenant through circumcision? What does it represent, symbolize and signify? An in depth and sensitive review of this fundamental Mitzvah. In this little masterpiece of wisdom–profound yet accessible, Rav Pinson reveals the deeper meaning of this essential rite of passage and its eternal link to the Jewish people.

....

THE GARDEN OF PARADOX:
The Essence of Non Dual Kabbalah

This book is a Primer on the Essential Philosophy of Kabbalah, presented as a series of 3 conversations, revealing the mysteries of Creator, Creation and Consciousness. With three representational students, embodying respectively, the philosopher, the activist and the mystic, Rav Pinson tackles the larger questions of life. Who is G-d? Who am I? Why do I exist? What is my purpose in this life? Written in clear and concise prose, Rav Pinson gently guides the reader towards making sense of life's paradoxes and living meaningfully.

....

WRAPPED IN MAJESTY
Tefillin- Exploring the Mystery

Tefillin, the black boxes and leather straps that are worn during prayer, are curiously powerful and mysterious. Within the inky black boxes lie untold secrets. In this profound, passionate and thought-provoking text, Rav Pinson explores and reveals the multi-dimensional perspectives of

Tefillin. Magically weaving together all dimensions of To-rah;, Peshat, literal observation, to Remez, the allegorical; Derush, the homiletic, to Sod, hidden Kabbalistic, into one wonderful tapestry. Inspirational and instructive, Wrapped in Majesty: Tefillin, will make putting on the Tefillin more meaningful and deepen the experience.

....

INNER WORLDS OF JEWISH PRAYER
A Guide to Develop and Deepen Your Prayer Experience

An in depth exploration and explanation of the actual Inner Experience of prayer. What occurs or could occur, when we pray? And how do we enter into a prayerful posture or modality? With practical step-by-step wisdom on walking the path of meaningful and transformative prayer

ABOUT THE AUTHOR

RAV DOVBER PINSON is a world-renowned scholar, kabbalist, prolific author and beloved spiritual teacher.

He is widely recognized as one of the world's foremost authorities on authentic Kabbalah, philosophy & Jewish wisdom.

Through his books, lectures and seminars he has touched and inspired the lives of thousands the world over, and continues to serve as a spiritual mentor and guide to many across the globe.

He has authored over 25 books, many of which have been translated into various languages, such as Hebrew, German, Spanish, Russian and Portuguese

Among his published works are:

- Reincarnation & Judaism: The Journey of the Soul
- Inner Rhythms: The Kabbalah of Music
- Meditation and Judaism: Jewish Meditative Paths
- Toward the Infinite
- The High Holiday Reader
- Jewish Wisdom on the Afterlife:
  The Mysteries, the Myths, & the Meanings
- The Upsherin; Exploring a Boys First Hair Cut
- Thirty-Two Gates of Wisdom;
  Awakening through Kabbalah
- Eight Lights: 8 Meditations for Chanukah

- The Purim Reader: The Holiday of Purim Explored
- The IYYUN Hagadah: The Hagadah Companion
- Reclaiming the Self: The Way of Teshuvah
- The Mystery of Kaddish: Understanding the mourner prayer
- Passport to Kabbalah
- The Four Species
- The Garden of Paradox:
  The Essence of Non–Dual Kabbalah
- Wrapped in Mystery: Tefillin
- A Bond for Eternity: Understanding the Bris
- Mystic Tales of from the Emek HaMelech
- Breathing & Quieting the Mind
- Inner Worlds of Jewish Prayer

Rav DovBer Pinson is the Rosh Yeshiva of the IYYUN Yeshiva and heads The IYYUN Center in Brownstone, Brooklyn NY.

www.IYYUN.com